To Nick:

Congratulations

it pay to be
intelligent —
Good Luck

Billy Mazer

YOU CAN'T HIT THE BALL WITH THE BAT ON YOUR SHOULDER

YOU CAN'T HIT THE BALL WITH THE BAT ON YOUR SHOULDER

THE BASEBALL LIFE AND TIMES OF BOBBY BRAGAN

BY BOBBY BRAGAN
AS TOLD TO JEFF GUINN

INTRODUCTION BY HOWARD COSELL

THE SUMMIT GROUP
FORT WORTH, TEXAS

THE SUMMIT GROUP
1227 West Magnolia, Suite 500, Fort Worth, Texas, 76104

Library of Congress Cataloging in Publication Data

Bragan, Bobby, 1917-

You can't hit the ball with the bat on your shoulder/ by
Bobby Bragan; as told to Jeff Guinn.
P. cm.
ISBN 1-56530-015-7

1. Bragan, Bobby, 1917—Biography. 2. baseball players—
United States—Biography. 3. Baseball—United States—
Managers—Biography. 4. Minor league baseball—United
States. I. Guinn, Jeffrey Mason, 1951- II. Title.

GV865.B7G8 1992   796.357'64'092
                     QBI92-963

Jacket & book design by Rishi Seth

Manufactured in the United States of America
First Printing 1992

For my mother, Corinne Roberts Bragan, and for baseball.

BOBBY BRAGAN

For Nora, Adam, and Grant.

JEFF GUINN

CONTENTS

ACKNOWLEDGMENTS

WE'RE GRATEFUL TO THE MANY MEMBERS OF THE EXTENDED "baseball family" who contributed their memories and opinions for our Between Innings segments: Hank Aaron, Bob Aspromonte, Al Barlick, Buzzie Bavasi, Carroll Beringer, Ralph Branca, Lou Brock, Lou Burdette, Roy Campanella, Orlando Cepeda, Harry Craft, Del Crandall, Tommy Davis, Joe DiMaggio, Leo Durocher, Al Gionfriddo, Dick Groat, Jerry Grote, Whitey Herzog, Tom Lasorda, Don Larsen, Vernon Law, Denver Lemaster, Denis Menke, John McHale, Cal McLish, Stan Musial, Billy O'Dell, Harry Ornest, Gabe Paul, Johnny Podres, Branch Rickey III, Blackie Sherrod, Duke Snider, Warren Spahn, Chuck Stevens, Bobby Thomson, Joe Torre, Lee Walls, Dick Williams, Maury Wills, and Don Zimmer.

Thanks to Howard Cosell for writing the foreword, and to The Summit Group for publishing *You Can't Hit the Ball with the Bat on Your Shoulder* (especially Clark, Bryan, Louie, and Norma Jean).

From Bobby Bragan: My wife Roberta proofread every page and made many useful comments; additional thanks go to Jim Beckman, Caroline and Bob Wighaman, and Dr. Barry Bailey. Continued love and respect are due to the memory of my father, George Washington Bragan Jr. and all the rest of my brothers and sisters – Sue, G.W. III, Walter, Lionel, Peter, Marian, Jimmy and Frank. And thanks to Jeff Guinn – without him, there would be no book.

From Jeff Guinn: My wife Nora and my sons Adam and Grant were brave to put up with me while this book was being written (and at all other times). Additional thanks go to Dot and Frank Lauden, Del Hillen, Felix Higgins Jr., Perry Perkins, Mike Hamilburg, Robert Fernandez and Gerald Zenick; to special baseball friends Larry Swindell, Mark Murphy, Rich Billings, and Zonk Lanzillo; and, from the distance of so many years, to my parents and sister. Of course, I'm also grateful to Bobby Bragan, who lived the colorful life it's been my pleasure to write about here.

FOREWORD:
HOWARD COSELL

BOBBY BRAGAN HAS A WAY of making a cliche´ sound utterly original and different. He will look at you from behind those somber brown eyes and say, with a deep Southern drawl that sounds like a series of "basso profundo" musical chords, "You can't hit the ball with the bat on your shoulder," and you find yourself nodding agreement as if you had never heard the statement before. Then, suddenly, his Indian-like face will be wreathed with a toothy smile that resembles a rabbit and you start to chuckle and you realize you've been had.

But this is Bobby Bragan, an original in the human species. I have known him for more than 30 years and we have been friends during all of that time. I watched him try to play shortstop for the Phillies and catch for the Brooklyn Dodgers. I saw him manage the Hollywood Stars and get national attention. I saw him manage the Pittsburgh Pirates and get fired, manage the Cleveland Indians and get fired, manage the Braves in Milwaukee and Atlanta and get fired. Always, I felt he got fired because he was ahead of all the others: too bright, too different, too daring, too challenging.

Bobby has never changed to this day. He is baseball's Music Man. If there are six pockets in a table, Bobby will hit every one. He is Elmer Gantry in uniform; legs like tree trunks, the exact opposite build of what one would have expected an athlete to be.

There are so many things I remember about Bobby: the day in 1940 when he hit two home runs in one game against the great Bucky Walters. When Bobby talks about that day, the words come out like relish on top of a hamburger. There was the time he joined a certain coterie of Brooklyn Dodgers who revolted and didn't want to play on the same team as Jackie Robinson. Then there was the time in 1956 when Bobby Bragan looked at me and proudly said, "I've got more black players on my team than any other manager in the major leagues." Together we'd visit Jackie in his home in North Stamford, Connecticut and Bobby and Jackie would embrace because they had become firm friends. This is another thing about Bobby, the capacity for growth at any age.

I remember Bobby always putting on the writers. That day at spring training in the era of Mays, Mantle, and Snider, and Bragan looking solemnly at the press and saying, "I've got the best center fielder in the business. His name is Bill Virdon." His Pirates of 1956 were a woebegone lot, too young, too old, destined to finish last. But, incredibly, it was the end of May and there were the Pirates in first place. Bobby came into the old Polo Grounds, faced an assemblage of writers and with perfect seriousness said, when asked if his team was for real, "They've got to catch us, we don't have to catch them." And they believed him.

In 1957 Bobby was at my Manhattan apartment playing the piano and singing "Mack the Knife." The phone rang and I took the call. It was Joe Brown, general manager of the Pirates calling for Bobby. Bobby left the piano and came back maybe two minutes later and started signing, "Oh, the shark has, pretty teeth, dear...", right back into "Mack the Knife." I said, "What did Joe want?" and he kept singing "Mack the Knife is back in town, Joe Brown just fired me."

That's Bobby Bragan and the spirit of he man. The whole feeling of him is in this book. Anecdote after anecdote, told in the Bragan way. I have watched managers come and go, appear and reappear, a game of musical chairs. For my money, there's one chair that will always be empty because Bobby Bragan no longer manages and baseball is the loser.

Fortunately, now baseball has a winner in *You Can't Hit the Ball With the Bat On Your Shoulder*. Mack the Knife is back in town. Welcome home, Bobby. Be at the studio at six, we'll have a hell of a show.

JACKIE

IN 1947, THE BROOKLYN DODGERS held their annual spring training in Havana, Cuba. Besides our major league team, the camp also included our top minor league club, which played its regular season games in Montreal. Every day we'd play the Montreal team. Our spring training facilities in Havana weren't anything like the fancy setups all the major league clubs have now. We just had one field, El Gran Stadium, that seated 35,000. We slept at night at the Hotel Nacional, and I remember seeing bullet holes in its stucco walls from old revolutionary days. We didn't live at poverty level, but we were just as far from enjoying luxury. Branch Rickey, who ran the Dodgers in those days, didn't believe in spending a penny more than he had to.

Mr. Rickey's decision to hold Brooklyn's spring training in Havana was neither convenient nor inexpensive for other major league teams. Cuba wasn't part of the regular Grapefruit League circuit; teams playing the Dodgers in Havana had to purchase extra plane tickets and pay for overnight stays in Havana hotels. We also played some of our exhibition games in Panama. I don't know why. Many people questioned the choice of Havana as our spring training site. Only Mr. Rickey knew for certain why he'd chosen that city. With him, there was always the possibility economics was the overriding factor.

One particular day of that spring training stands out in my mind, and for good reason. We'd just finished a morning workout in Panama. I was still wearing my uniform and was feeling kind of sweaty. Panama was so hot, even in the spring, but before I could change T-shirts someone came over and told me Mr. Rickey wanted to see me. I wasn't surprised. I knew what he'd want to talk about.

The Montreal minor league team featured a second baseman who could do it all—hit for power, hit for average, field, throw, and run. During our spring games with Montreal it was obvious that second baseman was the best player in camp, including anybody on the Dodger team. His name was Jackie Robinson, and most of us on the major league roster suspected Mr. Rickey was waiting for the right moment to announce Robinson was going to become the first black major league player. Of course, we didn't say "black" then— we said "colored."

Some of the other Dodgers didn't seem to mind the idea of having a black teammate, but I sure did. Growing up in Birmingham, Alabama, I never mixed much with blacks. The only ones I ever talked to were the maid who helped my mother around the house and the men who'd come over every once in awhile to ask my father, who ran a road-grading crew, for an advance. I had never really had much conversation with a black person, much less eaten a meal or shared a train compartment with one. That's what I would have to do if Jackie joined the Dodgers, and I just wasn't going to stand for it.

Several other players, mostly from the South—Eddie Stanky, Ed Head, my roommate and good friend Dixie Walker—agreed with me that we couldn't have a black player on our team. The most outspoken player against Robinson joining the Dodgers, though, was Carl Furillo. "I won't play on the same field with one of those," he'd say, and we couldn't understand why he was so racially prejudiced when he was from Pennsylvania. But he was dead set against Jackie.

Anyway, on this particular day Mr. Rickey had already called one or two of the other dissenters in for a talk, and it was my turn. Now,

I respected Mr. Rickey above all others. He know more about base-ball than anyone else. He also had a way of cutting you down to size if he felt like it. After the 1947 season when we'd won a National League championship he gave everybody else on the team a little raise, but when my contract came it was for the same salary— $9,000—as the year before. I wrote him a letter saying I was insulted I hadn't gotten a raise, too, and he wrote me back a masterpiece. It said, "Bobby, if you can in any way help us to negotiate a trade for your contract, I'd be grateful for any help you could give us. Other-wise, sign this contract and send it back." I did.

In Panama, Mr. Rickey had rigged up an office for himself on the top floor of a gray, two-story barracks. I think he actually put a door across some boxes to serve as a desk. When I got there he was with Arthur Mann, a former writer for one of the New York papers. Mr. Rickey always liked to have someone following him around doing little things, and Arthur Mann was the one that spring. As usual, Mr. Rickey was in a suit and had one of his big cigars between his fingers. He gave me a stern look.

The first thing he said was, "It's been suggested there is a move on to keep Jackie Robinson off the Brooklyn club, that there's dis-satisfaction among some of the players. I want to get to the root of it. That's why I sent for you."

I wasn't just sweating from the heat. You have to understand Mr. Rickey was God so far as the Dodgers were concerned. If he wanted, he could have me out of the major leagues in a second.

He continued, "Let me tell you, in the first place nobody else is going to tell me who to play. If Jackie Robinson can do the job better than another player, then regardless of the color of his skin Jackie Robinson is going to play. Do you understand, Bobby?'

I took a deep breath. "Yes, sir."

I think Mr. Rickey believed the matter was closed. "And how do you feel about this?' he asked almost genially.

"I wouldn't want to be the scapegoat in all this, Mr. Rickey, but if it's all the same to you I'd prefer to be traded to another team."

He looked at me, and I wondered if I'd finish the day as a Dodger. "If we call Jackie Robinson up, will you change the way you play for me?" he finally asked.

That question was easy. I always played baseball the same way, all out, using my limited abilities to the fullest. "No, sir. I'd still play my best."

Mr. Rickey looked at his watch. "What's your schedule? All right, go ahead with your workout," That was it. It wasn't a lengthy meeting. Later that night all of us who'd been called in compared notes. We were sure Jackie was going to be promoted to the Dodgers. Dixie Walker said he thought he'd put his feelings in a letter so Mr. Rickey would absolutely know how set he was against it. All of us expected to be traded, and all the other guys were—after the season, after helping the Dodgers win another pennant.

But I wasn't traded. The next day Arthur Mann sought me out and said, "Bobby, Mr. Rickey was impressed with the way you levelled with him." And somehow after that I didn't think I'd be traded.

Mr. Rickey had a parting shot for me, though. He officially announced Jackie had made the Dodgers at a season kickoff luncheon at the St. George Hotel in Brooklyn, I think it was. After the luncheon he pulled me aside and asked me which of my teammates I thought should be sent down to Montreal to make room for Jackie on the roster. I told him Marvin Rackley, and that's who was sent down.

There was more confusion that day which didn't even involve Jackie. Leo Durocher was the manager then, and he was a big Jackie booster. I learned later that Mr. Rickey had asked him if he'd play Jackie should he join the Dodgers, and Leo told him, "He'd be my first baseman." And that's where Jackie played his first season with us. In 1948 Gil Hodges took over first and Jackie shifted to second.

Anyway, I believe it was that same day when the commissioner's office announced Leo was suspended for the 1947 season. It had something to do with his knowing gamblers. Anyway, we got a black teammate and lost our manager at the same time. Burt Shotton took over for Leo, and he was a lot less dynamic, a quieter type. If Leo had been with Jackie that first season, maybe Leo could have taken some of the heat off him. As it was, Jackie was on his own.

Shotton was maybe the last of the old-time managers who didn't wear a full uniform on the field. He'd lead the team from a seat in the

Dodger dugout, and he'd always wear a Dodger jacket over his street clothes. Shotton went to such an extent to avoid the spotlight that Clyde Sukeforth, the pitching coach, was the only one who ever went out to the mound to talk to a pitcher or call in a reliever.

We took trains on road trips in those days, and you spent more time with your teammates. I would say Jackie was immediately accepted by most of his teammates, maybe 20 out of 25. Pee Wee Reese, who was from Kentucky, was a close friend of Jackie's from the beginning. But the five of us who'd been called in by Mr. Rickey kept our distance. Oh, I wasn't belligerent. I didn't call Jackie names or insult him that way. I respected his ability, and it was clear to me like it was to everyone else that he was the best player we had. But on those first train rides I can guarantee you I wasn't going to sit at the same dining table with Jackie or even have a conversation with him.

Even having Jackie in our clubhouse at Ebbctts Field was sour for me. The clubhouse was under the right field stands, and we'd get to the dugout from there by walking down a tunnel. Even though the Dodgers were one of the glamour teams in baseball, our locker room was ordinary. Each player had a cubicle about a yard wide, with chain link fence stretching down from the ceiling to the floor. In front of each locker was a plain stool. There were also a few tin lockers in the middle of the room, ones that looked and opened kind of like the lockers you see in schools. Dixie Walker and Pete Reiser used those. I remember our clubhouse manager, John Griffin, had a joke about Reiser. Pete ran into the centerfield wall pretty regularly and sometimes was hurt badly. Mr. Rickey ended up padding that wall because of Pete. Anyway, at one point Griffin would walk by those tin lockers every day and say, "You all right, Pete?" The joke was that Pete was hurt and hadn't been there for two months.

My locker was on one side wall, next to Arky Vaughn's. Bobo Newsome was on the other side. Bobo was quite a gin player. He and Leo played often. My uniform number was 24, which wasn't special then. Willie Mays came along a few years later and now everybody wants to wear 24, but then I think the number signified I was the 24th player on the 25-player roster. Also, nobody asked you back then what number you wanted. You got what they gave you, and you were just grateful to have a major league uniform to wear.

On opening day in 1947, Jackie came into the clubhouse. He got a locker on the other side of the room. Pee Wee Reese was next to him. To Pee Wee's everlasting credit, he was Jackie's friend from Day One. Most of the rest of us just sort of ignored Jackie that day, but Pee Wee talked to him just as friendly as he did to the rest of his teammates. The atmosphere in there that day was a little strange, though. Oh, we'd all suspected Jackie would be joining us, had heard it officially from Mr. Rickey at the St. George Hotel, but now all of a sudden he was right with us and it was happening for real.

Jackie put on his uniform, that old flannel uniform we used to wear, and I saw he had number 42. My number, reversed. Somehow, even that stung me a little.

We went out on the field to play the game, which I think was against the Braves. We won, and I caught part of the game. I don't remember exactly how Jackie did, but I do know once the umpire hollered, "Play ball!" we got down to business. I don't think any of us during those nine innings consciously thought about history being made.

Speaking of history, almost every baseball fan thinks Jackie was the first black player, followed by Larry Doby in late '47 and then Roy Campanella in '48. But that's not true. Mr. Rickey added another black player to the Dodger roster in 1947. His name was Dan Bankhead, and he was a pitcher. He joined us late in the year, and during the '47 World Series when I hit a double Dan Bankhead was sent in to run for me. Bankhead never really did all that much in the majors. His record for the Dodgers in '47 was 0-0, and he was sent back down to the minors the following spring. He came back to pitch for us in 1950 and went 9-4, but dropped to 0-1 in 1951 and never pitched in the big leagues again.

So while Mr. Rickey deserves—and gets—credit for bringing the first black player to the majors, he also ought to be remembered as the first owner to have two blacks on the same team.

But Bankhead came up later in the season, after Jackie had made the full tour of National League cities and had taken the first full wave of abuse from fans and members of the other seven teams. Some cities were worse than others for him.

When we played in Philadelphia, it was ugly. The worst example of someone attacking Jackie with slurs was Ben Chapman, the Phillie manager. He'd keep hollering to us Southern boys in the Dodger dugout, telling us to get up and let Jackie have our seats. The direct racial slurs Jackie heard mostly on the field itself; he'd be on base and first baseman would say something ugly, or a baserunner would call him a nigger. And Jackie was so proud, so self-confident. They'd insult him and he'd get a hit or steal a base and get even that way.

We watched. I learned. Not fast, but I learned. In fairness to the others, within a month everybody was fighting to sit next to Jackie on the train, because he'd earned such respect for his playing ability and dignity to deal with his tough situation.

Personally, I didn't talk to Jackie Robinson at length, didn't have what you might go as far as to call a real conversation with him, until the next spring training in 1948 in Vero Beach, Florida. The Dodgers were very family-oriented and would always have a screened-in breakfast area where families could be together and have cereal and orange juice, things like that. Jackie was there one morning with his wife, Rachel, and I came in with my wife, Gwenn. We had this four-way conversation about all sorts of things, not baseball, and I left thinking that this was a very special man and woman and I wanted to be their friend.

And I was. Jackie and I became close and stayed that way even after I left the Dodgers and beyond to when we were both no longer in uniform. We talked about everything. He was bold but not belligerent. He and I were both friends of Howard Cosell, and the three of us often went out together. We always had a good time.

Most people don't remember this, but Mr. Rickey considered several players before choosing Jackie to break the color barrier. There was a big guy named Jim Pendleton, who did go on to play in the majors after Jackie got there first. He was a hell of an athlete. And there was a Cuban player named Silvio Garcia. He was a great player, but Mr. Rickey decided against him because he couldn't speak English. In all Mr. Rickey scouted maybe 20 players before deciding on Jackie.

He made the right choice for baseball and, as it turned out, the right choice for Bobby Bragan. I learned so much from the time I spent with Jackie. Later on when I managed, I always had good rapport with black players. Despite my upbringing, I learned black people are just like anyone else. That might seem like something odd for a man not to know in 1992, but society was very different in 1947.

After knowing Jackie and coming to respect him so much, I was able to transfer that respect to other black people. My own family had some trouble understanding this. In 1948 I left the Dodgers to become the manager of the Fort Worth Cats, another Dodger minor league team in the Double A Texas League. Down in Fort Worth with the Cats I had a black clubhouse man, Alex Thomas. Alex had been with the club 15 years before I got there. He was a Cats team fixture. I hadn't been managing Fort Worth for a month when my brother Walter came to visit me. When Walt walked in the clubhouse I immediately introduced him to Alex, and it was only after my brother backed up a couple of steps that I realized he didn't want to shake hands with a black man. It left me dumbfounded.

That's how much Jackie affected me. Just two years after meeting him, I couldn't believe any white man wouldn't want to shake hands with a black man.

Of course, Jackie went on to have a long and great career with the Dodgers. We stayed in touch. Then in 1956 I was back in the major leagues as the manager of the Pittsburgh Pirates, and we had a below-average team which eventually finished dead last in the National League. On the last day of the season we played a doubleheader against the Dodgers, who had to win both games to beat Milwaukee out for the pennant. As much as I loved the Dodgers, I did everything I could to beat them twice, and we came pretty close to doing it. I recall the Dodgers won both games by a single run. And after the last out of the second game, Jackie made a point of coming over to the Pirate clubhouse to tell me he'd never seen a manager do any better than I had that day. It meant so much to me, coming from him. Jackie was not a man to give compliments out too easily.

In 1957 Jackie was at the end of the line, and the Dodgers traded him to the New York Giants. Jackie refused to go. He retired right there rather than go play for another team.

And that was just like him, even after his years with the Dodgers he wouldn't do something like let them trade him if he didn't want to go. So he retired and went to work for Chock Full O'Nuts, a big company, and did very well there.

Jackie did a hell of a lot of work for the NAACP after his retirement. He never gave up the good fight. I'd run into him at airports or at sports dinners and we'd visit and he'd tell me how he was working to eliminate this or that racial injustice. I was always delighted to break bread with him. He was a very intelligent, interesting man.

Irony of ironies, I went with Jackie to Mr. Rickey's funeral in St. Louis in 1963. Jackie and I sat together in a pew. Somehow I think Mr. Rickey, wherever he was, got a big kick out of that.

I wasn't surprised some years ago when Jackie died. The last few times I saw him I could tell he was aging, and not aging well. He had diabetes, for one thing, and I think maybe that fire burning in him was so hot and strong it just burned him out a little early. I didn't attend his funeral. I watched it on television, and saw my friend Howard Cosell go right up on the church steps and ask Rachel Robinson for an interview. I like Howard, but I thought that was too much. But I'll tell you this, the last time I saw Jackie alive was at an airport, and he was close to the end. He was so sick, but he still walked standing up straight, his eyes looking right ahead, ready to take on anybody or anything he had to. He was such a great man.

I always say that of all the people I've known in baseball, I respect Branch Rickey the most. Oh, I had great admiration for Leo Durocher and Whitlow Wyatt and many more, but above all there was Mr. Rickey. I'd have to put Jackie up there on top with him. Mr. Rickey was a genius, and Jackie Robinson is the best proof of that genius. Thanks to the two of them, I was able to overcome my racial prejudice.

That lesson is just one of many I've learned in my nearly seven decades in baseball. My days with the Dodgers and Mr. Rickey and Jackie are among the highlights, but it all got started in Birmingham, Alabama, where I was just one of millions of kids who grew up thinking baseball was the surest way to a better life.

B	E	T	W	E	E	N
I	N	N	I	N	G	S

AL GIONFRIDDO: I was traded from Pittsburgh to Brooklyn during Jackie Robinson's first season with the Dodgers. Bobby Bragan wasn't the only man against Jackie. My locker and Jackie's were side by side. Jackie and I had a few conversations where he'd name to me who he thought was with him on the club and who was against him. I won't say who he named. Oh, it was the Southern boys. Dixie, Bobby, some others.

HARRY ORNEST: Branch Rickey had planned and orchestrated the whole thing from Day One. Rickey told me that he deliberately had the Dodgers hold spring training in Cuba the year Jackie joined the club, because if they'd done that in the South, in Florida or someplace where other clubs had spring training, the pressure on Jackie would have been too much. But in Cuba where half the population was black, well, Jackie didn't draw as much notice while he was being worked onto the team.

Of course, Branch Rickey was well aware that he couldn't control how Jackie's new teammates would react, or what players on opposing teams might do once the regular season started. But at least it was possible to make spring training a little easier for Jackie by holding it in Cuba.

Once the season started, Jackie was really going to have to make it on his own.

BUZZIE BAVASI: Mr. Rickey didn't choose Havana just for Jackie. Keep in mind the Dodgers didn't have anywhere specific to train. We were building Vero Beach but it wasn't ready until 1948. Havana made a very lucrative offer to have the Dodgers hold spring training there. So call the choice of Havana a decision made on behalf of Jackie and economics both.

RALPH BRANCA: The way I remember Jackie Robinson joining the club is that it was a matter of individuals. The guys from the South had their ways, their mores and morals. They did with Jackie what they did at home. Guys from up North who'd played with blacks and lived with them had no problem.

Once Jackie established himself as a premier player he earned the Southerners' respect. Some of the other teams in the league rode him unmercifully. He got more than a double dose of abuse from them. But listen, in those days all rookies, especially the ones with the reputations for being pretty good, they all got it.

BOBBY THOMSON: Hell, as far as I was concerned (Jackie Robinson joining the Dodgers) wasn't even an item. I came up at the same time, I played in the same minor league he played in. He was with Montreal in '46 and I was with the Jersey City Giants. So in his first major league game, here he was—this was history, I guess—but hell, to me it was Thomson playing in the major leagues with 25,000 people in the stands. I was playing center field for the Giants. Somebody hit a ball to right center and I couldn't get my damn legs to move to get the ball because I was so nervous.

With Jackie there were some little things I heard secondhand. Like Jackie would swing and throw his bat. Or he'd swing it and bang Walker Cooper, our catcher, back there, swing so he'd catch Cooper on the shins with his bat. Cooper said to him, "Next time you do that, you know what I'll do with that bat." And Jackie hollered to the umpire, "He can't say something like that to me!" Sure.

On the other hand, Herman Franks, an older guy, was coaching for us at third, and Jackie might be playing third. Sometimes they'd get into words. Jackie came on more positive with Herman Franks than he did with Walker Cooper.

DUKE SNIDER: Don't ever believe Jackie was the one who started any trouble. I saw guys from opposing teams trying deliberately not to step on first base, but to step on Jackie and spike him instead. I won't say who—it's not important, and some of them are still alive. The whole thing is, Jackie learned to get off the bag kinda quick after he caught the ball.

STAN MUSIAL: When Jackie came up there was a story in a New York newspaper that the Cardinals would boycott our games with the Dodgers if Robinson came on the field for them. That really wasn't true. We hadn't had a team meeting or anything. We were really the team of the South, got a lot of our support from Georgia and Mississippi and Alabama, but there was nothing official organized. What did happen involving me was that a lot of the guys on our team knew I had played against Robinson. After the '46 season I'd played on a team of major leaguers who'd gone to California and played some games against Satchel Paige's barnstormers. Robinson played for Paige. Hell, I told the guys Robinson did everything stiff-armed; he swung the bat stiff-armed, chopped at the ball, fielded everything with his arms stiff. I wasn't impressed. I said, "He's nothing we're going to have to worry about. There's nothing to him." Think that tells why no team ever asked me to be a scout? Sure, we got on Jackie. We got on every rookie. Why the hell wouldn't we? I guess he took more but I thought we just rode him like we rode all the other new ones.

GIONFRIDDO: Jackie took so much from other teams he needed all the support from his teammates he could get. Why, Ben Chapman, the manager of the Phillies, flat advised his pitchers to throw at Jackie and told his players to call Jackie names.

SNIDER: When Jackie joined the Dodgers in '47 I was only a rookie, and in those days rookies stayed to the side and kept their mouths shut, which is what I did. So I never got directly involved with a lot that year involving Jackie, but I saw everything. What I remember most is Pee Wee Reese, a great man. Once on the field in Philadelphia Ben Chapman and some of the other Phillies were really riding Jackie, screaming at the other Dodgers to get up and let Jackie have their seats on the bench and worse things, much worse. Right there in front of everybody, Pee Wee went over to Jackie and put his arm around his shoulder. That was a great gesture, especially since Pee Wee himself was from the South and everybody on both teams knew it.

DICK WILLIAMS: I know from experience the Dodger veterans could be rough on any rookie. Some of them treated you like shit for the hell of it. Carl Furillo was like that. Later on he was my friend, but Carl just said 'way too many things that he shouldn't have. He had a big mouth.

ROY CAMPANELLA: I almost feel sorry for those people who tried to humble Jackie. Jackie was a man who would not be humbled. He burned like a fire, always.

THOMSON: As Jackie stayed in the league and did such a great job, he handed out more than he received. I'm sure it must have been tough for him. I don't know what he went through. But the Jackie Robinson thing, he was so good, but he was like any other Dodger. I'd say Gil Hodges was the only guy on that team universally admired and respected for the type person he was. Jackie was so quick, but he was a cocky guy. He wasn't overly modest.

JOE DIMAGGIO: We all learned from his first year in the major leagues that Jackie Robinson was a hard player, no doubt. I recall a specific incident in the World Series. Robby was on first base and the next Brooklyn batter hit a ball to our second baseman, who relayed it to Phil Rizzuto for the start of what everyone else would have assumed was an automatic double play.

But Rizzuto was hit hard by Robby, knocked up in the air, in fact, and Rizzuto wasn't able to make the relay for the second out. The take-out slide was all fair, the umpire had nothing to say about it, but it was still a case of Robby doing something potentially injurious to our shortstop that other baserunners would not have done. So it almost started a melee; I remember telling people, "Let's just get back and play ball." And things settled down again. But that's the way Jackie Robinson played–hard.

SNIDER: Jackie was a thinker. Everything he did on the field was calculated to give him an edge. Pitchers always pitched him inside, especially in that first '47 season when everyone was brushing him back, trying to see if he'd scare. Well, Jackie used a bat with a real thick handle, an S100 model, so that when he got jammed he could still swing, get enough wood on the ball and muscle it into the outfield. Some poor pitcher'd try to knock Jackie down and the next thing he'd know Jackie had blooped a single into center and was laughing at him from first base. And then Jackie'd steal second.

GIONFRIDDO: I can tell you from being there that during that season Jackie proved he could be a big league player, that he was an asset to the club. By the way he played he helped us white boys to pull together with him, and eventually we really all did become like family.

BIRMINGHAM

I USED TO HEAR PEOPLE REFER TO BIRMINGHAM, Alabama, as "the Pitts-burgh of the South." There was a lot of iron ore around Birming-ham, a lot of coal mines. These products were the basis of the local economy. Kids who grew up in Birmingham and stayed there had a good chance of ending up in the mines or in the factories. I was born in Birmingham in October 1917, the fourth child and third son of George and Corinne Bragan. Eventually my folks had nine kids, seven boys and two girls. Big families were more common in those days, and I can't say growing up with so many brothers and sisters left me with bad memories. I loved being part of such a big group, though we all had to learn to share. My father had his own company, Bragan Brothers. He'd put in sidewalks, gutters, and curbstones for the city and private contractors. He also had a small tin shop and did roofing and heating systems. We were by no means rich, even by the standards of those days. I would say we were average or a little above, by which I mean we got those three square meals a day, sufficient clothes to wear to school and a little lunch money or a peanut-butter-and-jelly-sandwich to eat while we were there. Plenty of other kids we knew weren't nearly so lucky. I'm going to tell a little bit about life in Birmingham in the 19-teens and '20s and '30s, not so much out of nostalgia as to share the way life was back then. If you want to understand baseball, how it's been and how it's changed, you have to understand the times in which the game has been played. Today it's immensely popular, still the Great American Game, but back then it was really the only professional sport kids could hope for a career in. Football and basketball were essentially college sports, not something you could do for a living. So kids who loved being outdoors playing a game, who wanted to carry that activity into adulthood pretty much knew they'd be pro baseball players or nothing.

Up to a certain point in baseball history, most of the really great players came from working class backgrounds. Babe Ruth learned to play ball in a Baltimore orphanage. Joe DiMaggio's father was a fisherman. Stan Musial's people worked in the Pennsylvania coal mines. Ted Williams was raised by a widowed mother who took in laundry. Don't you suspect that when those four played baseball as kids they dreamed of the sport as a way to make money for them- selves and their families? And don't you suppose they practiced and played harder than kids from finer homes and better circumstances?

The generation into which I was born also was hit by the Depres- sion, the impact of which is being forgotten more and more. For people like my father working hard to support big families, it was sheer hell. I remember him pacing back and forth on the porch, doing this night after night. We kids got scared and asked Mom what was troubling George, which is what we called him.

My brother Lionel was two years younger than I and one of those kids who talked and acted like an adult early on in life. When Lionel was 12, we were all sitting around finishing supper when my father asked him a question, concluding, "What about it, old man?" Lionel coolly replied, "I guess it's true, George." Everybody laughed, and afterwards we always called our father by his first name. The cus- tom carried over to my mother as well; from then on, to all of us she was Corinne.

George worked much more than a 40-hour week. Mom ran the roost. We lived in a big two-story house with a red tin roof. We had what we called a "sleeping porch," a screened-in porch with some windows where we could fit two beds. We kids shared beds, of course. I always slept with my brother Walter, who was almost exactly one year older than I. I never did get my own room at home. Never thought about having one, actually.

George was light-complected with blue eyes, very soft-spoken. My mother was just the opposite. She was dark and liked to talk all the time. I took after her. She was quick-witted but could have a very sarcastic tongue. I remember one day a boy named Herman Harris came over to the house to play marbles with Walter and me. I guess we were 12 or 13 years old, but Herman weighed something like 160 pounds and he wasn't all that tall. Anyway, we played marbles and Herman was losing, so all of a sudden he grabbed all the marbles and started running. Walter grabbed a broom and hit him in the legs, and I guess we got all over him for awhile. His mother showed up five minutes later and said to my mother, "Your boys hurt my baby." "You mean your baby elephant," my mother shot right back.

We had a big back yard, the kind you can't usually get now the way houses are built right on top of one another. It was a fine yard. With so many boys we could always get a ball game going there, and there were also lots of trees—mulberry, pear, and peach trees. I remember the peach trees well, because that's where the switches came from my mother would use on any of her boys who got out of line. I got many a switching. I don't believe they did me any harm, and maybe they did some good.

It was such a different time from now—I wonder if younger people realize how much. Every morning my mother would get up and bake—from scratch, you understand—40 or 50 biscuits. She did this 365 days a year. I can still see my daddy cut those biscuits in half with his big knife, and then we'd pour syrup on the biscuits from a big gallon can. That was breakfast in those days, and it always tasted good. We never wasted food. One Sunday morning I remember going in the kitchen and finding a dead mouse floating in the syrup can. We threw out the mouse but not the syrup.

Every Monday morning my daddy put $35 on the table. That was for my mother to cover the week's living expenses. Everything she bought—food, clothes for the kids, whatever—would come from that $35. He didn't tell her how to spend it. It was understood her responsibility was to get good value for every penny. On Saturdays sometimes if business had been good he'd put another $20 on the table, saying it was "for Corinne." God, she kept going 24 hours a day. She was president of our school PTA and always busy with some project or another.

All of us kids had jobs, too. In those days it was more common for a boy, even in grade school, to have a part-time job than not. My older brother George was a wheelboy for a long time. He worked for a drug store. People would call in prescriptions and George would get on his bicycle and deliver them. When he got too old to do that, he passed on the job to Walter, who at that time then bequeathed me his paper route. We all knew Daddy's unspoken rule that if you worked for a man, if you took his money, then you worked as hard as you possibly could.

The money we earned wasn't much, a dollar or two, and unlike many other kids we didn't have to contribute our earnings to help support our family. Instead, we could enjoy treats. If we didn't earn much, the treats didn't cost much, either. A Coca-Cola—which, of course, we called Co'cola—was a nickel. At school, four fresh cinnamon buns were a nickel. You could eat a couple, share with a friend, and look like a big man.

Though there were so many of us, Papa was not any closer to one of us than another. Unlike Corinne—and me—George was very reserved. One of my nicest memories of him involves the movies. Theaters in downtown Birmingham would change features maybe three times a week. George loved the western heroes in movies of that era—Hoot Gibson, Tom Mix, and Buck Jones especially. So every week on Tuesday night two or three of us kids would put on our best sweaters and come to the dining room table where George and Corinne would be sitting. We'd stand there until George would say, "Who is it tonight?" "Hoot Gibson," we might say, and he'd immediately reply, "We're going." It only cost a dime apiece to get into the show. We had a four-cylinder Dodge and we'd climb in and drive to whatever theater had the cowboy movie that night. I also remember that one night a year there'd be "Pony Night" when some kid at the show would win a horse in a drawing. Every year on that night, Walter and I would get into a big argument about which one of us would ride the damn pony home if we won it, but we never came close.

Movies were a big part of my childhood, but nothing like base-ball. I got a catcher's mitt when I was 12 and probably got a very commonplace fielder's glove when I was 13 or 14. I think my first glove was supposed to be modeled after the real one of Bill Doak, a pitcher. Having the right glove was very important to youngsters back then. Baseball occupied my mind constantly. School would be out at three o'clock, and during the baseball season the Birming-ham Barons would often play afternoon games at Rick Wood Field, which was seven miles from the school building. Every time they were scheduled to play there on a spring weekday I'd leap up as soon as the final bell rang and head for the ballpark. I ran until I got too tired and would walk the rest of the way. I never really cared if the game was over by the time I finally got there, because the real thrill was waiting around to see professional ballplayers as they left the park. I remember their names and faces clearly: Hal Willet. Andy Moore. Guy Sturdy. Yam Yaryan, who weighed maybe 270 pounds. I looked at them and felt like I was looking at God.

I remember one special day hurrying to the ballpark and kicking something in the grass. I reached down and picked up a baseball, one that had been used in a real professional game and fouled out of play and lost. I never wanted to stop holding that baseball. I thought if I held it long enough some special kind of force would flow into my fingers and body and make me a good enough player to play some-day on a real field on a real professional team. Who knows? Maybe it worked.

Anyway, like most other boys in Birmingham I played baseball from the time I was big enough to pick one up. When I was 14, I remember playing on a city league team. A local drycleaner, M.J. Leonard, bought our uniforms for us. There was a sidewalk in front of his joint and sometimes he'd want me to take a ball and bounce it back to myself on a short hop. He'd tell passersby, "Bet me a half dollar this boy can't catch 25 in a row." It was easy for me, and from the time I started in organized games I was always one of the two or three best players on any of my teams. I could always catch the ball and throw the ball. I never could run very well.

By the way, lots of people ask me now if I think all the organized youth league teams and YMCA leagues and so forth are the best way for modern kids to learn baseball. I guess it's better, in these times, for kids to have a scheduled place to be with adults around to keep watch over them. But I think maybe there's too much pressure now, that it's almost too organized. Even when I played in city league, the best games were at home with my brothers and friends. We'd play until dark and argue who was safe or out, but the important thing was we played and played and played. In baseball there's no such thing as ever becoming perfect, but the more kids practice the better they'll get.

When I started at Phillips High School in Birmingham I was appalled that the school had no baseball team. After a year, I talked my mother into letting me live in Memphis with my uncle and aunt, Sam and Laura Pritchard. Then I was able to play baseball for Memphis Technical High School. I made the All-Memphis High School baseball all-star team as a sophomore, but then Phillips High back home resurrected baseball, so I moved back home even though after I got there the coaches at Phillips told me I was ineligible to play for their team.

For me and most kids then, baseball really was the only game in town. Basketball and football offered us more or less just college heroes. I really felt at home with a glove on one hand and a ball in the other. Even today, that's how you can usually tell the kids who have a chance to make it in the pros. They're the ones who always want to practice just a little bit more, the ones who'll play with the other kids until everybody else quits, and then stick around tossing the ball up into the air and catching it all by themselves. Lord, I remember how for hours and hours I'd play catch with myself by the stairsteps of our house, angling how I threw the ball so it might come back on a line one time and high in the air like a pop fly the next time.

And it was a big advantage to me to have six brothers. There was always somebody around to throw with, always just about enough for some kind of baseball game. Until city league age of 15 or 16, we didn't have organized youth leagues in which to play, nothing like that.

So we'd go play on Saturdays at North Haven City Park, and we'd use big rocks for bases. Sometimes when we got lucky we could play on a semi–pro diamond built for a company team by the North American Cast Iron Pipe Company.

There were never enough gloves, balls, and bats to go around. We shared what we had. When we'd change over between innings we'd just leave our gloves on the ground so the kids on the other teams playing the same positions could use them. I can even remember that, during summers, if I woke up and looked out the window in the mornings and it was raining I'd probably start to cry. Really. Playing baseball meant that much to me.

I'm sorry to say school didn't, and now I understand better the importance of all youngsters who want to play pro ball still getting a complete education. Oh, my high school grades were all right, though I usually got below average grades for conduct because I'd talk too much in class. I had no college plans as such.

During summers I was in high school, I played on a local semipro club. In 1936 we went to a tournament in Wichita, Kansas, that was eventually won by a team from Bismarck, North Dakota, featuring a pitcher named Satchel Paige. We refused to play that team, because we wouldn't get on the same field with black players.

Even then, Satchel was a wonder. During that tournament, I remember he'd call his outfield in to sit in the dugout and just play with a catcher and infielders. He was that good. God only knows what kinds of records he could have set if he'd been allowed to play in the major leagues for a full career instead of just a couple of seasons when he was already well into his 40s—if you believed him —or his 50s—if you believed the record book.

I was playing shortstop then, and during that tournament I made a play I still remember, one that made me think I could really play ball well enough to make it in the major leagues someday. It was a line drive I lost in the lights. I just reached up and it was in my glove, a fast play made both on instinct and knowing how to position myself properly. It was just one out in a game otherwise forgotten, but it made a big impression on me—and my glove. I never did it again.

My best asset as a player was how well I could throw. I think I owed some of that ability to my paper route. I had to throw hundreds of newspapers every afternoon. You had to feel sorry for the last four or five houses on my route, because riding my bike there always took me past a ballfield where kids would be playing. I'd stop and get into the ballgame, and the people in those last houses would call the paper to complain they weren't getting their afternoon paper delivered until after dark.

Nothing got in the way of playing baseball, nothing at all. Once my mother took me with her to Nashville for her father's funeral. I was eight then. We took a taxi from the railroad station to his house, and on that ride I saw a field two or three blocks away where boys were playing baseball. So the minute I got out of that taxi, I disappeared. They came looking for me to take me to the funeral and found me in the park on second base.

STAN MUSIAL: Hey, every boy who grew up in those days wanted to be a baseball player. It wasn't like today, when the good athletes can choose to play professional baseball or football or basketball or tennis. If we wanted to make our livings playing a game, it had to be baseball. So we all dreamed that dream, and nobody had an easy time making it come true.

WALTER BRAGAN: Robert and I were closest in age among the kids, so we were the closest friends. We never did quarrel, except one time about a pony given away at the show. On that occasion we had a knock-down-and-drag-out. We were fighting over who would ride the pony home, and our father suggested we win it first and fight about it after that. But we had a brawl over it.

Robert and I always got along. We would skate together, play baseball together, play football together. When we got older we would go to dances together, always double date together.

When Robert was supposed to start high school in Birmingham, we had an uncle who worked for the railroad in Memphis, and he got transferred. He wasn't going to be at home sometimes and my mother didn't want our aunt to be alone, so Robert had to move to

Memphis to live with them and take care of our aunt while our uncle was away. It tore us up, Robert and me. It liked to have killed me, having him gone. I believe he was two years getting back to live at home and to go to high school in Birmingham.

JIMMY BRAGAN: Bobby took after Momma. She was such an influence on us all. Papa was more laid back. George and Corinne Bragan gave their children good training. We learned right from wrong, and we attended Sunday school and church. I certainly think we had the dream way to grow up. And best of all, there were enough of us to always have a Bragan brothers baseball team!

PRO BALL

From the time I owned my first mitt, I was sure I'd be a major league ballplayer some day. That didn't make me very special. Almost every boy I knew in Birmingham had the same plan.

The first real sign I got that my dream might not be the pipe variety was when I was 15 or 16 playing amateur ball. One of the managers in the league was a fellow named Dukey Hamilton, who'd been in the majors himself. I don't remember which big league team he played for. But after one game he came up to me and told me I had a chance to make it to the big leagues if I kept working hard.

Then I recall very, very vividly playing a game in Birmingham the next year. I guess I was 16 then, in American Legion ball. The umpire behind the plate that day called me aside and said, "Bobby, if you'll leave whiskey and women alone you've got a chance to go to the big leagues." He made quite an impression. I never did have a drink.

In those days I was playing shortstop pretty much exclusively, and I was starting to gain a reputation at 22 as one who knew the game and who played hard and smart. This same umpire later told me, "Bobby, if you want to go to the majors you'll have to make it as a catcher. You don't run well enough to be a big league shortstop."

I was still young, and I thought I had the speed I needed to stay at short. And, eventually, I did make it to the Phillies as a shortstop. But after I got to Philadelphia I saw immediately I couldn't handle the ball the way Marty Marion of St. Louis could, or the way Pee Wee Reese of the Dodgers could. All those years before, that umpire had been right.

I hadn't planned to go to college. Most kids didn't back then. But when I graduated from high school I got a call from Billy Bancroft, who'd been an outstanding college player at Howard College in Birmingham. It's called Samford College now. Anyway, Billy, who had gone on to play for the Birmingham Barons of the Southern League, offered me a scholarship to play baseball at Howard, and I took it. It wasn't that I wanted some kind of fail-safe if I didn't make it professionally as a ballplayer, but even then we knew a young man with a college degree had some advantages other guys his age didn't. Not that I was a college student long. I did last one semester.

The summer before I started college I played semipro ball, and a man named Bill Morrell was my manager. After that summer season he got hired as manager of a minor league club in Panama City, Florida—Class D ball, as low in the professional ranks as you could get. Just as I was finishing my first semester, the fall semester, at Howard, Morrell called me long-distance and said if I wanted to play pro ball he had a job for me.

I left college right away, and my parents encouraged me to do it. With the chance to play major league baseball as a career, college just didn't appeal to me as much and my parents understood that. I signed with Panama City that winter. The contract paid me $65 a month. I thought I'd have to wait until spring training to get my hands on that money, and would have looked around for some kind of temporary work in Birmingham. But Morrell said, "Come on down now. We're just building our ballpark. You can help with the labor, and I'll pay you the $65 a month starting right away." So I went down, and that was really my first position as a professional baseball player—a painter!

These days I guess newlysigned young pros would think building the very stadium they'd later play in to be menial work. I sure didn't. Morrell had a couple other players there to help out, too. I remember once some pitcher and I fell off a scaffold and bounced about 10 feet when we hit the ground. But we were young. We loved every second, and mostly we loved being able to say we were pro ballplayers. I know I told everyone I met, and I did my best to meet lots and lots of people.

To get to Panama City, I took the Greyhound bus from Birmingham. I think the ticket cost $15. I didn't have much luggage, just the pants and shirt I was wearing and a suitcase big enough to hold two or three pairs of underwear, an extra pair of pants, three shirts and some socks. I also had a little satchel that never left my sight to hold my glove and bat. One of each, with no money for new ones. Anyway, I took an early bus that left Birmingham at 6 A.M. and I got to Panama City that night. Eighteen years old, I was. Felt like a man, probably looked like a little boy.

In Panama City I did what the rest of the players did and lived in a boardinghouse. I think the best word for it would be "unfancy," if there is such a word. It was just a set of rooms on the second story over a store. A dozen of us lived in the five or six rooms, everybody 18 or 19 or possibly 20, though if you were still in Class D ball at age 20 you likely weren't a prospect for the majors.

We had to go out to eat, and we didn't dine on health food. We'd each get a hamburger or hot dog, something that cost just a quarter. Real dinners were out of the question financially. I'd daydream about my mother's home cooking. And my room made me miss home some, too. It was plain vanilla, with a narrow old-fashioned bed to sleep in. There was a little box at the bottom of the bed for me to put my clothes in, and a community bathroom at the end of the hall. It was hot, very hot, but if we opened the windows the mosquitoes came in to dine.

For the first six weeks I was in Panama City we were waiting for spring training to begin. There were just two or three other players helping Bill Morrell and me work on the park. One was Carl Stinson, a lefthanded pitcher who could throw a wicked curveball, which made his fastball all that much more deceptive. We called him Red because of his hair. He'd gone to the same school in Birmingham as I had, a couple of years ahead of me. He took great delight in challenging other boys to stand up against the school wall and catch a ball he'd throw at him. Sometimes when he missed the kid you'd hear the ball pop against the brick wall and think, "I'm glad he wasn't throwing at me." Except sometimes he did pick me, and even though I didn't do very well at least he respected me because I was game enough then to try to catch him.

In my first pro season at Panama City we didn't win the league championship, but we held our own. I could field and throw as well as most other players I competed against, and I hit decently. The big star of the league that year was a pitcher named Virgil Trucks, who played for Andalusia. Later on he went to the majors and pitched two no-hitters. We're still friends. But that year if there was one player in our league everyone knew would make it to the big leagues, he'd be the fellow.

Bill Morrell was a very sensitive man, as I recall. He never cussed. When we'd go on road trips, Mrs. Morrell would ride on the bus with us. That's the only time I ever recall a manager bringing his wife on a team bus. Bill was a graduate of Tufts College, and having that degree gave him a well-deserved reputation with his players for being smart. And he'd pitched a bit for the New York Giants, and we looked up to anybody who'd made it all the way to where the rest of us hoped to be going.

It was a solid season for me. I would bat sixth or seventh in the lineup. Maybe I wasn't a big star on offense, but I was durable. I played every game. Remember, there were hundreds of minor league teams then and just 16 major league clubs. Competition was always on your mind. If you were too hurt to play, somebody on some team somewhere who played the same positon might be getting four hits and making spectacular fielding plays and moving up the ladder ahead of you. It was a risk I wasn't going to take. We had 140 games to the season—the majors played a 154-game schedule.

In Panama City, a guy named Charlie Saliba was a big supporter of our team. He owned a pool hall, and I was able to get in with him sufficiently so he'd let me work concessions there, getting customers drinks and snacks. This was a way for me to make a few extra dollars to go with the $65 a month from the ball club. I saved every cent I could because I knew in the off-season I'd go back to living at home, and I wanted to bring back some money to contribute for my keep.

At the end of the season I proudly gave my father $150, or maybe $175.

It was also time at the end of the season to get a better idea of how I stood as far as having a chance to make it to the big leagues. H.L. Suddeth, a real estate man, owned the Panama City team and it was an independent club—not affiliated with any of the major league teams. I knew if I was really a prospect he'd be trying to sell my contract after the season to another team a little farther up the minor league ladder. I felt I had the statistics necessary for that to happen. Off the top of my head—exact records weren't always kept, so you mentally kept your own—I probably hit four or five home runs, batted .275 – .280. I was fielding good, throwing good. I didn't steal many bases. I was beginning to realize that damn umpire was right about my lack of speed. But I was a solid player otherwise.

After the season was over, my contract was in fact sold by Suddeth to the Pensacola Flyers, a team in the Class B Southeastern League. It was a big step up, but Pensacola was also an independent team. This meant I still wasn't under any kind of contract binding me to a major league team. I got notified about being sold through the mail, in a letter from either Suddeth or Morrell, I don't remember. I guess the Bobby Bragan sales price was $500, but the big number for me was the $110 I'd get a month—a huge raise, the way I looked at it.

I spent the winter at home, and of course I had a winter job. I worked for Birmingham's "Railway Express," which was kind of like UPS today. Railway Express would get a package and put it on a truck and deliver it. I'd spend the day sitting around with the other drivers and wait until they called my name. Then I'd get the packages and drive three or four hours until the stuff was all delivered. I spent a lot of hours sitting and a lot of hours driving, which gave me plenty of time to think about what it would be like in the big leagues. I thought about that all the time.

I ended up working three off-seasons for Railway Express. My Uncle Sam was on what we used to call the Frisco Railroad, making the trip from Birmingham to Memphis and back. I think he spoke to the Railway Express people about giving me the job. I gave everything I made back to my parents to help out with household expenses. I made the going minimum wage back then, though there wasn't yet a law to regulate how much it had to be. As I recall, I worked for 90 cents an hour.

As soon as time for spring training came, I was thrilled to head for Pensacola. The Flyers played some road games in Alabama, and my parents could make the trip to Gadsden or Anniston.

And we had some great players at Pensacola. Three of us ended up going to the big leagues and lasting a good while, and some others at least got a look at the majors. There was Big John Hutchings, a pitcher who went on to play for Cincinnati. Phil Seghi, someday to be a major league executive, played third base. I played shortstop. Our center fielder was a guy named Harry Walker, whom I'll discuss in detail later.

In Pensacola, like the other players, I lived in a place called Ma Falker's Boardinghouse. It was better than where I'd lived in Panama City, mostly because you got to eat at this one. In Panama City I paid $3 a week for a place to sleep. At Ma Falker's I paid $1 a day, and we were fed very well, homestyle meals with all of us sitting around the dining room tables and passing the bowls of food. Ma Falker—all the ballplayers loved her. I guess we would have loved anybody who fed us nice meals.

Whatever time we had to spend at the boardinghouse wasn't spent listening to the radio, and television wasn't around yet. There was another diversion. One of our players was named Bubba Floyd, who went on to play a little for the Detroit Tigers. I would watch him roll dice on his bed, gambling with the other guys. I myself played very little—I was timid in that area, and I wanted to save all the money I could for my parents. Most of the other players weren't so cautious, and chose to take Floyd on. All of 'em liked to play, but I'd guess only half of them knew what they were doing, if that many. Nobody had much money so they really weren't playing for any big stakes. The big winner might get $10 or $12. More often than not, that was Bubba Floyd. Nobody ever accused him then, and I can't say for sure if he did, but now I wouldn't be surprised if he didn't cheat a lot. He had to, to win all the time.

So far as on the field was concerned, I was playing for another good team. Wally Dashiell was the Pensacola manager, and I've always said he was the best I played for except Leo Durocher. And

Leo was in a class by himself, so it's really not fair to compare anyone else to him. Dashiell wasn't the same kind of father figure to his payers Bill Morrell had been. He was tough on us, but we all felt he was fair. Even if he hadn't been, none of us would have complained to him or about him. If we were to move up further in the pros, he'd be the one to recommend us. Remember, there was all kinds of competition all over the country with thousands of minor league players trying to win a handful of major league jobs. You did *not* cross your manager if you wanted to have a chance.

For me, Class B ball was a huge step up in every way. Today, no minor league player would accept having to perform under the kind of conditions we did. It was a spartan life. There was one goal for the players—to make it to the majors. There was one goal for the team management—not to spend too much money.

On road trips we went on a bus. An old bus. A very old, rickety bus. There were days we pushed that bus farther than we rode in it. The bus would stall or get stuck and everyone would jump out and push. Nobody complained about having to do this. It was just part of minor league life.

We had two uniforms, a white one for home games and a gray one for games on the road. They got dirty fast—we dove for every ball and slid every chance we got to prove we were willing to hustle. The ballclub cleaned the basic uniforms, the jerseys and pants. We ballplayers had to wash our own sweatshirts, sliding pads, jock-straps, socks, and sanitaries. As you might imagine, we didn't wash clothes as frequently as our mothers might have had they been there with us. If a fan yelled, "Your team stinks," he might not have been referring to our play on the field.

There was someone we referred to as the clubhouse "boy," a man named Paul Raibon. He was, as you might expect, black. A Negro, people might have called him then. More likely we referred to him as colored, or, not thinking to be offensive, as a nigger. He doubled as clubhouse boy and bus driver. I have no idea what salary they paid him, but it couldn't have been very much. Anyone who depended on us impoverished players for tips had to be just a step out of the poorhouse.

The clubhouse in Pensacola was in no way a palace. The player stalls were 18 inches wide and separated by chicken wire. Occasionally two of us would have to share a stall. You hung your street clothes on nails pounded into the wall. One stool was shoved into each stall. You wanted to get to the park early so you could have the stool to sit on instead of the guy you might be sharing with. And after games there were two shower heads to go around among 20 ballplayers. Many times you wouldn't want to wait for your turn, so you'd go back to the boardinghouse without showering.

And every second of it was fun for all of us. We loved it. We thought nothing about the difficulties and all the time about how lucky we were to be playing baseball and through some miracle getting paid for it. All the players felt this way. After the games, we'd congregate in a restaurant in downtown Pensacola called the B&B. The place stayed open until 1 A.M. and we'd each get a sandwich or a hot dog and Coca-Cola and visit a bit. In the minors then, your friends were your teammates. We were all about the same age, 19 or 20, except a few older players kept around by management to be good influences on us younger ones.

In that first season of 1938 I played pretty well. I know I hit close to .300, maybe .297. I still was as good as anyone I played against when it came to throwing and fielding. I truly believed I was going to make it to the major leagues, which again was the same thing all the rest of my teammates believed about themselves, except the older guys who knew they had absolutely no chance but were grateful to be playing ball instead of working in a factory somewhere.

Though Pensacola was an independent minor league club, Wally Dashiell did have this working agreement with the Philadelphia Phillies. The Phillies would pay Pensacola $4,500 a season, which you can believe paid for the salaries of several players. Then at the end of each season the Phillies could select one player from the Pensacola roster. Philadelphia didn't have to take a player automatically—the $4,500 was for the right to get first pick if there was somebody especially worth choosing. After, 1938 season they picked somebody else. I made up my mind that after the 1939 was over the Phillies would be picking Bobby Bragan.

B	E	T	W	E	E	N
I	N	N	I	N	G	S

LOU BROCK: The minor league system from Bobby Bragan's day is just not there anymore, really. Now colleges are the ones producing the players for the majors. Players aren't willing to spend years in the minors just playing baseball. Instead, they get intensified work with videotapes and diagrams and lectures, usually from a college coach. Well, baseball is maybe reliant on a college training ground now, but the fundamentals are just not taught well.

LEW BURDETTE: Nowadays teams draft some kid number one out of college and send him straight to the big leagues. Hell, I scouted for a season in 70-something, scouted college teams. Maybe it's just another opinion, but that whole year I never saw any college coach who even knew how to hit infield grounders the right way.

BROCK: All those years ago, through the '50s and into the early '60s, you knew going in it took a long time to get to the major leagues. Being a pro player at all was the first big reward. That provided the satisfaction during the years of apprenticeship in the minors. It began to change in the '60s with expansion. You got up faster. Me, I ended up only being in the minors for a year. I didn't even know how to flip sunglasses when I got to the major leagues. Somebody had to take me and show me.

JOE DIMAGGIO: No matter how glittering your record in the minor leagues might have been, there was the sense you had to wait your turn. I was sold by the San Francisco Seals of the Pacific Coast League to the New York Yankees in 1934, but with the understanding I would play with the Seals through 1935. Time for furthering my minor league experience was built right into that deal.

BURDETTE: When I played, players knew the game better and it wasn't any damn accident. I spent five, six years in the minors just learning the game. By the time we got to the majors hitters had had about 2,000 professional at-bats and pitchers had thrown 1,000 innings. We knew what to do on the field. Major league fans wouldn't have accepted anything less. Neither would the owners, the ones who signed the paychecks.

ALMOST THERE

I WASN'T REALLY SORRY TO SPEND A SECOND SEASON AT PENSACOLA. I knew I was playing well, and with another good year I'd be the likely player to be signed by the Phillies. Besides, both the town and the team were as much fun as any young guy could handle.

When I think about the 1939 season, what I remember most is how all of us would go to the beach during the day, swimming and getting suntans and having a great time. Then we'd go to the ballpark at night and beat some other team decisively. Because we all spent so much time together and became each other's best friends, we had real team chemistry. You always knew what the other guys were thinking on the field, what they'd do in each situation. I'm convinced major league teams would play better today if management insisted that players spend more time together off the ballfield as well as on it.

Some of the memories probably seem a little cruel today, but it was a tougher world back then. Cruder, if you want to call it that. I'd describe it as more direct.

One of our players was a guy named Johnny Roberts. He'd been a star college football player at Alabama, but he was trying to play pro baseball. One time our team was on our way back home after a night game. Most of us lived at Ma Falker's, but a few of the older guys stayed at a place called the San Carlos Hotel. Anyway, we were on the team bus and Paul Raibon was driving. It was 1 A.M. and we were getting back from a night game in Jackson, Mississippi. Roberts hollered at Raibon to take the rest of us back to Ma Falker's first so the guys who didn't live at the San Carlos wouldn't have to walk an extra mile home. But Raibon was pretty tired himself, I guess, and just drove everybody to the San Carlos. We all got out of the bus and walked into the San Carlos lobby, where Roberts didn't say anything. He just reached back and laid a good one on Raibon's chin, and I can still see Raibon sliding across the floor of the lobby. The rest of us walked to Ma Falker's, and the next afternoon in the clubhouse nobody said anything about the incident, including the guy who did the hitting and the guy who was hit. It was a minor incident, part of everyday life, and quickly forgotten.

It was a playful time, too, a chance for us to be a little silly. Big John Hutchings, our best pitcher, weighed a good 265 pounds. He was as big as a hog but he was still a great dancer. He could do the most popular dance steps of the day—the lindy hop and the jitterbug. Hutchings was married to this little tiny girl named Ann; I remember she had coal black hair. Anyway, Manager Wally Dashiell got a great big bang once a month or so out of asking Hutchings and his wife to dance the jitterbug on the roof of our dugout between innings. The fans loved it, and some of them would come to games just in hopes that Hutchings and his wife would be dancing that night.

Dashiell loved anything that brought in a few extra bucks. He was team owner besides team manager, and he cut every corner and made every two-bit deal he could. I've mentioned the team bus, which probably was the worst team bus in the history of organized baseball. Nothing about that bus was first-class, or even 10th-class, except for a picture of Pensacola Beach on both sides of it. When the bus would stall and we'd have to jump out and push it, Dashiell didn't want anybody blocking the pictures of the beach. We finally figured out he was getting some money for the advertising, probably from the Pensacola Chamber of Commerce or somesuch. Dashiell was a nice man, a brilliant baseball guy, but he'd do anything for an extra buck—as I'd find out at the end of the season.

But we certainly had all sorts of characters playing for the team. One little righthanded pitcher was named Charlie Cuellar. Charlie's English wasn't so good, but he tried hard to communicate. Unfortunately for him, his pitching was at the same level as his English. He got pounded nearly every time he walked out on the mound. After one particularly bad outing he joined some of the rest of us at the B&B after the game, where we all ordered coffee and got the early newspapers to read the sports section. And there it was on the front sports page—"Cuellar Sold to Greenwood," a Class C team in Mississippi. Nobody wanted to get moved down a notch, and Cuellar was ready to cry. ""When did I went to Greenwood?" he hollered, and we tried not to laugh at his grammar because we all worried in the backs of our minds that we might be the next ones moving down the minor league ladder.

And there was Harry "The Hat" Walker. He was one of the greatest hitters I've ever seen, or that anyone's ever seen. Harry was on loan to Pensacola from the St. Louis Cardinals, so he was really one up on the rest of us. Teams would sometimes lend minor league players around to be sure all their top prospects got to play every day. Harry was a treat to watch when he was hitting. I'd say he was a lot like Rafael Palmeiro of today's Texas Rangers, a guy who sprayed his hits from foul line to foul line. Palmeiro does have a little more power. But he and Harry both could hit a given pitch to any part of the field. That's a tremendous advantage to a batter, and pitchers can't ever find one pitch or location the guy can't handle.

Harry could do one other thing as well as hit—talk. Lord, the man could talk. Later on in his career he was a National League batting champion and then manager of the Pittsburgh Pirates and Houston Astros. But people forget that. What they remember is how much Harry talked about hitting or fielding or anything else whether it had to do with baseball or not.

I think the first day he was with us in Pensacola he was hit in the throat with a ball and rushed to the hospital. The doctors said the injury would affect his speech forever, and it did—but only the quality, not the quantity. Harry's voice has been rather hoarse since, but never silent. When you had a conversation with Harry, you started by saying "Hello," and then left the rest to him.

But Harry Walker was no clown. God, I remember how hard he worked to improve as a hitter. There was no doubt he already was good enough to play in the majors, but Harry wanted to be absolutely the best hitter possible. So he'd spend hours in the batting cage every day before games, practicing hitting in various game situations. He'd spend all one day just working on hitting pitches to the right side of the infield so that during games he'd always be able to move a runner from second to third if there were no outs. He'd bunt 500 times in a row until he felt he'd gotten the roll just right. He hit sometimes until his hands bled.

We all did. There were 45 minor leagues in operation then, not like today at all. If you didn't produce for your team, you were gone. Minor league managers wouldn't forgive you for ignoring ways to help the team—not bunting when ordered to, not giving yourself up as a hitter by moving the runner over with a grounder—with the idea of improving personal statistics. Do that once too often for Wally Dashiell in Pensacola, and if you were lucky you might get another roster spot in Gadsden, a step down. I always reminded myself that if there were 45 minor leagues, maybe of eight teams each, that meant 360 other shortstops were trying to get to the major leagues ahead of me. To beat those kinds of odds, you committed yourself to playing your best on every play in every game.

As a result, the fans of minor league teams always saw hard-played games even if the overall quality wasn't quite up to big league level. You really developed close, friendly relationships with the folks who'd come out every night to see your home games. One of my first big thrills in baseball involved a young family who lived not too far from Legion Park, home of the Pensacola Flyers. This husband and wife came by the ballpark one day and asked if I'd come home with them to see their kid. I went over—they had this little place, nothing fancy—and there was a little boy maybe two years old. "Say something," his mom told him, and he said, "Bobby Bragan." Those were his first words. It was great for my ego.

Our second baseman with the Flyers was named Norris Sims. He was a little guy, a singles hitter who could play good defense like Ozzie Guillen of today's White Sox. Anyway, like lots of the players Norris found a girlfriend in Pensacola. The young single girls liked to meet the ballplayers, and vice versa. I think the girls hoped to marry players who'd make it to the big leagues. It was their way of moving to the big city just like playing ball hopefully would be ours.

Anyway, Norris's girlfriend was the daughter of the Pensacola haberdasher. All men wore hats in those days, so this guy made a pretty good living. He also liked to do some pretty heavy drinking, and every time we had a home game he'd show up to cheer for Sims. Dad had himself a loud voice, and he'd sit in the stands and get a few beers in him. Then when he was soused enough he'd start to cheer for Norris, and he'd always holler the same thing: "Get two, Norrie." He yelled this even if the other team didn't have anybody on base. It got to be the biggest joke of the season for the players. If you called up Harry Walker today, and hollered into the phone, "Get two, Norrie," he'd know exactly what you were talking about. And he'd laugh again.

Those are the sorts of things you remember.

This is probably the right time to confess I was noticing the girls myself. In Pensacola there was one girl in particular I liked named Toody Crim. I had several dates with her, and between the 1938 and 1939 seasons I corresponded with her when I was home in Birmingham for the winter. Her letters were nice and I ended up inviting her to visit Birmingham and meet my family. This was serious business in those days.

When she got to Birmingham, naturally Toody didn't stay with us at our house. That would not have been considered correct behavior for a nice girl. On the Sunday during her visit I was supposed to pick Toody up at her hotel to take her to Sunday school and church. When she met me, she was wearing this coat with a fur collar. It looked like a rat was wrapped around her neck. I was ashamed of her then, to tell you the truth. I had no desire to escort her to church while she was wearing that particular garment. Right there I lost all the desire to spend time with Toody. The romance, if you'd call it that, ended.

Well, when I got back to Pensacola and baseball I had the kind of strong 1939 season I'd hoped for, and as it ended I felt pretty certain the Phillies would buy my contract. This wasn't just guesswork. During the season the Phillies sent a scout, Patsy O'Rourke, to look

Pensacola over a few times, and from his conversations with me and from the questions he asked other players about me—trying to get an idea about my character and work habits, I guess—I knew they were interested.

If the sale was going to happen, I knew it would take place at the winter baseball meetings. They were held that year in Atlanta, not that far from where I was spending the winter in Birmingham, so I went to Georgia and looked around until I found Wally Dashiell. Harry Walker was with me, hoping to hear he was going to move up to the Cardinals.

Anyway, Dashiell said very matter-of-factly he'd sold my contract to the Phillies, who would be in touch with me to let me know when I should report to spring training. Then Dashiell handed me a check for $100. See, Dashiell had made an agreement with me that I'd get 20 percent of whatever my contract sold for, so I figured the Phillies had paid $500 for me, which was low even then.

I was thrilled, of course, to have a chance to go to the majors, but the $100 figure kind of stuck in my craw. After I calmed down I remembered that the Phillies paid $4,500 a season to Pensacola for the right to choose one player at the end of the year, and even though my math wasn't the best I knew 20 percent of $4,500 was a lot more than $100.

It wasn't until sometime in the 1940 season when the Phillies were playing the Cubs in Chicago that I got the money that was coming to me. I was walking down Michigan Boulevard with Benny Warren, a Phillie catcher, and he said, "Hey, Judge Landis has his office in this building." Judge Kenesaw Mountain Landis was baseball commissioner in those days, and his word was law. You read today about owners telling the commissioner of baseball what to do. It was the other way around back then.

If I'd really thought about it I believe I wouldn't have had the nerve, but instead I just walked right into Landis's office and said, "Judge, I want to talk to you about something." I told him about Dashiell and our agreement for me to get 20 percent of what my contract brought him, and he listened and seemed very amused. He told me he'd look into it.

The next thing I knew, I got a phone call from Dashiell. He yelled, "Bobby, what the hell have you done now? Leslie O'Connor from the commissioner's office has come to my office, taken my keys and locked me out while he looks through all my correspondence. Jesus, what have you done to me?"

And soon after I got a check for $800 with a note from Judge Landis, saying he'd found evidence I'd been promised 20 percent of the contract sales price, and that $800 plus the $100 Dashiell had originally given me made up the right amount.

Now, I don't consider Dashiell a bad man or a real crook. I learned a lot of baseball from him, and he was just one to cut every corner financially that he could. I had to deal with much worse managers and owners over the next several decades. But I'm also glad Judge Landis got the rest of my money for me.

I went back to Birmingham for the rest of the winter. George and Corinne were proud of me, as were all my brothers and sisters. It was a big thing to have someone in the family with a chance to play in the major leagues.

And it was still just a chance. Sure, the Phillies had purchased my contract, but undoubtedly they'd purchased the contracts of lots of other minor leaguers, too. Going to spring training with the team only meant I'd have a chance to make the Philadelphia roster. If I didn't, I might find myself back in Pensacola or somewhere else in the bush leagues.

In 1940, all the best professional athletes in America were baseball players. Professional football and basketball were hardly thought of. Realistically, I knew I had physical limitations other better athletes didn't. And I really felt some pressure when I got word that winter that the Phillies would pay me $2,500 for the season if I made the team—big money back then. I had no dreams of making the Hall of Fame. I just wanted to put a big league uniform on and see what I could do, and make a good living besides.

So besides my fulltime winter job, every day I walked from my house in north Birmingham across the city to the south side, where there was this big statue called "Vulcan," emblematic of the steel industry that made up the city economy. The statue was tall and hollow, the same idea of the Statue of Liberty although on a lesser scale. And every day I would go to the staircase inside the statue and walk all the way up, then all the way down. Then I'd jog up, jog down. Run up, run down. I would do this for about two hours. Often Harry Walker, who also lived in Birmingham during the off-season, would come and work out with me, but Harry really didn't need to. He had strong legs already and could run fast. But me, my legs were heavy, built for slow movement.

To make it as a shortstop in the big leagues I would have to be quicker, and I enjoyed every sweaty step up and down that statue because I knew it was helping me get to the majors. If a rookie did that kind of thing today people would say he was crazy. *Sports Illustrated* would probably do an article about him. But in the winter of 1939–40 all I knew was lots of other would-be Phillie shortstops were getting in shape. I had nothing to take for granted.

RALPH BRANCA: Minor league success was in no way a guarantee of ever playing in the big leagues. Many guys against their will made careers out of playing in the high minors. This was a danger unless you were so obviously outstanding, a Snider or a Musial or a DiMaggio. The guys heading up the organizations thought having veteran players around on the Triple-A teams and lower ones was good for the young kids. If you played for an independent (minor league team) it was even tougher. You might know in your heart a big league club ought to pick up your contract, but nobody had an obligation to do it.

WHITEY HERZOG: My first year I hit .351 in D ball and the next year I went to C ball. No shortcuts then.

STAN MUSIAL: No matter how good you were, you waited. Harry Walker's a good example. Just hit the hell out of the ball for every minor league team he played on, and after every season he'd end up in the minors again. When he finally made it to the majors he won a batting title. And then there's Harry Brecheen, the Cat, just a great pitcher. But he must have been in Triple A for five years.

HERZOG: I remember in '52 Moose Skowren was player of the year for the Kansas City Blues, the Yankees' Triple-A club. Son of a bitch hit .338, had 140 RBIs and he didn't even go to the next spring training with the Yankees.

TOM LASORDA: It became clear after awhile I just wasn't going to break into the Brooklyn pitching rotation. We had 26 farm teams, Brooklyn was a great team, just an unbelievable club to crack into. God, think of the Hall of Famers from just a few seasons—Robinson, Campanella, Reese, Snider, that great manager Leo Durocher who ought to be in Cooperstown with them. And how does somebody like me replace Carl Erskine or Don Newcombe or Clem Labine or Johnny Podres? It couldn't be done. Not that I wasn't a hell of a pitcher in my own right. The way the level of competition is today, I'd pitch a lot of years and win a lot of games in the big leagues.

DUKE SNIDER: Tommy Lasorda said to me the other day that you'd hit .350 with St. Paul or Montreal and just hope to break camp the next year as one of the big club's 28 players. See, in those days the major league teams could leave spring training with 28 players and after a few weeks they had to reduce the roster to 25. So if there were too many better players ahead of you, the best you could hope for was to be the 26th, 27th, or 28th player for three weeks to at least be able to say you were a major leaguer for a little while. Once, Lasorda said, the Dodgers had to choose between him and Sandy Koufax for the 28th spot. "How could they choose Koufax instead of me?" Tommy said he asked at the time.

Listen, Lasorda is a great example of one of those guys who almost had enough talent but not quite. He'd win 18 for Montreal and know he was going back to Triple A the next season because the Brooklyn team just didn't have any room for him. It was hopeless. Bill Sharman and Gino Cimoli—guys waited and waited. Sharman's got some kind of record; he was the 28th man once and never did get to play before he got sent back down, but he did get run out of one major league game for yelling at the umpire. Sharman was the only guy who never officially got in a game but still got thrown out of one.

JOE DIMAGGIO: Though being in the minor leagues then was sometimes a drawn-out process, it could eventually prove beneficial.

In 1935, for instance, the extra season I had to wait to move from the Seals to the Yankees, my manager Lefty O'Doul gave me some very fine tips, a good amount of advice about playing in the major leagues and particularly about Yankee Stadium.

O'Doul said that to hit home runs in Yankee Stadium I'd have to hit the ball straight down either of the foul lines. Well, at that time I was a spray hitter in the sense I hit the ball to all parts of the park. But during this final season O'Doul had me, because he knew where I'd be playing in the major leagues, he taught me to be a pull hitter right there in the Pacific Coast League. This is why, in 1936, I could be a pull hitter when I joined the Yankees. As good minor league managers did in that time, O'Doul saw his specific purpose with me as the responsibility of teaching those particular skills necessary to what would be my eventual major league situation.

5

MAJOR LEAGUER

I REPORTED TO THE PHILLIES' SPRING TRAINING CAMP in Miami Beach, Florida, on March 6, 1940. Though I can't remember exactly, I probably got there by taking the bus from Birmingham. I sure didn't consider myself a big leaguer yet—the bus was plenty good enough for me, and a lot cheaper than buying myself a car and driving down to Miami Beach.

I knew, of course, that the Phillies were a last place team in the National League. Unlike the Dodgers and the Giants and the Cardinals, for instance, Philadelphia didn't have any tradition of fielding all-time great ballclubs. But I didn't give that a second thought. Don't make the mistake of thinking a last-place team in the National League of 1940 was a bad team with poor players. This was before the major leagues expanded so many times. There were just 16 major league teams, eight in the National League and eight in the American, with hundreds of minor league teams hustling to provide them with players. If you got to one of the big 16, you had to be pretty damned good to begin with.

I'm not saying that if the 1940 Philadelphia Phillies could some- how magically compete in 1992 we'd whip Oakland and Los Angeles and sweep the World Series in four straight games. But we'd be competitive, and we sure wouldn't finish last.

But that half-century ago I saw my spring training with the Phillies as a real opportunity to find out what I could do when competing against the very best baseball players. I was to learn later that the Phillies were in such a sad financial plight the owner, a man named Gerry Nugent, was forced at the end of every season to sell his one or two best players to other major league teams. He needed the money he got for them just to make Philadelphia team ends meet. Because of his sell-'em policy, the Phillies were never going to have a chance to develop a roster of star players from top to bottom and consistently compete against those teams who regularly contended for National League pennants.

Being the manager of such a team took a man with patience and the ability to get what he could from the players he did get to keep. The Phillies' skipper was Doc Prothro, whose son Tommy later became famous as a college football coach at UCLA and then in the NFL coaching the Rams and San Diego. Now, before coming to the Phillies Doc Prothro had managed a number of years at Memphis in the Southern League, so I knew of him by reputation. He was reputed to know baseball inside and out, and I was eager to learn as much as I could from him. All rookies back then felt that way, that they should learn as much as they could about baseball from the manager and his coaches. Later on when I became a manager myself I always felt my proper role should be teaching more than anything else. That's especially true in the minor leagues and when working with rookies and young players in the majors.

Prothro was a pudgy sort with very short arms. In his playing days he'd been a third baseman and shortstop for the Washington Senators, Cincinnati Redlegs, and Boston Red Sox. When I reported he told me he was happy to have me with the team and that I'd get a fair chance to make the club. It was all I could ask for.

I'd say the Phillies only had 50 or so players in their spring training camp, with maybe 35 having any real chance of making the regular season's 25-player roster. Other rookies that year included Danny Litwhiler, who became a good friend of mine, and Ike Pearson, a good college pitcher at Mississippi State. I looked at those guys and wondered if I was really good enough to make the club.

The Miami Beach facilities were fine. There was just one diamond, but at night we stayed at the Miami Beach Hotel, which was nice. Cy Johnson, a veteran pitcher, was my roommate. In those days most clubs usually roomed raw rookies with veterans, and the older guys were expected to take us under their wings, so to speak. Mostly what I remember about Johnson is that he and Walter "Boom-Boom" Beck played pinochle all the time.

Beck was a star, and Johnson had played in the majors for 17 years. They knew their way around. I looked up to and respected them both. I was lucky they took an interest in me and gave me advice on how to act the part of a major leaguer.

Being in the big leagues, even in spring training, took some getting used to. For instance, at the hotel we could sign for our meals. You ordered whatever you wanted to eat, and all you had to do when you'd finished eating was to sign your name on the tab. Lots of rookies got carried away with this and ordered all sorts of rich food at every meal. They'd get stomach problems or gain too much weight too fast and end up not playing their best during spring training, meaning they'd eaten up their chances to make the major leagues. I was careful to eat sensibly.

The club even gave us money—I can't remember how much, but, knowing the Phillies' financial situation, I'd say it was just a couple of dollars or so a week—to use for tips at the hotel. I felt like a big man being able to tip the waitresses in the hotel restaurant.

The first day I was in camp I remember going into the clubhouse and looking for my locker. Philadelphia had a red-headed fellow named Leo Miller who was the team equipment manager and assistant trainer. He would greet rookies and new players and show them to the right locker.

I couldn't believe what Miller showed me. I had my own locker, and my name was on a sign over it. "I'll be furnishing you with your sanitaries and cleaning your uniform for you," he told me. "We've got cold drinks in the ice box over there—just put a check by your name on the list there whenever you take one."

Remember, I'd been playing on clubs where I had to do the washing myself, and where I hung my street clothes on a nail pounded in the wall. So with the Phillies I was in hog heaven. I felt like I had arrived, and I was determined to play hard enough and well enough to stay.

My uniform was white flannel. Today's players would think it was too heavy and too baggy, but to me it shone like it had some kind of strong light reflecting from it. Strangely, I couldn't tell you what number was on the back of the jersey. Numbers weren't as important then. They'd only been on jerseys for about a decade when the Yankees started the tradition. They gave Babe Ruth number 3 because he batted third in their lineup; Lou Gehrig got 4 because he hit fourth.

My first number with the Phillies was in double digits, probably between 10 and 20. Anyway, the number meant less to me than having my own personal locker. It was the first time I didn't have to share one.

Looking around the locker room I recognized some of the players there. Even back in 1940, *The Sporting News* was the bible for young ballplayers. Now I saw in person some of the guys I'd spent years reading about—Chuck Klein was there, and Johnny Rizzo and Kirby Higbe. The players I didn't know were the younger ones who were trying to make the club like me.

And I sure recognized George Scharein, because he was the Phillies' regular shortstop whose job I would be trying to take away. I was 23 and he must have been 29 that year, middle-aged to my young way of thinking. George was very thin and tan with curly hair. I was worried he'd dislike me because I was out to take his job from him, but George was a very laid-back type who treated me well from the start. We got along fine, and during spring training he gave me advice about positioning myself against other clubs and their hitters.

Scharein had started 146 games at shortstop for the Phillies in 1939, hitting I think around .240 or .230. I guessed going into spring training that the Phillies wanted me or somebody to take the shortstop job away from Scharein. The club wouldn't have bought my contract if they didn't think I could play for them. But those first spring training games literally scared the hell out of me, because I got to see up close just how good the other shortstops in the National League were. Pee Wee Reese at Brooklyn and Eddie Miller with the Boston Braves were great fielders. I'd watch them and know deep inside I couldn't do some of the things they were doing every game. But I did think I might be a better shortstop than George Scharein.

In one of the first spring training games, I remember going up to Fort Myers to play the Cleveland Indians, who trained there. Bob Feller pitched that day, and I had to hit against him. Feller was known, of course, for his fastball, but what I remember from that day is how great his curveball was. I think I hit the ball pretty solidly against him, but nothing fell in.

Besides Feller, one of the best pitchers I hit against that spring was Bobo Newsome. He could throw almost as fast. After you had some at-bats against fireballers like that you'd head back to the dugout wondering what you were doing trying to compete with them.

The first 10 days of camp, though, were spent just with other Phillies players and coaches working on fundamentals. We'd start around 10 A.M. and keep on going until three in the afternoon, with a short break for lunch in the clubhouse. On the field we'd take batting practice and fielding practice, and every activity always had a specific purpose. We'd go through rundown and pickoff plays, develop a defense when other teams would try a double steal against us, specific game situation practice like that.

Hans Lobert was Doc Prothro's right-hand coach, and he was in charge of lots of the training drills. Lobert was a great baserunner in his day, and he wanted us to be just as good. The Miami Beach practice field had sliding pits filled with sawdust. We'd practice sliding over and over, and afterwards we'd have a couple pounds of sawdust each in our shoes and inside our sanitaries.

We bunted a lot. There were drills on hitting the right cutoff man. Fundamentals were constantly stressed. If you screwed up in practice or in a game by throwing to the wrong base or not getting a sacrifice bunt down properly, you were made to feel embarrassed. It bothers me today seeing hitters miss bunts or throw to the wrong base and then grin about it. We didn't grin then, I guarantee you.

We also would practice the hidden ball trick, which was used quite a lot in those days. As a shortstop, I probably pulled it successfully on opposing runners a half-dozen times a season. I'd pretend to hand the ball to Pinky May at third and he'd take a few steps toward the mound and pretend to hand it over to the pitcher. Some other players used to enjoy having the ball hidden and sneaking up behind unsuspecting runners, then whispering, "Look what I've got", before tagging them out. I didn't have the audacity to do the same thing; if I caught somebody with the hidden ball, I'd just tag them and get on with the game. I do remember, though, pulling the trick on Brooklyn's Dixie Walker—Harry's brother—at Ebbetts Field. That was one of my biggest kicks ever in the major leagues.

Always in those spring practices of 1940, I'd have to field a lot of grounders. Another reason I thought the Phillies had me in their season plans was that in infield practice I was constantly paired with Ham Schulte, Philadelphia's regular second baseman. The idea was that the everyday second baseman and shortstop should practice together in spring training so they'd work better together in the regular season.

After practice every day, our time was pretty much free.This was where some earlier musical training back in Birmingham came in handy for me.

A black man named Frank used to work for my father as a tinsmith, and he was a good one. Frank could cut those lengths of tin into elbows for vents as nicely as other artists could sculpt clay. Frank could also play the piano, and on Saturdays he would come to our house, mow the yard, and then around noon come in and show my brothers and me how to make chords on the keyboard of the piano we had. Frank played on the black keys primarily, in the key of G Flat. He loved music, and the first song he played for us was, "My Task," and the first words were "To love someone more dearly every day." I can hear him singing it like it was yesterday.

After Frank got me interested in piano, I ended up sending off to a guy named Leroy on the radio who promised for a dollar he'd send a book that would teach anyone to play well. I sent my buck and got a book that taught by the numbers, where you'd have an octave scale or eight notes and hit keys 1-3-5-8, let's say, to make a certain chord. Eventually all of us brothers learned to play; I think Jimmy was probably the best. I got so I could play popular songs by ear—

to this day, I still can't read a note but I can play just about anything after hearing it once or twice.

Anyway, there was a piano at the Miami Beach Hotel and every day after practice Cy Johnson and Boom-Boom Beck would order me to entertain them. I played the familiar songs of the day—Who's Sorry Now, In the Good Old Summertime, I Want a Girl Just Like the Girl Who Married Dear Old Dad. Most of the time I enjoyed playing for Beck and Johnson, and I didn't let on the few times I didn't feel like doing it. Rookies were expected to be respectful to veterans. I think one reason the older players accepted me so fast was that I always kept that rule in mind.

And in the afternoons and evenings we also spent a lot of time just talking baseball. The usual group I was in included Ben Warren, a catcher; Art Mahan, a first baseman; and Merrill "Pinky" May, the Phillie third baseman. We talked about stealing other teams' signals and tried to think up signals for ourselves the other team couldn't steal, or work out new pickoff plays—inside baseball. And, always, we talked about how we each could improve.

The idea was that no matter how good you were, no matter how long you'd played in the major leagues or whether you were a star or just a bench player, you should do everything you could to become better. If one evening I'd told Pinky May, for instance, that I didn't feel like talking baseball, he would have straightened me out fast.

On the field in games against other teams, George Scharein and I split time at shortstop. I did well with the glove, and I remember one game against the Washington Senators when I hit a home run in an early inning. John Welaj hit one for Washington to win it in the ninth. But Scharein had always been what we called then a Punch-and-Judy hitter. When he got on base it was usually with soft singles. And his throwing arm was just mediocre—that's where I really had the edge. After a few exhibition games I began to feel I'd gained an advantage over George.

Not that I was overestimating myself as a ballplayer. Looking back, I was lucky in that I was in the right organization at the right time trying to win a job at the right position. Had I tried to beat out Pinky May at third, I'd have failed because he was simply better than I was. The same thing would have applied to Ham Schulte at second base. But I was a shortstop and George Scharein was the competition.

During the last week of spring training we began a series of exhibition games, playing our way back up north to start the regular season. It was during that week before a game in Georgia or North Carolina, I forget which, that Doc Prothro came up to me and said, "You're my shortstop." And with that I was a big leaguer, and all those childhood dreams back in Alabama had come true. I don't think I cried, either then or when I was alone that night, but I was truly moved and couldn't wait to call George and Corinne to share the good news with them.

George Scharein had sensed what was happening, and he was a gentleman to the end. After Prothro made it official, Scharein came over and wished me good luck. He wasn't cut from the club right away—in fact, he started the first few games of the season because Prothro wanted me to get my feet wet gradually.

On Opening Day of the 1940 major league season, the Philadelphia Phillies played the New York Giants at the old Polo Grounds. I was just overwhelmed to be there. Prothro pinch-hit for Scharein and I went into the field in the sixth inning as a defensive replacement. I came up to bat for the first time in the eighth inning. Walter "Jumbo" Brown was pitching for the Giants. He was a giant himself, a right-hander who weighed 270 pounds. I hit the first pitch back to him on one hop and he threw me out easily. My knees were shaking and I was just glad to get out of the batters' box. I did field all my chances at short cleanly, and I started the second game of the season and every game after that. Following the seventh game of the season, George Scharein was sent down to the minor leagues and, as far as I know, never played in the majors again.

From the Polo Grounds we went on to Pittsburgh. Ken Heitzelman pitched for the Pirates in that game in old Forbes Field and I got my first major league hit against him, a ground ball single to center field. Naturally, I didn't ask for the ball as a souvenir. If you were good enough to play in the major leagues, the feeling was, then getting a hit was no big deal. I wondered for a moment whether I'd ever get another, but then the game went on and there was no time to stop and enjoy the moment too much.

As the Phillies played the other seven National League teams that season, I was awed by the great players.

Stan Musial, Enos Slaughter and Johnny Mize made the St. Louis Cardinals a top team. Cincinnati was tough with Johnny Vandemeer Ernie Lombardi, and Bucky Walters. Whitlow Wyatt was the best player for the Chicago Cubs. Mel Ott was with the Giants, and Bill Terry was the team's manager. He was the last player to hit .400 until Ted Williams did it in 1941, a year after I made it to the majors.

And Casey Stengel was managing the Boston Braves without much success. When a cab driver ran over Casey that season and broke his leg, a lot of Boston fans wanted the cab driver named National League Most Valuable Player.

Pittsburgh meant the Waner brothers, Lloyd and Paul. "Little Poison" and "Big Poison." Both of them were voted into the Hall of Fame. Rip Sewell was a Pirate star too, and Al Lopez was the Pittsburgh catcher.

Arky Vaughn, another eventual Hall of Famer, played shortstop for the Pirates. I do remember Arky Vaughn well. When he slid into second base, he'd have one leg reaching for the base and the other trying to cut the other team's second baseman or shortstop. It was a hard game in those days—no quarter asked or given.

But almost everybody was friendly—or at least I thought they were. The first time I came into Pittsburgh with the Phillies, I was thrilled that Honus Wagner was a Pirate coach. Honus Wagner and I were on the same field! At Forbes Field, the visiting team had to get to the playing field through the home team dugout. When I first came out there, Wagner was already on the field hitting practice grounders to the Pirate infielders. I got a big thrill by walking up and saying to him, "How are you, Honus?" He answered back, "Hi, kid. How's the weather?"

I told everybody I knew that I'd talked to Honus Wagner, and I couldn't wait until the next time I saw him to renew our acquaintanceship. I went right up to him and said, "Hi, Honus," expecting a conversation, and he just said, "Hi, kid. How's the weather?" It turned out he'd always say the same thing to everybody.

It was about this same time during the early 1940 season that I had to change my baseball nickname. From the time I was a kid, I was always called Robert and not Bobby. When I started semipro ball in Birmingham, some of the coaches thought I resembled an older player named Nig Yates, so I got the nickname Nig Bragan. I never thought the name might be offensive to anyone.

The Hillerich and Bradsby Co., the people who make Louisville Slugger bats, had a custom at that time of going around the minor leagues and signing young players to lifetime contracts to use their names on bats whether or not the youngsters ever made the big leagues, with the understanding only a certain percentage of the signees would achieve that level. I think the company would give players a set of golf clubs or something in exchange for the rights to print their names on their bats someday. Anyway, when I got to the Phillies a representative of Hillerich and Bradsby came to me and said I needed to start signing my bats as Bobby Bragan instead of Robert "Nig" Bragan, which I'd used in the minor leagues. I guess it's obvious why—the major leagues were so color-conscious they didn't want any reference to a minority race, even if it was just the nickname of a white player.

I had no objection to being called "Bobby." What a small price to pay for continuing to use a Louisville Slugger in the major leagues!

B	E	T	W	E	E	N
I	N	N	I	N	G	S

LOU BROCK: One thing that prohibits today's players from having fun is that years ago all the players in spring training had to stay together in headquarters, some hotel. Teams would have a midnight curfew and since nobody was sleepy we'd all lay around in bed talking baseball. You ate all your meals together, took the bus to practice together, just plain got to know each other.

Some of us didn't agree with the way things were then and went to get the rules changed. I was part of that, I admit, when we said we wanted players to get out of the dormitory situation. We got it, but now I think we were wrong. After that, the way it turned out was you only saw your teammates at the ballpark. You didn't get to know and care about each other as much. In football they still go to training camps away from their families and live together for four weeks or six weeks. Baseball ought to go back to that. It would help what they call team chemistry.

BOBBY THOMSON: During spring training the veterans could get a little tough on the rookies, but mostly it was all in fun. Fun, I'd say, with an underlying sense that every rookie who made the club took away some veteran's place in the big leagues.

Warren Spahn used to kid that way. Spahn was such a great pitcher, but he intended to play in the major leagues forever. When I was with the Braves with Spahnie, in spring training he'd go up to young left-handers in pepper games and say he was going to whack the ball at 'em and put 'em out of the business. Of course he never did, but some of those kids sure did think he might.

DICK WILLIAMS: Expansion has diluted the talent that's still available, but back in the '40s and '50s every player from Double A up who was brought to spring training had enough talent to play at just about the highest level. If Bobby Bragan beat out some guy in 1940 to be the Phillie shortstop, I'll tell you that today whoever it was he beat out would probably have a multiyear, multimillion-dollar contract with some major league club.

It's sad to say you're probably seeing the best rookies available making major league clubs these days. I wouldn't be surprised if in four or five years the Japanese couldn't regularly beat any major league club America could put on the field.

Rookies in those days were supposed to hustle at all times and keep their mouths shut. It didn't hurt anybody to have it that way.

BROCK: If you were a rookie in spring training who got out of line in the old days, the manager would talk to you tough or, if necessary, some of the veterans did it. Today's rookie runs to his agent. It's like telling your mom as a kid that other people are being mean to you.

ROOKIE YEAR

BEING A MAJOR LEAGUER WAS EVERYTHING I'D HOPED IT WOULD BE. I struck up a really strong friendship with Phillie first baseman Art Mahan, another rookie who'd been a big baseball star at Villanova. We decided to be roommates and found a nice place on 21st Street, Mom Keyburn's Boardinghouse. Shibe Park, where the Phillies played our home games, was on the corner of 23rd Street and Lehigh, so we just had to walk a couple of blocks to the ballpark.

Mom Keyburn's was a warm, cheerful place. We weren't the first ballplayers to room there. Schoolboy Rowe had lived at Mom Keyburn's the year before us, and a couple of the American League's Philadelphia Athletics had also lived there. Art and I had separate bedrooms upstairs, and when we weren't on the road we ate breakfast and lunch at Mom's. I think we paid $75 a month total.

For me, one of the real perks was that Art and I were treated as celebrities by the other boarders. Sometimes we would also walk outside and sign autographs for everybody who was in the neighborhood. Mom's son Bill, who was 20 or 21 years old, owned a flashy red Buick convertible, and he was always proud to drive Art and me where we needed to go, so we didn't even have to spend money for transportation.

Mom Keyburn's was one in a series of row houses, the kind where they all stand together and all look alike. It wasn't unusual for somebody in that neighborhood to take a long visit at the corner bar and then, heading home, walk into one wrong house after another. There was a real sense of community.

It was a very happy time for me. I was making big money with the Phillies—$500 a month for five and a half months, just over $2,500 for the season. In every game I got to wear a first-class flannel uniform and the ballclub furnished and washed our sanitaries, baseball underwear, and sweatshirts.

The only thing that kept the season from being perfect was, the team was bad. Really terrible. It was a ballclub where you expected you'd lose most of the time. It wasn't a question of if we'd drop the game that day, just of who would be that game's goat. I earned the horns my fair share.

In one game at Cincinnati, the score was tied with one out in the Reds' half of the ninth. The bases were loaded and big, slow Ernie Lombardi hit a ground ball to me on the left side of shortstop towards second base. That easy double play ball went right between my legs, and the Reds won the game. We came back to the visiting team clubhouse and poor Doc Prothro threw up his hands and said, "I knew we couldn't hit, but at least I thought we could field!"

I partially atoned a couple of weeks later when we played Cincinnati at our home park. This was the team that would win the league championship that season because of its great pitching—Bucky Walters, Paul Derringer, and Johnny Vandermeer. In this particular game we were behind 1-0 in the seventh inning when I hit a solo home run off Bucky Walters to tie the game. Then in the bottom of the ninth I hit a two-run homer off Walters and we won. In our clubhouse after the game, Doc Prothro sent a Coca-Cola to my locker. That was my bonus for hitting two home runs.

The next day at the batting cage, Bucky Walters wandered by, tapped me on the shoulder and said, "Hi'ya, Babe," referring to Babe Ruth. The next time I faced Walters I went oh-for-4, and when he greeted me after that he said, "Hi'ya, Bobby."

In my heart that whole season I knew I wasn't as good a shortstop as others in the National League. I saw Marty Marion, Pee Wee

Reese, and Eddie Miller on a regular basis, and the idea began to come to me that if I was to stay in the majors long-term it would have to be as a catcher. But for then I was just happy to be in the big leagues, and if the Phillies wanted me at short that was where I was happy to play. And I wasn't bad there. I got most of the balls I could reach, and I had a sufficient arm.

I saw and heard a lot in those colorful times. Baseball was rougher. It wasn't out of the ordinary for arguments between opponents or even teammates to get settled physically.

In one game Rube Melton, a right-handed pitcher, was sitting in our dugout watching Lee Grissom no-hit the Dodgers for five innings. At the end of the fifth, Grissom took a seat in the dugout next to Melton and Rube remarked to him, "The Dodgers haven't had a hit yet, have they?" It was considered the ultimate bad luck to tell a pitcher he had a no-hitter, and sure enough the Dodgers shelled Grissom in the sixth. Doc Prothro took him out of the game, and when Grissom came into the dugout he headed straight for Melton and slapped him as hard as he could. Rube jumped up ready for fist city but they were separated and the fight was stopped. That meant nothing. In the clubhouse after the game they went for each other again.

During a game in Pittsburgh, Mickey Livingstone was our catcher and batting eighth and Melton was pitching for us and batting ninth. We were having our usual lousy game and everybody was in a bad mood. Nick Strinceovich was pitching for the Pirates, and in one inning he first struck out Livingstone, then Melton. When Melton got back to the dugout he said, "That last curve must have broken two feet." Livingston, putting on his catching gear, looked up and said, "Rube, you're crazy. The ball he struck me out on only broke about five inches." Rube snapped back, "Maybe he thought five inches was all it would take to get *you*." And they were ready to go at it.

Merrill May, our third baseman, was maybe the most intense competitor. He hated losing, which we did regularly, so most of our games were just excruciating for him. We were playing the Cubs in Wrigley Field and John Podgajny walked a guy. We had an infield that liked to talk a lot, and May hollered to John, "Make them hit the ball. Let us help you." Podgajny walked another one. May yelled at him some more to let them hit the ball. Podgajny walked somebody else. "Throw strikes, John!" May hollered. John called May over, grabbed him by the shirt and screamed, "Maybe I could throw a strike if you'd shut up!" They got into a fight right there on the pitcher's mound.

Through it all, Doc Prothro was low key, all business and fun to play for. And we'd have a real celebration every time we won. We were just usually overmatched in a league with so many great stars. Mel Ott, Arky Vaughn, Enos Slaughter—I remember a game where Slaughter hit a hot ground ball to our second baseman. There was a runner on first and one out, so I took the toss at second for the force and fired it to first, only to see Slaughter already had crossed the bag. He had such great speed, but after that inning Boom-Boom Beck, who'd been on the mound, cornered me in the dugout and said, "How hard does a ground ball have to be hit for you to turn a double play?"

Cincinnati's Paul Derringer and Johnny Vandermeer were the toughest pitchers for me to hit. Vandermeer threw as hard as was humanly possible, like a Bob Feller from the left side. Derringer threw hard and also had a great curve. Whitlow Wyatt with Brooklyn gave me trouble, too. I did prefer hitting against southpaws as long as Vandermeer wasn't one of them.

I kept in mind as the season went along that the Phillies always had to sell or trade somebody every year to get money to pay the bills. Hugh Mulcahey and Danny Litwhiler went that way, and I thought if I kept improving I could be another one who became attractive to a different team. I would have been happy to go to any club besides the Boston Braves. I was a boy from the South, and we played in Boston on June 30th and it snowed. That convinced me I didn't want to play in that climate.

So I was trying hard to establish myself as a major league player who would be around a long time. With my limited skills, it wasn't easy. I would look for any edge. I remember one day in Boston when the Braves sent a knuckleballer named Jim Tobin against us. Tobin was a good hitter—I once saw him hit three home runs in a game and bounce a fourth shot against the top of the fence for a double —

but from his pitching motion I thought I could bunt against him. In this game I bunted down the third base line and beat it out. It worked there, and in our next series against Chicago I picked the right spot against a Cub pitcher and beat another bunt out. We went on to St. Louis and I got a bunt hit there. By the end of my rookie year I'd beaten out at least one bunt against every team in the National League. This was the type of thing that would get word out about a rookie, that he might have something extra to offer.

At the end of the 1940 season, Doc Prothro gave me assurance I would be his shortstop again the following year. This made it nice going home to Birmingham. I could anticipate another full season in a big league uniform, and I'd saved almost $600 to give George and Corinne. My part-time job at Railway Express was waiting for me, and that winter I also took a fling at selling life insurance for Massachusetts Mutual.

I got home to find I'd gained some recognition in Birmingham. I gave interviews to the three local papers. My younger brothers appeared to have gained some respect for me. I took pride in going down and working with some promising players at my old high school. Harry Walker came down to help with that. He was still in Triple A because the Cardinals had so many established outfielders on their major league roster ahead of him.

But that winter I had more than baseball on my mind.

I'd met Gwenn Best in 1939, and I started courting her again in the winter of 1940. She was a senior in high school. Her parents had separated years before, and she lived with her grandparents, Dr. and Mrs. Frank May.

Gwenn and I started going steady in the 1940 sense that we went to dances on weekends and to church together on Sundays. We talked about getting married, and finally I told her that if she'd wear a black dress to church I'd do it—I loved the way Gwenn looked in a black dress. Well, she wore a black dress three weeks in a row and nothing happened, so the fourth Sunday she wore a flowered dress. What she didn't know was that I'd acquired a marriage license, and that Sunday we went to a minister's house in Hueytown outside of Birmingham and got married in a secret ceremony.

We had to keep it secret because it wasn't considered right for a girl in high school to get married. I went back to George and

Corinne's and she went back to her grandparents', but we were happy to be man and wife. We were going to tell everyone after she graduated from high school in the spring.

But the secret didn't last quite that long. Gwenn's grandmother worked in the probate office of the county courthouse, and one day somebody who worked with her said, "I see by the marriage license records that granddaughter of yours got married." Mrs. May said that wasn't so, but then was shown the records. She came home that night and told Dr. May. I was off with the Phillies for the 1941 season by then, and that night I was talking to Gwenn long-distance. Dr. May heard the news and said, "That young man has got to assume his responsibility," so I started sending more money back to Birmingham to pay for Gwenn's upkeep.

Gwenn graduated from high school, and my brother Lionel good-naturedly drove her and her belongings from Birmingham to Philadelphia. When they arrived, they were told the Phillies were in Brooklyn playing the Dodgers. Lionel and Gwenn got back in the car and drove to Brooklyn. Lionel left her and the car and took the train home. Gwenn and I spent our honeymoon night in Brooklyn, and when the Dodger series was over we drove back to Philadelphia to begin our married life together.

AL BARLICK: I remember Bobby first when he came up at shortstop for Philadelphia. I'll say this—even then he knew the game. But I wouldn't want to talk too much about whether he had much ability as a player.

STAN MUSIAL: Bragan was slow, one of the slowest guys I ever saw in the major leagues. That's what I remember most about him from those days.

The Philadelphia organization wasn't terrific, but the Phillies teams themselves were mostly made up of good guys who clearly were close-knit. Every team was, in those days.

Any ballplayer from my generation will tell you that teammates would be together on trains, in hotel lobbies, we'd socialize with one another. We spent time talking baseball. We enjoyed it. There was just something about being a big league ballplayer. It was a thrill and a privilege, and we all appreciated that. Take today, though, nobody even has a roommate on the road anymore. With us, you and your roommate would go to bed and lie there and talk about what happened in that day's game. Today they fly someplace and put on headphones and nobody talks. They go to their own rooms and talk to their agents on the phone. I doubt they even take cabs to the ballpark together. They're missing something important, but probably they don't realize it.

7

LOSING

WHEN I REJOINED THE PHILLIES in Miami for spring training in 1941, I felt a lot more at home. I had a job. I'd been the Philadelphia shortstop for a year and Doc Prothro had promised me I'd be out there regularly again. It was nice to have a feeling of security.

But in baseball, nothing's really secure. My roommate Art Mahan was gone after one season, sent back to the minor leagues for more seasoning. Ham Schulte, my double play partner at second base, was gone too. Replacing him was a guy named Danny Murtaugh, who would also be a presence later on in my career.

The rest of the team faces were mostly familiar, which was good and bad. It was good in that we had a real sense of togetherness. We'd played ballgames together, travelled together, learned about each other's families and troubles and dreams. If I needed a favor I could ask any guy on the roster. I'd do the same for any of them.

But it was also bad for that exact reason—we had the same team. Hope springs eternal every spring training, but with the 1941 Phillies there was no way to avoid being a realist. In 1940, we'd had the worst talent in the league, and owner Gerry Nugent wasn't in a financial position to improve us any. Truth to tell, as people we were wonderful but as a team we knew in our hearts we were a dog. The Boston

69

Braves were just about as bad as we were. Everybody else was going to feast on us for another year.

When you play for a sorry team, you end up setting individual goals. Why not? Mine in 1941 was to play in every game and stay off the rubbing table, which was the extent to which any injuries got treated in those days. If you hurt anywhere, you got a rubdown. It didn't matter if the injury was a charley horse or a torn rotator cuff —except we didn't know about torn rotator cuffs back then.

Even lying on the rubbing table had a negative stigma. The idea was that if you were a real athlete and team man you played with pain. To lie down on the table was to have all your teammates walk by and say loudly, "Ooh, how is she feeling today? Is she hurting?" with the emphasis on the word she. There was no sympathy to be had.

So during that second spring training with the Phillies I tried to come to terms objectively with what I could hope to accomplish for my own career. I knew my ability was limited—probably more limited than Phillie management yet realized. On the field, my speed was still nonexistent, but now I had the advantage of having played in the National League for a year. I knew the opposing hitters and our pitchers, so I could better position myself at shortstop. This meant I got to a lot more balls by covering shorter distances.

I considered myself rolling in the dough, too. I'd gotten a $2,000 raise to $4,500 for the season. Even though Art Mahan was no longer around, I moved right back to Mom Keyburn's when the Phillies broke camp and returned East to start the year. After Gwenn graduated from high school and joined me in Philadelphia, we rented a small row house on Wynncote Street on the north side of town. It was two blocks from the very last stop on the subway line, which is how I got to and from the ballpark. We paid $110 a month for rent, which included furniture. At no time did we think about buying a car, which for many families was still a luxury.

1941 turned out to be my best year in the majors. I improved my 1940 average by 20 points to .271, and it seemed like every hit I got was a double. I soon considered myself among the upper half of the players on the team. Merrill May, I guess, was our established star if we had one at all. Me, I hustled. All the time and every time, because I hoped other clubs were watching who might make Nugent a good offer for me. One veteran, Ben Chapman, was quoted as saying, "Bragan has less natural ability than anyone I've ever seen in the big leagues." I hoped he meant it as a compliment.

It seemed like we lost every day. Through it all we stayed friends. Free agency didn't exist then, so for many players you stayed on the same team your whole career. You had to get along, because you might not be going anywhere else. And baseball was truly fun in those days, especially going on the road to play the Giants and Dodgers and getting to see the sights of New York, competing against famous players and inwardly enjoying seeing them do great things, even if they did happen to be doing them against us.

After games in Philadelphia, I'd go home to Gwenn. On the road I'd congregate with the other guys in the hotel to talk baseball. We all would spend hours on the front steps of the hotels or in hotel lobbies, wherever we could find spots to sit down and talk baseball. If kids happened by and wanted autographs, well, we were kind of proud to be asked and would always oblige. No matter how bad we were as a team, we still enjoyed being major league ballplayers.

And that was a danger. We weren't complacent, but I learned that season how easy it is to get accustomed to losing. When there's little hope of winning, ballplayers can lose an edge. After a game if you got two hits or made a nice play in the field, you'd feel good about that instead of grinding your teeth because it was a 10th straight loss. Doc Prothro did his best to keep us focused on winning, but Nugent wasn't ever going to give him a quality team and we all knew it.

We were so bad, we didn't have players who could carry out basic plays. One pitcher, Tommy Hughes, could make the 180-degree pivot necessary to pick runners off second base. Only Hughes among our pitchers had the simple coordination to whirl and throw. None of the other guys could, and word got around the league. This meant runners on second got bigger leads and could score easily on short singles. Weaknesses like that just kill a club's chances over a season. If players have physical abilities you can usually teach them the necessary techniques. But if they can't do the job physically, there's no way they can play at a major league level and win.

Sometimes I'd daydream about playing somewhere else. Like any player in baseball at that time, I would have loved to play for St. Louis or Brooklyn. They were known as class ballclubs, teams with management committed to excellence and willing to take whatever steps were necessary to achieve it. Cincinnati was desirable, too. The Reds had won the National League pennant in 1940 and had a strong roster from top to bottom. In depressed moods I pondered a move to the Boston Braves where I'd have to field and hit during snowstorms, but when I'd shudder at that prospect I'd try to make myself consider the alternative. Rather than going back to the minors like Art Mahan, I would gladly have played for the Braves.

So I enjoyed my own relatively good season and relished the chance to see the great players on other teams up close. I loved visiting St. Louis, where Musial, Enos Slaughter, and Johnny Mize performed. I enjoyed going to the Polo Grounds and watching Bill Terry manage, trying to keep one step ahead of his opposite number. I admired Ernie Lombardi in Cincinnati and Arky Vaughn at Pittsburgh, but mostly in 1941 I envied players on the Brooklyn Dodgers. Leo Durocher was the manager at Ebbetts Field, and he was so aggressive. His team took advantage of every opponent's weakness, which is why I can't remember Philadelphia beating Brooklyn once that year. The Dodgers ended up winning the 1941 pennant, and even with all their fine players like Pee Wee Reese I believed Leo was the catalyst. In those days you'd drift by when he talked to reporters just to hear what he had to say. If you saw Leo off the field he was always immaculately dressed in expensive clothes and seemed comfortable in any situation. Honestly, Leo became a hero to me.

On and on that 1941 season went. Different guys' behavior fell into patterns. Hans Lobert, the coach, would play his coffin trick on porters every time we took a train for road trips. He'd corner porters in the passageway and say his sister had just died. Her insurance policy had gotten her one coffin, and he'd gone out and bought one, too, so there was an extra left over. Would the porter like to buy it for $10? "It would be real comfortable to sleep in," Lobert would assure the horrified porter. At some point somebody must have complained, because Lobert got a letter from the Commissioner's office telling him to stop it.

Some guys drank. That's no secret. I will say I don't think anyone was drinking so much he couldn't perform properly in games. It would be the veterans who imbibed. I remember Chuck Klein, in the twilight of a fine career, liked to have a few drinks, as would Cy Johnson. They wouldn't be really open about it, but some nights you could smell the liquor on their breath.

Most of the team played a lot of pinochle on the train and in hotels. I never learned the game and never did like playing any form of cards. But cardplaying for small stakes and occasional drinking was as far as it went. This was an innocent time. For recreation on the road, it was not unusual after day games for teammates to have a nice, leisurely dinner and then take a walk down Michigan Blvd. in Chicago or visit Times Square in New York.

We finished dead last in 1941, which didn't surprise anybody. After the season Gwenn and I went home to Birmingham. We spent that winter living with my parents; young married couples often did this in those days. It was a traumatic time because of the war. That winter my older brother Walter enlisted in the Air Force, and when we heard the news all the rest of us just laid down on the floor and cried. Honestly, I had no desire to interrupt my baseball career to go fight. Instead, I took my winter job at a defense plant, American Cast Iron Pipe Company. My job was making steel in an electric furnace. I'd start at 5 A.M., melting down scrap iron. After 45 minutes of heat, the scrap became hot molten iron. I'd call over a crane, which swung in a red-hot ladle to scoop the stuff up and take it to another part of the factory to be shaped into pipe. Then I'd do the whole thing over. We called each batch a "heat," and we'd do about four heats a day. For this I made $80 a week.

Everybody at the plant talked about the war. I thought about being a Phillie again in 1942. Since I worked in a defense plant and was married I got a draft deferment for the time being. Gwenn was pregnant, too. Our first child, Bobby Jr., would be born on May 11, 1942.

I certainly didn't love melting scrap iron the way I loved baseball. It was a relief to go back to spring training. There were some differences with the 1942 Phillies, the most important being Doc Prothro had been fired by Gerry Nugent. Prothro never had a chance. The owner didn't give him a team that could win and then that same owner fired him for not winning.

This is the way it worked then and still works now. Later I'd learn firsthand the manager gets the blame no matter what.

Hans Lobert, fresh from pretending to sell coffins, was the new manager. He didn't have a chance either, but he did his best. Lobert was usually a quiet competitor, though he had his moments. During one home game he went into the upper deck trying to get at a fan who'd been riding him, and everybody on the Phillie team went right after Lobert to protect him if it became necessary. The Phillie fans, of course, had been stuck with a losing team for years and knew as well as the players did there wasn't much chance for improvement. They resented the situation and weren't shy about saying so, especially from the stands. But I didn't feel sorry for them, because the worst hecklers in the world were in Philadelphia. People in that town have always been hard to please under the best of circumstances. It's no coincidence that shows wanting to get to Broadway open in Philadelphia. The idea is that if you can succeed in Philly you can succeed anywhere.

Though I hadn't realized it, 1941 was to be my first and last decent season as a regular player. 1942 found pitchers figuring out what I couldn't hit—namely, curveballs. I never did care how hard left-handers threw, but mediocre right-handers could drive me away from the plate with curves. I took more batting practice, I talked to myself between pitches, and it only got worse. Finally, it became more a mental than physical thing. When a ballplayer gets it set in his mind he can't do something, then it's certain he won't. Maybe today a team would take a young player like I was then and get him to a sports psychologist for counseling. Fifty years ago it was, "Damn it, Bragan, quit bailing out."

I don't remember falling into any complete depressions. I did ask Danny Litwhiler, one of our outfielders, to throw me extra batting practice while I tried switch-hitting. It didn't work for me, but it did give me an idea many years later when I became the minor league manager of another good-field, no-hit shortstop named Maury Wills.

In an effort to keep a big league job, I finally got the nerve to suggest I could be a decent catcher. The 1942 season was a month old when both our catchers, Benny Warren and Mickey Livingston, were injured. We were scheduled to play an exhibition game in Allentown, Pennsylvania, and I told Hans Lobert I could get behind the plate and catch that day without any problem. I caught all nine innings and we won.

Shortly after that, with the season already given up on by Phillie management, we had a home game scheduled with Cincinnati. Very few people had been bothering us by buying tickets and sitting in the stands, so as a special promotion Nugent advertised that Earl Naylor, one of our outfielders, would pitch for the first time and that shortstop Bragan would make his regular season debut as a catcher. I don't think that sold many extra tickets, but Naylor pitched four or five decent innings and we got a rare win, 4-2. The Reds had a very fast player named Lonnie Frey, and twice during the game I threw him out on steal attempts. After that Lobert would alternate me, playing some games at shortstop and others behind the plate.

I got something else for catching that first game—the return of a $50 fine. Now, in those days players didn't make a lot of money and any fine hurt. Usual fines might be $10 for missing a sign or getting to the ballpark late. I generally managed to stay on the straight and narrow, and my $50 fine earlier in the 1942 season seemed both harsh and unnecessary to me.

A very pregnant Gwenn was in Elizabeth, New Jersey, on May 10 visiting family and went into labor with our first child. The Phillies happened to be in Boston at the same time, playing the Braves in a doubleheader. When I got the word about Gwenn, I asked Hans Lobert for permission to leave the team temporarily and be with my wife for the birth. He replied, "Bobby, babies are born every minute. There's no need for you to worry about being there for this one of yours. I can't give you that permission."

After the doubleheader, the team went back to our hotel room. Cy Johnson was my roommate then, and when I poured out my story, he said, "Bobby, go ahead to New Jersey if you feel you must. All Hans can do is fine you a little for leaving the team." I went, and was there to see Bobby Jr. born.

I reported back to the team in Philadelphia on May 12 and Lobert immediately relieved me of $50. I suspected he took the cash and

75

immediately passed it on to team owner Gerry Nugent. That must have been true, because after the game when I caught for Naylor, Mr. Nugent told me he would order Lobert to give back the $50 I'd been fined.

God, that season got hard on me. Lobert tried all kinds of pep talks and threats to get me to stay in the batters box and swing at curveballs thrown by sidearming right-handers. It wasn't a matter of swinging and missing the curve. It was a matter of swinging with my ass out and popping the ball up or hitting easy grounders. In those days there just wasn't any taking of a called third strike. You didn't do it. There was a certain amount of shame involved. Teammates wouldn't speak to you afterwards, except to say something unfriendly. I'd tell myself I was a major leaguer making the princely sum of $5,500 a year, and that I just had to learn to hit the curve. The more I'd worry, the more curves I saw.

As a catcher, I could and did tell myself over and over I didn't have to hit much to be an asset to the team. I used all the baseball knowledge I had to call good games, and after each game I'd go back to the hotel and go over every pitch, trying to remember which hitter missed what so I'd have an advantage the next time we played the same team.

If I helped the Phillies much as a catcher, it didn't show up in the final season record. We finished last again, and, as much as I hate to admit it, I was letting myself get accustomed to losing. My goal was more to stay in the majors than to win. When Gwenn and I went back to Birmingham for the winter I was glad the 1942 season was over.

I took my winter job in another defense plant, Bechtel-McComb, this time in the relatively nice job of running a warehouse. It was cleaner work than melting scrap iron. Then one night at home I got a phone call from Gerry Nugent.

Maybe in one part of my mind I expected to hear Nugent say I was finished in the majors, that I was going back to the minors where slow players who couldn't hit the curveball belonged. Instead, he said simply, "We've traded you to Brooklyn. It'll be a break for you. I want to wish you good luck."

Nugent didn't have to wish me good luck. He's provided it himself. The next call I got was from Buzzie Bavasi, a Dodger executive.

He told me they'd given up Jack Kraus, a left-handed pitcher, and some cash for me. Players always want to know who was traded for them. The better the other player or players going to your old team, the more your new team wanted you. Well, hearing Kraus's name didn't give me much comfort. I think he pitched one year for the Phillies and then was gone from the majors forever. And Bavasi didn't say how much money changed hands, though that had to be Nugent's chief consideration.

The war affected everything, even the way I thought about what future I might have with Brooklyn. There was some elation in going from a doormat to a winning organization, but like every other club the Dodgers were losing some of their best players to military service. They also were known to turn a tidy profit each season.

So my first two assumptions were that since Pee Wee Reese was gone to the war, I probably would be the starting shortstop, and that because the Dodgers were a rich organization just by joining them I would get a healthy raise.

Both assumptions were wrong; a man named Branch Rickey was the reason why.

STAN MUSIAL: The Bobby Bragan-era Phillies were bad, real bad. They would always finish last. They didn't have any outstanding players, or, if they ever did come across a couple, the owner would sell 'em right away to get operating money. How good can a team be if all its best players just hope they'll get sold somewhere else where they might have a chance to win?

DON LARSEN: For a long time there weren't usually surprise teams coming out of nowhere to win pennants. You knew if you got to one of three clubs—the Cardinals, the Dodgers, or the Yankees—you would probably end up getting World Series money pretty regularly. Bad teams, though, stayed bad.

I got lucky. I was pitching for the Orioles, a bad team at the time, and went 3-21. A year later I'm with the Yankees, same stuff, same pitcher, and I'm 9-2 and in the Series. Guys on bad teams really wanted the same thing to happen to them.

DICK WILLIAMS: The minute a player accepts his team losing, he becomes a loser himself. It's dangerous. When I took over the Red Sox and the Padres, the first thing I had to do was get everyone determined to win for a change. The pennants wouldn't have happened without that first step. A losing tradition is often impossible to shake.

LARSEN: Going from the bottom of the standings to the top through a trade is like, well, getting born again. I don't know, it's like colors are suddenly brighter.

MR. RICKEY

Visitors to my office on the West Side of Fort Worth are often struck by a signed photograph on one wall. In this picture, an older man with pursed lips and a very stern expression regards the world from behind polished eyeglasses. He wears a dark blue suit, and a rather jaunty blue bow tie with white polka dots.

He fills the left side of the photograph. On the right side, hung behind him, is a framed passage from the Bible:

"He that will not reason is a bigot; he that cannot reason is a fool; and he that dare not reason is a slave."

The signature reads, "To Bobby Bragan, one of my choicest friends—Branch Rickey."

Mr. Rickey. To me, he was one of the greatest baseball minds ever, and I don't think you'd be wrong if you took out the word "baseball." It's almost impossible to tell people who never met him what he was like, because Mr. Rickey was unique. There were so many facets to his personality. Branch Rickey was an intellectual, a preacher, a trader, a visionary, a rulemaker, and a rulebreaker. Above all, he was a teacher. Being traded from the Phillies to the Dodgers meant more than an elevation in the quality of the team for which I played. It also meant I'd have the privilege of being exposed to the Branch Rickey way of building and maintaining a ballclub, which is to say the best way it's ever been done.

When I came into the National League in 1940, Mr. Rickey was general manager of the St. Louis Cardinals. He'd become a legend there by building the first extensive farm system that gave a major league team the luxury of grooming young players for several years. When rookies finally made it to the Cardinals, they'd learned all the baseball basics through repetition and hundreds or even thousands of minor league games. So if it took Cardinal farm hands longer to get to the majors, it also meant they were ready to play well as soon as they arrived. Harry Walker was a good example; he'd been my teammate in the minors for a couple of years and clearly was the better player, but I went to the Phillies pretty quickly and Harry had to wait his turn before joining the Cardinals—and he won a batting title once he got there.

Mr. Rickey himself had been a very marginal major league player, hanging on for a few years in the early 'teens as a second string catcher. He'd managed some in the majors, too, without much success. This undistinguished record meant many people were surprised at his spectacular achievements with the Cardinals, and, later, the Dodgers, but those who really knew the man understood why he succeeded at a higher baseball level after failing so much on the way there. See, Branch Rickey was an administrator. It was his gift to create new plans, and his talent to choose other people to carry them out successfully.

With the Cardinals, for instance, he built a team based on pure speed. To Mr. Rickey's way of thinking, other baseball skills could be learned, but speed was something a player naturally did or didn't have. So he mandated that his scouts hunt for the fastest players, and sign them before anyone else. Mr. Rickey was the one who came up with the idea of using the 60-yard dash in tryout camps. Maybe 150 hopefuls would show up, and the first thing Mr. Rickey would have his scouts do is make everybody run a few 60-yard dashes. That way he'd eliminate 150 of 300 prospects in the first half hour. Sure, occasionally he might lose a Hank Greenberg or Ralph Kiner who could hit the ball a mile but not jog a few yards, but most of the time he got the very best athletes.

Once he became general manager of the Cardinals and, later on, when he ran the Dodgers and Pirates, Branch Rickey never once entered a team's clubhouse. He didn't feel that was his place—again, an example of how he let the people who worked for him do their jobs. Now, he wanted the manager to come see him every day before the games, but in Mr. Rickey's mind the front office was the domain of the general manager and the clubhouse belonged to the manager.

Mr. Rickey even approached trading players differently than anyone else. It was the habit of most club executives to call each other up in a chummy way and come straight out offering one specific player for another. Mr. Rickey's favorite maneuver was to give the other general manager a choice of players, one usually better than the other. That way there was always a chance the other guy would choose the player Mr. Rickey really didn't want to keep. One time when he was running the Cardinals, outfielders Enos Slaughter and John Rizzo were both having excellent years in Triple A. Mr. Rickey had a player he wanted on the Pirates, and he told the Pittsburgh general manager he could take either Slaughter or Rizzo in return, being sure to make it seem as though Rizzo was the better prospect and someone Mr. Rickey was reluctant to part with. Naturally, the Pirates wanted Rizzo. He ended up having a few decent years for Pittsburgh; Slaughter was a star at St. Louis and eventually was elected to the Hall of Fame.

When I was traded to the Dodgers in 1942, Larry McPhail was Brooklyn's general manager. But soon after I became a Dodger over that winter, Brooklyn lured Mr. Rickey away from the Cardinals by offering him a 25 percent ownership in the ballclub. Though Mr. Rickey was a religious fellow—he never once would go to the ballpark on Sunday, saying he'd promised his mother to keep the Lord's day sacred—he also had an abiding interest in money. The chance to own a good chunk of one of the most profitable teams in professional baseball was enough to make him leave the relative security of his job in St. Louis.

And that's how, in the spring of 1943, I went to the Dodger training camp in Bear Mountain, New York to have my first meeting with the man who was going to influence my life more than anyone else.

The Dodgers held spring training at Bear Mountain that year because it was close to the U.S. Army Academy at West Point. It was considered patriotic to work out with the plebes and do baseball's part to keep up the spirits of military officers-in-training.

My spirit was already up. I travelled to New York state from Alabama humming all the way and feeling pretty sure I could be the starting Dodger shortstop. I knew for a fact I was due a sizeable raise, too.

I got to Bear Mountain and immediately went to Mr. Rickey's office to request an appointment. Soon enough, his secretary ushered me into his office. I immediately felt a little awed; Mr. Rickey was such an imposing man. His eyes glittered; you felt like he was reading your mind, which he probably was.

"We're really glad to have you with us," he said in a friendly fashion. "You hit a great number of doubles with Philadelphia. That was an impressive amount of extra-base hits."

I thanked him for noticing; I didn't yet realize Branch Rickey made a point of noticing everything. Since he seemed to admire me so much, I decided it was time to turn the subject to money—specifically, what my salary would be above the $5,500 I'd made in my final year with the Phillies.

"Mr. Rickey," I said, "'I'm coming from the poorest club in baseball to one of the richest. That in itself should warrant some kind of raise, don't you think?"

I learned immediately what a great psychologist Mr. Rickey was. He smiled gingerly, furrowed his brow just a bit, and waggled the cigar he always held, often unlit, between his fingers.

"Bobby," Mr. Rickey responded, "You've got it all wrong. Now, in Philadelphia you played every day, didn't you?"

"Yes, sir."

"Well, over here you're going to be on the bench so much, everyone will be calling you "Judge." So I suggest you sign this new contract with us for $5,500."

I signed. And I really wasn't offended. You can't be when somebody smarter than you so obviously gets the upper hand.

With St. Louis, Mr. Rickey had built a reputation as someone who believed you won championships by keeping your players hungry.

The way he would explain it was you played for him at the salary he thought was right, but if you played baseball the way he taught you, more often than not you'd come into extra money at the end of the season for playing in the World Series.

Among people who didn't deal with him every day, Mr. Rickey was nicknamed the Mahatma, a term for the top dog of a foreign country. It was said with respect, like the way in that movie Don Vito Corleone was called "Godfather."

To his face, all his players and subordinates simply called him Mr. Rickey. You didn't dare call him anything else, not because of fear he'd get mad but simply out of respect for his genius.

Leo Durocher was the one person who called him "Branch." They ended up not liking each other. I'll go into all that in a later chapter. I often wondered how men who were two such opposites could have worked together for as long as they did. Mr. Rickey was a man who enjoyed attending church on Sundays and sometimes even preaching. Leo thought Sunday mornings were to get over the hangover from Saturday night's drinking. Mr. Rickey never swore, certainly never ran around on his wife. He was a devoted family man. Leo—well, I remember once when Leo was managing the Giants and I was managing the Pirates. We were together one night trying to work out a trade, and we each had somebody from our respective team's front office with us. The trade talks went on and on, and finally somebody said, "Let's quit for now and get back together tomorrow morning." Leo stood up and barked, "I don't know about you other three, but tomorrow morning I'm going to be back in Beverly Hills having a good time with a woman!" Actually, what he said was a lot blunter than that, and I don't doubt for a minute that's exactly what Leo did. In the same position, Mr. Rickey would have gone right to bed while hoping the representatives of the other team went out partying so they wouldn't have clear heads when trade negotiations resumed the next morning.

But as I say, that was one of Mr. Rickey's gifts. He didn't expect his manager to be exactly like him. As long as Leo could get the Dodgers to produce, he had Mr. Rickey's support.

And Leo knew he did. Mr. Rickey would prove it when necessary. When I arrived in Brooklyn, our best pitcher was Bobo Newsome.

In the first part of '43 I think he'd won nine games and lost only four. Then in one game against Pittsburgh, I was catching Newsome with the bases loaded and a 3-2 count on Elbie Fletcher, the Pirate first baseman. Maybe Bobo dripped some sweat on the ball accidentally, but all I know for sure is that he wound up and threw me a wet one without telling me it was coming. The damn pitch broke two feet and got by me all the way to the backstop. I ran to retrieve it, but of course the winning run scored from third. When I picked up the ball and turned around to throw to the plate, Bobo was just standing there with his hands on his hips, his posture saying loud and clear in front of everybody, "How could you have missed that pitch?"

Well, we went into the clubhouse and Leo and Newsome immediately got into it. Leo made sure everyone could hear him tell Bobo, "I don't mind my pitchers throwing a spitball, but the catcher's got to know when it's coming!" Bobo yelled at him, Leo yelled back and the insults got more and more personal as the rest of the team gawked. Leo's last words to Newsome were, "I'm going to suspend you for insubordination!"

Within a week, Mr. Rickey traded Bobo to the St. Louis Browns. The same man who was always ready to outsmart the other general managers had this time given away his best pitcher and gotten very little in return. I can't even remember what player we got for Newsome.

A day or two after the trade I happened to see Mr. Rickey. He said to me, "Bobby, I appreciate your keeping your mouth shut during the argument between Newsome and Leo. Leo was totally in the right; I can't imagine a player trying to show up the manager like that in the presence of his teammates. Well, young man, if you think you ever saw a person that was busy, you should have seen me trying to get rid of that fellow Newsome. Really, I would have given him away for nothing. That was no way for a professional baseball player to act."

Some of the other players actually resented what happened to Newsome. I recall Arky Vaughn, whom I admired very much, walking to Durocher's office and throwing his uniform jersey in through the open door, yelling, "Here's another one you can have." But Arky would never have said the same to Mr. Rickey, and Leo could afford to ignore what Arky did because Mr. Rickey had already sent the message that the manager of the Dodgers had the authority to discipline his players.

There are so many Branch Rickey stories to tell. Though he never swore, when upset he'd often blurt, "Judas Priest." It was a catch phrase to use where other people might holler, "Jesus Christ." When things didn't go Mr. Rickey's way, "Judas Priest" would echo off the walls.

Mr. Rickey always wore a bow tie and, more often than not, a hat. He was a very formal person in most ways. Usually someone was hired to follow him around taking care of the small details Mr. Rickey was too busy to think about. Kenny Blackburn stayed with Mr. Rickey for years.When they'd get to a railroad station or airport, Mr. Rickey would want to buy a cigar and Blackburn, a skinny guy with bad teeth, would always have to come up with a quarter to buy him one because the boss never carried any money. And as Mr. Rickey chewed up the cigar, he'd deposit the wet bits in his coat pocket. I always felt sorry for whoever had to go through his pockets before sending those coats out to be cleaned.

If he'd been of a political bent, I believe Branch Rickey would have been a U.S. Senator or even President. Even his leisure time was spent trying to understand everyone around him. Mr. Rickey's favorite parlor game was to gather a dozen people around him and give each one a sheet of paper and a pencil. Then he'd tell you to number the paper from 1-10 down the left side. With that done, he'd ask questions of the group in general, things like, "If you could have any car made, what would you drive?' and "If you were in the hospital and had a semi-private room, who besides a family member would you want in the other bed?" When all 10 questions were asked and answered in writing, he'd call for the papers, read out the responses on each sheet, and then guess who had written what. He was usually correct.

Later on when I became a manager in the Dodger minor league chain, I learned that every night during spring training Mr. Rickey would hold meetings for all his managers, coaches, and scouts from every level of the organization. The manager of the lowest level farm club sat shoulder to shoulder with the Dodger manager. When everyone had arrived, Mr. Rickey would talk for an hour or two hours.

His lectures took many turns. Sometimes he talked baseball strategy. He'd tell us the best way to evaluate our players was to take our lineups before a game and compare them position by position to the other team. In comparing first basemen, for instance, we should look at the opposing player and ask ourselves, "Do I want him playing for me or against me?" and then ask the same question about our own player. If in making that comparison we regularly would have preferred the player on the other team, then it was time to get rid of the player we had.

He talked to us about how much sense it made to bat our best hitter first in the lineup even if he was a slugger. "It's unreasonable to deprive the finest hitter of an extra chance to bat in a game," he'd say. To give an example using modern players, if you managed the San Francisco Giants, would you rather have Will Clark or Robbie Thompson get up an extra time during a game? Later on I would use this philosophy with great hitters like Hank Aaron and Roberto Clemente.

When the time came during spring training for managers to cut players from their roster, Mr. Rickey would suggest we use his "lost at sea" scenario.

"If you're trying to choose between two pitchers like Rex Barney and Hal Gregg," he might say, "If you must keep one with Brooklyn and send one back to the minor leagues, pretend you're in a boat with those two fellows. If the boat capsizes and you have just one life jacket to spare, which do you save?"

Mr. Rickey cautioned us about how and when to give players advice. The best teaching technique in the world won't help if someone doesn't want to learn, he'd say over and over.

What we called his "Uncle John Nance" story was Mr.Rickey's favorite. Even if you'd managed for him for 10 years, he'd make sure you heard this tale once every spring training.

"Be patient with your players, even if they've gone 0-for-15," he'd begin. "You must let people prove to themselves that they can't get the job done in their own way.

"My uncle, John Nance, was an avowed atheist," Mr. Rickey would continue. "Yet in his old age, Uncle John's doctor came to him and said, 'John, it grieves me to tell you, but with you it's just a matter of hours.' It was then for the first time that this now-sick man looked at the ceiling and cried, 'God help me!'

"And that, Mr. Manager, is the way it must be," Mr. Rickey would conclude. "Until your batter proves to himself he can't hit in his own way, and that his professional life is about to expire, then leave him alone. If you force him to do something before he is ready he will probably fail miserably, and point the finger of guilt at you. But if he is the one who comes to you saying, 'Mr. Manager, help me,' then he is ready to accept your good advice. He will do better, and trust your judgment the next time correcting must be done."

Mr. Rickey never took it upon himself to offer a player advice on how to hit, field, or pitch better. He knew it was proper for managers and coaches to do that. He did spend his spring training and regular season days at the ballpark, though, seeing everything that happened with everybody in a Dodger uniform.

The only time he would intrude on daily activity would be to step in and help someone emotionally, especially youngsters in camp for the first time. Mr. Rickey truly cared about young people, and wanted them to be happy if possible. Many is the time I saw Mr. Rickey go over to some 18-year-old rookie or other in spring training and, after spending some time talking with him, ask, "Son, are you homesick?" The boy might say, "Yes, sir," and Mr. Rickey would respond, "Go in and tell Fresco Thompson I said you could go home for three days. But then come right back—the Dodgers need you!" And off the boy would go, excited about seeing his mother but also thrilled because Branch Rickey had said the Dodgers needed him.

That was Mr. Rickey—the rawest Dodger farmhand in Class A ball was as important to him as Leo Durocher, which the farmhand undoubtedly appreciated but Leo didn't.

For 20 years Mr. Rickey was my mentor, my teacher and, I don't mind admitting, my idol. I think of him very often. Among all the great men I have met, in baseball and in the rest of my life, he remains Number One, and there's a big gap between him and the second rung.

There will be many more Branch Rickey stories in the next chapters, including triumphs and failures like when he was forced out of the Dodger hierarchy. But our relationship was pretty well set from our meeting at my first Dodger spring training. We might disagree sometimes in the future, but I never again tried to outmaneuver him, especially where money was concerned. Except once.

Even though he'd made it sound like I'd spend every game collecting bench splinters instead playing, at one point in that first Dodger season I caught 80 straight games. Since it had been Mr. Rickey's point I wouldn't get paid more because I wouldn't play much, I thought I'd go by his office and point out his prediction hadn't been correct.

After that 80th game, I went to see Mr. Rickey. His secretary, Jane Jones, greeted me and heard my request to see the boss. She went into his office and came back in a minute saying, "Mr. Rickey can't see you today, Bobby, but he wants you to come back tomorrow at noon before the game."

I returned at noon as requested, and Jane told me to go right in. As I entered his office, Mr. Rickey stood up and greeted me with a somewhat concerned expression.

"Bobby," he said, "My secretary told me you came by to see me yesterday, and I've been wracking my brain ever since wondering what this young man might want to talk to me about. I prayed to God it wouldn't be a request for more money, Bobby, because either you're the kind of man who can live up to a contract or you're not. Isn't that right, Bobby?"

"You're exactly right, Mr. Rickey," I said, backing toward the door. "I just dropped in to say hello. Good to see you." And I went on my way.

B	E	T	W	E	E	N
I	N	N	I	N	G	S

ROY CAMPANELLA: I always thought that Branch Rickey was a genius. This was something I figured out the very first time I met the man. I was playing in the old Negro League and we had an All-Star game in New York, I think maybe in 1945. Somebody came up to me before the game and asked if I'd come to the Dodger offices at 10 that Saturday morning.

That was the next day. I went to the Dodger office and was introduced to Branch Rickey. He immediately told me he wanted me to be with the Dodger organization. Right there on his desk he had a scouting report on me, and it must have been three inches thick. He had me sit down and he read it all to me. This man had information on every part of my game, he was telling me things about myself as a player that I didn't even know. Mr. Rickey must have had his scouts following me around for the longest time. I was flattered to know he had so much interest in me.

So this is how it all began. I was going to play winter ball in Caracas, Venezuela, and Mr. Rickey wanted my address there. He said someone from the Dodgers would contact me and I would then be invited to their spring training. He had plans for me, Mr. Rickey said. He'd taken care to make sure I was exactly the player he needed. All this, and he did it without me even knowing it.

STAN MUSIAL: The concept of making a player fundamentally sound before he gets to the majors went back to Branch Rickey. You can't praise the man enough. He was the father of the farm system, and not just because he was the first to use sophisticated techniques to find the best players. He also picked managers who were good teachers. The kids learned from quality professionals who were also good fellas.

Sometimes people don't agree that under Rickey the Cardinals and Dodgers had the best farm systems for developing players properly. I say, look at it this way: along with the New York Yankees, those three clubs have more players in the Hall of Fame than any other teams. That's not a coincidence.

LEO DUROCHER: He always wanted everybody to call him Mr. Rickey. I called him Branch. He didn't like it.

BUZZIE BAVASI: You've heard the story of how Mr. Rickey promised his mother he'd never go to the ballpark on Sundays, and it's true he didn't. But it's also true that while he was home on those Sundays, he'd call me sixteen or seventeen times a game at the ballpark wanting to know about attendance and how the game was going.

DICK WILLIAMS: I still thank God I was signed by the Dodgers and went through the Rickey system. That Rickey influence on sound fundamentals was passed on by him to Bobby Bragan and by Bobby Bragan to me, and you can spend hours listing all the people whose lives were touched and influenced by Branch Rickey. Think of all the managers—Leo, Walter Alston, Gil Hodges, Roger Craig, Gene Mauch—we tried to count them up one time and I think in the last four decades there were maybe 30 major league managers who learned directly from Mr. Rickey. Some of them may have eventually gone their separate ways with other organizations, but they taught the game the way it should be taught because of what they learned from Mr. Rickey, even if a few of them never would admit it.

MUSIAL: Mr. Rickey was way ahead of his time. He could have been anything he'd wanted to be. He was the first one to be experimental in that he changed the positions of lots of players. He could look at a guy once and know he was better suited to second base than third, and so forth. And he was as cheap as they say.

AL GIONFRIDDO: Mr. Rickey was one of the first owners who knew how to make money out of the game. He's the one who really made baseball a business.

MUSIAL: When I came up in '41, Mr. Rickey signed me for two years. I took it as a compliment he wanted me for that long. Later on I realized he figured I'd have a big rookie year and then want more money for my second, so signing me cheap for two years cost me a big raise. Branch Rickey didn't believe ballplayers and money should mix. He'd always say to us not to worry about the season salary and talked about how we'd make extra money in the World Series. And for a few years while he was running the Cardinals, that did happen.

DUKE SNIDER: The way Mr. Rickey was, he'd mold his managers and players into his image whether they liked it or not. But if they liked to win, they generally grew to accept he knew best.

BROOKLYN

IN 1943, BROOKLYN WAS A NATIONAL JOKE. Not the Dodgers, but the borough. "Borough" is New Yorkese for "suburb." People living in Brooklyn were considered, well, different by everybody else. Brooklynites were even supposed to have their own dialect—"dese" for "these," "dem" for "them" and so on. To live in Brooklyn was to be considered an exotic, if not sophisticated, breed of human being.

There were three major league baseball teams in the area then, and each drew its own special set of fans. The New York Yankees were the aristocrats. When their fans came out to Yankee Stadium, they sneaked away from $50,000-a-year jobs in skyscrapers on Wall Street. New York Giants fans were the traditionalists, priding themselves on decades of wonderful ballclubs and heroes like John McGraw and Christy Mathewson.

Brooklyn Dodger fans had one simple quality: They loved their team no matter what. Win, and they rejoiced with you. Lose, and they sympathized. I ended up playing in Brooklyn for most of four seasons with a two-year interruption for military service. In all that time, I never really heard Brooklyn fans boo their Dodgers. If somebody made an error in a crucial situation there might be a collective groan or sigh in the stands, but nothing worse.

"Dem Bums," they called us, but affectionately. The players returned that affection. We lived near Ebbets Field, we knew the regulars at the ballpark, and we often called our fans by name. After playing in Philadelphia where so-called Phillies fans found their pleasure most in berating the home team, Brooklyn was paradise for me.

Of course, it was tough at first for an Alabama boy to make some lifestyle transitions for the big city. The first thing that hit me about Brooklyn was that I didn't need the car I'd so proudly purchased in Birmingham over the winter. I'd paid $600 for a Plymouth, the first car I'd ever owned, but when Gwenn and I went apartment hunting in Brooklyn we quickly discovered there was no place to park a car when you weren't using it. We found a garage on Flatbush Avenue where we could store the Plymouth for $20 a month. Sometimes in the evenings we'd take a walk over to the garage to visit the car. We never drove it from the beginning of the season to the end.

Gwenn and I ended up paying $125 a month for a place on the corner of Ocean St. and Church Ave. The apartment was 15 blocks or two subway stops from Ebbets Field. I'd take the subway to the games and walk home down Flatbush Avenue afterwards. Dodger pitcher Hugh Casey owned a restaurant on Flatbush between the ballpark and our apartment, so I might meet Gwenn for supper there. And Dodger players Ed Head, Mickey Owen, and Kirby Higbe all lived in the same apartment complex Gwenn and I did, so there was plenty of company and good baseball talk in the evenings. We found our apartment by talking to those teammates. Clubs didn't help with relocation back then. You had to pay all your own moving expenses and find your own place to live.

All of us on the Dodgers used to enjoy strolling around Brooklyn. The nickname "Lords of Flatbush" was true. It didn't make any difference to Dodger fans whether you were a star pitcher or, as I was destined to be, a second-string catcher. I was pleasantly delayed by autograph-seekers just as much as Dixie Walker, Whitlow Wyatt, or Billy Herman. In a restaurant or on a subway, people would come up with scraps of paper and say, "Bobby, would you sign this?" That is, adults would say that. Most kids would call players "Mr. Bragan" or "Mr. Wyatt" when asking for autographs. All of us signed all of the time. We enjoyed the attention.

There were lots of perks for Dodger players. Fans who owned grocery stores might give you steaks. Haberdashers who loved the team enjoyed giving hats away to any players who wanted them. Gwenn and I made close friends with Harry and Millie Weissinger, a couple who lived in the same apartments. Harry owned Hannah-Troy, a ladies' dress manufacturing company. In exchange for tickets to the games he'd always give healthy discounts to wives of Dodger players.

I immediately felt very comfortable with my new Dodger teammates. Ed Head was from Louisiana, Kirby Highbe was from North Carolina, and Mickey Owen came from Arkansas, so there were several good ol' Southern boys for me to make friends with. And when I arrived at Bear Mountain for my first spring training, I was delighted that Dixie Walker had arranged for me to be his roommate. Dixie, of course, was Harry's brother, and since we both were from Birmingham we had lots of other friends in common. Besides the good company, being Dixie's roommate had other advantages. He had connections with businesses in every city where we played. In Cincinnati, for instance, he'd take me with him to visit the Beau Brummell Tie Co. and the Palm Beach Suit Co. Nice items were to be had there for substantially less than everybody else paid in stores for the same clothing. In New York, Dixie had friends in the discount jewelry business. So we got lots of goodies.

Being a Dodger was different from being a Phillie in just about every baseball way you could imagine, too.

From the minute you entered the Brooklyn clubhouse, you knew who was in charge. Leo. Some managers like to think they're really a 10th player on the field, but with Durocher it was true. He wasn't one to stay back in his clubhouse office and call players in to see him. Leo mingled and mixed, constantly talking to somebody. 1943 was Leo's first season not to be a player-manager, and you could tell he was having a little trouble adjusting. He wanted to grab a bat and take batting practice, and to field practice grounders instead of hitting them. His energy level was unbelievable. He never stopped.

My meeting with Leo on the first day of spring training was very crisp and brief. "Nice to have you with us, Bobby," he said. "You're going to enjoy being a Dodger." That was it. I thought he might tell me where he figured I'd fit in, but he didn't. It was just hello and let's get on the field.

In one respect the Dodger camp mirrored that of the Phillies. Emphasis was on practicing the fundamentals, not on learning them. It was expected that knowing what to do in which situations had been imbued in every player during his stay in the minor leagues. You were already supposed to know that if you were four runs ahead in a late inning you would get the sure out instead of trying for a double play if the ball was hit to you. Even rookies would be aware that if they got on base with the team three runs down they would run conservatively and not get picked off or thrown out trying for an extra base.

The Bear Mountain facilities were first class. There was an indoor facility for batting and fielding practice in case of bad weather. We stayed at the Bear Mountain Inn, a fine hotel run by a wonderful man named John Martin. The team took all its meals together. Afterwards we might sit around talking baseball or gather around a piano. Dixie Walker liked to sing and, as usual, I accompanied him. This was a very important time, because, to use a modern word, the team "bonded."

No detail during daily camp activities was too small to escape notice by Leo or Mr. Rickey. One day I was asked to help with the workout of a free agent pitcher. Free agents then were not the star players looking for multimillion-dollar contracts we have today. Instead, they were raw youngsters hoping to show some stuff and get signed to a contract by any major league team that would invite them to try out. In this case, the free agent pitcher's name was Rex Barney. He started throwing in the indoor facility, and I estimate his pitch speed averaged between 90 and 100 MPH. That was excellent, but what wasn't was Barney's inability to get most of those pitches in the strike zone. I might not have done more than thank Rex for his time, but Mr. Rickey came to watch and told our scout, Clyde Sukeforth, "Go with this boy to his home town in Omaha, and don't let him out of your sight until you sign him." Other free agents were signed, too, though none were as good as Rex Barney. Every team in 1943 was signing players it otherwise wouldn't have been interested in, because the war was draining baseball of many of its quality players.

Even in spring training I could tell everyone associated with the Dodgers expected to win. Not hoped to win—expected to. There was a cockiness, a confidence both on and off the field. The Dodgers knew they were going to win in the same way the Phillies felt we'd have to be lucky if we didn't lose. In 1941 Brooklyn won the National League pennant, and in '42 the team had finished second to Cincinnati. The Reds won 106 games and the Dodgers won 104. In Philadelphia, 104 was about how many we'd lose every year.

I was enthralled to be on the same team with great players I'd been admiring from the other dugout. In the future I wouldn't have to try to hit Whitlow Wyatt or Kirby Higbe. Arky Vaughn, who was deservedly voted into the Hall of Fame a few years back, had a hardnosed work ethic that inspired everybody else on the team. Billy Herman was a true star, sparkling at bat and in the field.

And there was Mickey Owen, the starting catcher. In the 1941 World Series, it had been Mickey's passed ball on a third strike to the Yankees' Tommy Henrich that kept a New York rally going and led to Brooklyn's eventual defeat. If Mickey is remembered today, it's for that passed ball, but in truth he was one of the game's most outstanding catchers of his era, much like Mike Scioscia of today's Los Angeles Dodgers.

As regular catcher, Mickey wore jersey number 10. At that time, all starting catchers wore that number, and this was now my goal - to beat Mickey out of a job and wear #10 myself. That was my aspiration, but the Dodger plans for me were evident when I was assigned #24. Later on Willie Mays made it one of the most popular numbers to wear, but then it just meant I was 24th on a roster of 25 players.

The exhibition season went along smoothly. After listening to some Phillies players criticize Doc Prothro or Hans Lobert behind their managers' backs, I was shocked that not one Dodger at any time during the spring, or the regular season, for that matter, ever second-guessed one of Leo Durocher's moves during a game. Oh, lots of players bitched about Leo disciplining someone or maybe that he favored one player over another unfairly, but as far as knowing what to do while the game was on we all understood Leo was a master. He saw everything; his mind was like a computer in that he'd think five or six batters ahead and like a crystal ball because he always seemed to know what the other manager was thinking, too.

After games, Leo would sit down with the writers and go through all 27 outs for both teams pitch by pitch. He'd say that in the third inning Billy Herman took a fastball high for ball one, a curve over the outside corner for strike one and then hit a high slider into short left-center for a single. It was amazing. I never knew any other manager, coach, or player who could do that without consulting a scorecard or pitching chart.

I played in every spring training game, though mostly as a backup to Mickey Owen. I was hitting the same way I did when I was with the Phillies, which was to say not very well. I still was confident against left-handers, but moving to Brooklyn hadn't increased my confidence with right-handers who threw curveballs.

During the season, though, having Dixie Walker as my room-mate paid off in ways other than discounts on clothes and jewelry. Like his brother Harry, Dixie was a fine hitter. I finally got up the nerve to ask him how, as a lefthanded batter, he was able to stand in so well against breaking pitches from left-handers. He said, "Bobby, I have to make myself go into a pitch; I have to force my front foot in." Knowing it was tough for someone who could hit as well as Dixie somehow made it a little easier for me. I hit .264 in 1943, one of my best batting averages ever in the majors.

When the regular season started I was introduced to the joys of being the home team in Ebbetts Field. The field was cozy and close —the stands hung down over the field; you felt like you could reach out and shake hands with the fans in the cheap seats. When the Dodgers first took the field to warm up a couple of hours before game time, there was always a welcoming committee of fans already in their seats to greet you. It soon got to be like seeing friends every day. Nobody yelled, "Hey, number 24!" Instead it was, "How you doing, Bobby?" The fans were very prideful about their relation-ships with us. They not only knew our names, they hoped and expected we'd get to know their names, too.

I spent lots of Ebbetts Field game time in the Dodger bullpen, warming up relief pitchers and trying to make myself useful in any other way needed. One fellow came to the bullpen during games without fail and would yell, "Chiclets, Bobby?" He'd give me gum, and then pass some out to Rex Barney or Hal Gregg or whoever else might be there, always addressing the players by name. That was his reward, you see, calling players by their given names one by one and knowing they'd respond to him. Even now if I run into Rex Barney, the first thing he'll say is, "Chiclets, Bobby?"

Then there was the matter of players giving away tickets. For each game, each team would give a player four tickets. They could then be given to your family or friends. If you needed more you could ask the manager for some, or get a couple from a teammate who wasn't using all of his. When I joined the Dodgers I told Ralph Branca, Rex Barney, and Dixie Walker about the ticket system at Philadelphia where Hans Lobert required players to give him the names of all the people they wanted game tickets for. Bennie Warren, one of the Phillie catchers, always asked for two for Scroggin, a friend of his. Scroggin must have gone to every Phillie game, home or away. Same thing with Ike Pearson. Before every Phillie game he would tell Hans he needed two for Chatfield. Some of my Dodger buddies thought that was so funny they'd go around before games asking for tickets for Scroggin or Chatfield, and to this day Branca calls me Chat or Scroggin.

I liked giving tickets away to fans. Why not make somebody happy? I knew that as a kid I'd have cried with joy if a major leaguer had given me a ticket to a game, so I made a point of having my four handy. The Dodger bus might pull up to the hotel in St. Louis or Pittsburgh, and I'd see some guy looking like he'd love to talk to a ballplayer. Our eyes would meet and he might say, "Bobby, could you leave me two tickets?" and I'd reply, "Sure, what's your name?" and leave them at the Will Call window. On the next trip, the same guy would probably meet you. And sometimes people would come up to me and say they were from Birmingham, or were friends with somebody I knew who'd told them to say hello to me. After they'd pass along a greeting, they'd inevitably ask for tickets—and I'd always find them a couple. Later on when I was managing the Braves, Milwaukee travelling secretary Donald Davidson told me, "Bobby, you leave passes for some of the seediest people I've ever seen." Well, as far as I'm concerned, anybody who likes baseball can't be all bad.

Sometimes a gift of two tickets would grow into a warm friendship. At Forbes Field I once gave passes to a guy named Jim Laffey. We got to be such friends that when his son was born he was named Bobby Bragan Laffey.

I caught some in '43, but during the regular season most of my game action came at shortstop. Pee Wee Reese was in the military and Leo really didn't have a regular shortstop to replace him. We finished third, a leap upward from what I'd been used to in Philadelphia but a comedown for the veteran Dodgers. The war was taking its toll. As it dragged on, more and more veteran players were being drafted. Because the heart of the Dodgers had been older guys—Herman, Vaughn, Owen, Dolph Camilli, Augie Galan, Frenchy Bordagaray—it took longer for the draft to sap the roster. But it was starting to happen, and within another season it would result in a brief Brooklyn tumble into the National League's second division.

But '43 found the team still more than competitive. I mean the Dodgers hated to lose. In one game I was playing shortstop when Les Webber, the #4 starter, was getting battered around. The other team got four straight hits off him, all solid singles and doubles. When the fifth hitter came to the plate, Webber reached down past the resin bag and got a handful of dirt and pebbles. He put the ball on top and threw the whole mess at the batter. That's the first and only time I ever saw that happen. Today the commissioner would probably suspend him for a week, and TV replays would show the incident for months. In 1943, it was just part of a hard-played game. Nobody said anything and play went on.

The older Dodger players approached the game with intensity but not nervousness. Paul Waner was on the club as a pinch hitter, and he put no importance into the size or weight of a bat. When called into the game he'd close his eyes, approach the bat rack, and put out his hand. The first bat he touched was the one he'd use. He'd pull out this bat at random and then announce, "I'm going to hit a line drive down the left field line." And then he'd do it. The ball might not always be fair, but it would go in the general vicinity that he'd predicted.

Arky Vaughn was another old-timer who kept things in perspective. He didn't play regularly anymore, and games would often find him on the opposite end of the bench from Leo. If Leo wanted Arky to pinch hit, somebody would have to go wake Arky up. That's how worried Arky was. He always had the potential to do something great, too. Once when he was with the Pirates, Arky was picked to play in the All-Star game even though another player, Alf Anderson, had taken over his position at shortstop. Arky went to the All-Star game anyway and hit two home runs. See, when Arky Vaughn played he was always very much awake.

I got up 220 times in that '43 season, catching every third or fourth game and filling in at short in between. I was still hopeful of becoming the starting catcher and getting that #10 jersey. Later on when I managed I insisted on wearing #10. To me, that number signified being successful.

Meanwhile, my fourth season in the majors had rekindled in me the excitement of being a big league ballplayer. By the end of the year I knew there wouldn't be any question about the Dodgers wanting me back. Gwenn, Bobby Jr., and I went to spend the winter in Birmingham, where I again took a defense plant job making that steel. Gwenn was pregnant again, and Cissie was born February 13, 1944. I called her "my little deferment."

I awaited my new Dodger contract with great interest. After my first experience with Mr. Rickey I knew for certain there would be no forthcoming gesture of financial generosity.

Whatever raise I got would have to be squeezed out of him. I eventually got a $750 raise because I had fulfilled what had been expected of me. My play was nothing great, but it had been adequate. I felt my new salary of $6,250 for 1944 would be fair, and was still quite a bit more than my peers in Birmingham received for their year-round jobs.

It was understood by the Dodgers that there was only one sure way to get a raise out of Branch Rickey, and that was to get married. Mr. Rickey believed married players were more settled and anxious to do a good job and provide for their families. All of us heard him approach single players any number of times and make the same offer—"You ought to get married, young man. If you do, I'll give you a $500 bonus." But I was already married, so that extra $500 was never available to me.

```
   ┌───┬───┬───┬───┬───┬───┐
   │ B │ E │ T │ W │ E │ N │
   ├───┼───┼───┼───┼───┼───┤
   │ I │ N │ N │ I │ N │ G │ S
   └───┴───┴───┴───┴───┴───┘
```

BOBBY THOMSON: The Brooklyn thing with the Dodgers was so unique. Brooklyn, the people there, took to the Dodgers as family in a way other fans didn't do with other teams. Brooklyn was really just a small community of people. Comedians used to mention Brooklyn in their routines to get a laugh. But in that time there was a closeness between the team and its community. Brooklynites lived and breathed for their Dodgers.

DUKE SNIDER: Every time I hit a home run in Ebbetts Field I'd sort of touch my cap while rounding the bases. It was a way of acknowledging the crowd. I wasn't signaling anyone in particular. Now, Gil Hodges used to like to throw a kiss to his wife Joan. But I was just thanking the crowd. They loved you when you hit a home run and hurt for you when you struck out. To be a Dodger was to be forgiven anything by the Brooklyn fans. Not to be a Dodger was to be an outsider trying to beat members of the Brooklyn family. The loyalty we had in Brooklyn was never equalled and never will be.

JOE DIMAGGIO: We Yankees certainly considered the Brooklyn Dodgers to be very worthy rivals. We believed our organization was superior and apparently Brooklyn players believed the same of the Dodgers. It made for some very good World Series play.

SNIDER: To be a Dodger, well, Lord, to have that uniform on. You tingled.

LOU BROCK: For the longest time up through my era, if you came into the Dodger, Cardinal, or Yankee organizations you had a tradition you were obligated to live up to. God, with the Cardinals I was aware I was part of the line of Stan Musial, Pepper Martin, back to Dizzy Dean and Frankie Frisch and the Gas House Gang. The Cardinals, Brooklyn, and Yankees instilled the organizational pride, say, the Cardinal way of doing things which from decade to decade proved to be the winning way.

The first day I put on a Cardinal uniform I thought, "Gosh, I'd better be good." When I was with the Cubs I guarantee you I never thought about that. You could walk into Busch Stadium, Ebbetts Field, or Yankee Stadium and besides the applause or boos you hear the footsteps of the past. Just the uniforms of those teams were symbols of success. They are the tuxedos of baseball. In my opinion, there's a lot to be said for that, in how it can positively affect a team even when the franchise has been down a while, like the Cardinals were from the mid-'50s to early '60s or the way the Yankees are today. They can always snap back.

I had a left-handed hitting teammate named Jerry Mumphrey, who was on the Cardinals for a bit and then played for the San Diego Padres for a long time. Eventually they traded him to the Yankees. I saw him then in spring training and asked, "Jer, is it true that Yankee uniform makes players feel 10 feet tall?" He answered, "This son-of-a-bitch makes me feel 20 feet tall, but nobody's pitching right-handers against us so I can prove it."

CAL McLISH: I spent a little time with Brooklyn when I was 18 and as green as they come. '44 and '46. Brooklyn at that time was four things: Mr. Rickey, Ebbetts Field, those fans, and Leo Durocher. The spirit of the team, its successes, seemed to flow from those four things. And Leo just dominated that clubhouse.

SNIDER: I was in awe of Leo Durocher when I first came up, because to me he was what baseball was all about—a very dedicated baseball man. Leo knew all the movie people and off the field he was nice and friendly to everyone, but once the game started it was like Jekyll and Hyde. He wanted to win at any cost and in any way he had to—and he never cared whose feelings he had to hurt while he was doing it. As a result, a lot of people grew to hate him.

BUZZIE BAVASI: Other managers thought an inning ahead. Leo was four or five innings ahead.

AL BARLICK: Leo was a great manager. He knew the game as well or better than anyone. He never made a foolish maneuver. Umpires notice these things. Sure, he would get on us. But I always felt each of his rages had a purpose. He never really lost control, and knew what he was doing at all times.

LEO DUROCHER: I was the best because I knew my teams better than the other sons-of-bitches knew theirs—and I knew their teams better, too.

SNIDER: Other teams hated Leo, and at any time several of his own players weren't crazy about him, either. He had his doghouse, and it was tough to get out of. Leo knew he was unpopular. He once said to me, "If our club gets into a fight on the field, I not only have to be careful of the 25 on the other team, I have to watch out for seven or eight of mine."

You could tell Bobby Bragan thought the world of Leo. He watched everything Leo did. Of course, Bobby had plenty of spare time because he didn't play all that much.

RALPH BRANCA: Bobby Bragan was a great teammate. He played shortstop for Brooklyn as well as catcher. To be truthful, he was not too swift a runner. But historically in baseball the guys who couldn't run became catchers. They were all that way—Bill Dickey, Gabby Hartnett, not to say Bobby was ever on a level with those guys. It's different today because the better athletes have figured out the fastest way to the major leagues is learning to catch.

DUROCHER: Bragan always played very hard for me when he got in games. He did his best. He was no star, but he understood how to fill a supporting role on a team. You can't have 25 stars. You need players who know their place.

BRANCA: Bobby was very smart. I was a young kid who really didn't know how to pitch. He understood the situation and when catching me in games he worked accordingly. That meant I could trust him to know how to set up batters. In my second year, '45, I was a better pitcher and could begin to think some situations through for myself. When I got to that stage Bobby knew it, and as my catcher he adjusted and let me go my own way a little more.

SNIDER: Bobby was very nice to rookies. He took us under his wing. I felt he was very special for doing that.

BRANCA: What I remember most about Bobby is that he had a baseball brain. I mean he was into the game of baseball, every nuance and potential situation. He loved talking about inside stuff, the tactics. In those days everybody on a team talked baseball a lot, but there were always one or two who were most fascinated by it. Bobby was one of the ones like that on the Dodgers, him and Eddie Stanky. Bobby was a student of baseball and because of that I always expected him to get into the managing end of it.

SNIDER: But whether you warmed the bench or hit cleanup, you felt great because you were a Brooklyn Dodger.

WAR

In 1944, Brooklyn finished next to last in the National League. It wasn't because we didn't have a good manager — Leo was as cagey as ever — but the war was definitely a factor. Dolph Camilli was gone, Billy Herman, Whitlow Wyatt, Arky Vaughn, Kirby Higbe. The rest of the teams in the league were hard-hit, too, but war attrition happened to them more gradually. They lost some top players before the Dodgers did, but had a chance to work new guys into their lineups. We lost all our best players at once, except for Pee Wee Reese, who'd gone into the service a couple of seasons earlier.

In that '44 season, St. Louis was clearly the class of the league. They won 105 games, and frankly I couldn't see why they didn't win another 20 or 30 on top of that. The Cardinals were a great team with all the best players in the league on their roster — Musial of course was the biggest star, but they also had the best shortstop in Marty Marion and annual all-stars like Whitey Kurowski, Walker Cooper, Max Lanier, and Harry Brecheen. These fellas all were about the same age, married with a couple of kids. The draft hadn't gotten all the way down to calling up married guys with families. No wonder Mr. Rickey wished we had more family men on the Dodger roster!

In Brooklyn we staggered to a 63-91 season record. With Pee Wee still gone I played most of the time at shortstop, batting .267 in 266 plate appearances. I had so many new teammates it was tough to keep all the names straight. Many would never have made it to the majors without the war taking away so many legitimate big-leaguers.

Even in '44, though, we had some quality players. Goody Rosen, for instance, was the center fielder. Goody was amazing—Pete Rose before Rose was ever thought of. I remember in every game when we were in the field that when the last out was made by the other team Goody would be in the Dodger dugout before our first baseman. He ran that hard just between innings. Rosen hit .325 that year, too. He was the greatest hustler in the positive sense that I ever saw play. Eddie Stanky took Billy Herman's place at second base. Mr. Rickey was the one who nicknamed Stanky "The Brat." And Stanky was. He'd make a fuss over everything, and wasn't shy suggesting he knew more about any subject than the next guy. But put Eddie Stanky on a baseball field and the man was amazing to watch. Not that Stanky was in any way a good or even average athlete. Mr. Rickey would say, "He can't run, he can't hit, he can't throw. All he can do is beat you." With the Dodgers, Stanky was considered just good enough to hold down a spot in the starting lineup until the real players got back from the war. After a couple seasons in Brooklyn, Stanky went over to the Boston Braves and was a big part of their championship team in '48. They really didn't appreciate him either and shipped him on to the New York Giants. If you watch the old newsreels of Thomson's Miracle Homer in 1951, you'll see Leo, who'd gone over to the Giants by then, dancing with Stanky in the third-base coach's box while Thomson ran by. Some people think Stanky grabbed Leo to keep him from hugging Thomson and maybe making him miss third base, because if that happened the Dodgers could have appealed and gotten Thomson called out. But anybody who knew Leo knew he was too smart to do that. Any major league manager or coach would have known better. This myth has irritated me for years. The truth is, Stanky loved Leo and was so excited that he wanted to share the special moment with his manager. It's farcical to think anything else.

In '44, though, Leo was still with the Dodgers. The season must have been hell for him, but he never let on. It's been said Leo was best at managing contending clubs, because his brilliance during games would get any team he led a half-dozen extra wins during a season above and beyond what the players themselves would have earned. But to me Leo was also gifted at running a club where the players needed to be inspired to perform at a higher level. With the Dodgers in '44, Leo could have made it plain he had a squad composed mostly of Triple A players, and that he was just biding his time until the real Dodgers got back from the war. Instead, he stayed absolutely the same somewhat loud, abrasive leader who'd holler at you one minute and pat you on the back the next.

If he thought it would help, Leo even let himself be the target of team humor. In '44 there was one incident on a train trip when Leo fell asleep in a lounge chair and a player, catcher Dee Moore, lit a hot foot on Leo's $85 tan shoes. Leo was a clothes horse and he was especially proud of those shoes. When the flames licked his foot and woke him up, he was less concerned about getting burned than trying to see if his shoe was permanently smudged—it was. Leo shouted, "I'll give anybody $250 if they'll tell me who the bastard was who ruined my shoe!" Well, no one would tell on Moore, and we all had a good laugh. It promoted a little player unity on a team going nowhere.

We were so bad that Roscoe McGowan, a veteran writer for the *New York Times*, wrote a song about us in his column. We'd been in a tailspin, losing 11 or 12 straight, and after each loss Roscoe would add a new verse to his song, which was based on the old standard "Bless 'Em All." For one game Mr. Rickey promoted a young supposed hotshot from the minors and put him at short. The rookie booted a crucial grounder and another loss was Brooklyn property. The next day McGowan wrote:
  "Lose 'em all, lose 'em all,
  Can this thing go on until fall?
  'Miksis will fix us,' said Rickey, the boss,
  Put him at shortstop and chalk up a loss..."

That's how bad we were. Of course, after being with the Phillies I felt right at home. Also, even in that terrible season of '44 I had the satisfaction of being on a team that still finished ahead of Philadelphia.

When you've got a lousy team, you have to try other means of getting fans in the stands. One night Mr. Rickey put us in slick, shiny satin uniforms. The other team, of course, was still in flannel. We looked like walking ads for ladies' underwear. And when we took the field and started the game, we found that these uniforms were very, very hot. We sweated until, by the ninth inning, even our gloves were soaked with perspiration. I can't blame the uniform, but in the ninth inning when the score was tied, the bases were loaded, and Leo had his infield in, I let a ground ball go right through my legs to lose the game. The great Brooklyn fans didn't boo, and never screamed anything in poor taste about the possible personal habits of ballplayers wearing satin uniforms. I shuddered to think what might have been yelled at me if I'd been in the same situation in Philadelphia.

In 1944 I first decided I would try to stay in pro ball as a manager. My reasoning was simple. Even in war ball, so to speak, I couldn't stay in a major league starting lineup. Playing at my best, I still was skilled enough only to be a reserve. And when the war was over and the best players got back, marginal players would quickly be cut. My luck was to be playing for Leo, so I could watch the best and learn from him.

For instance, I noticed Leo never, ever got on any player for a physical error. He knew nobody deliberately went on the field and screwed up. But I often saw him take a player's money for a mental blunder. It was Leo's opinion, and later mine, that major league ballplayers should know what was going on in games at all times. If a player doesn't care enough to concentrate, then he needs to lose some money to remind him where his attention should be.

Of course, even when you're near-perfect there are still things you could do better. I knew from experience Leo was making a mistake not having his game lineup posted before players got to the clubhouse. See, on any team there are always six or seven standouts who know they're going to be starting in almost every game, but the other seven or eight non-pitchers would like to know the lineup, too. A number of times when I played for Leo I assumed I wasn't starting, so I'd catch batting practice. Then I'd come to the clubhouse all worn out and sweaty to find Leo had decided at the last minute to have me catch the full nine innings or maybe play short. When I ran the Pirates, Indians, and Braves I always had my lineup posted before the first player arrived.

Besides the pressure of constantly losing, Dodger players in '44 also had to worry about being drafted. Uncle Sam was starting to call up married men with children, so those of us who'd been passed up before knew we stood a good chance of becoming soldiers. One fear for all of us was that we'd go to war, get wounded, and never be able to play ball again. We all heard about Burt Shepard, a pitcher for Washington, who was in combat and had his leg shot off. Shepard is a forgotten baseball hero. He came back to become the only major leaguer ever who played with an artificial leg. Can you imagine how famous some current player would have been if he'd fought in Desert Storm, lost a leg, and still come back to play in the big leagues? Well, times were different then.

By the end of the '44 season, guys up to age 30 were being drafted. I was 27, so my name had to be coming up shortly. It did while Gwenn, the children, and I were home in Birmingham for the winter, in January of 1945, I guess. As soon as I got the draft notice I contacted the Dodgers. The team sent me back a form letter wishing me luck in the war. My salary from the team stopped as soon as I was called up. The Bragans went from the relative comfort of $6,250 a year to the Army pay of $100 a month plus $20 for each child. Gwenn had trouble adjusting. Some of our family members had to step in and help out financially.

As a first step of joining the service, I got on a bus one day with the rest of the local recruits for a ride to Fort McClellan in Anniston, Alabama. We were put through some tests and sent home to make our goodbyes. On the ride to the base I remember a lot of joking. On the ride back everybody was quiet.

A couple days later I was ordered to Camp Wheeler in Macon, Georgia for basic training. I won't lie and say my experience there was the same as any other guy who'd just been drafted. Every basic training camp in the country had officers on the lookout for pro baseball players who showed up, and my group at Camp Wheeler had its share. Besides me there was Carl Shibe, a Philadelphia A's pitcher; Joe Dobson, a Boston Red Sox right-hander; and a 19-year-old named Johnny Logan. Logan hadn't signed with any pro team yet, but word was out in baseball circles that he was a sure-thing star. After the war he ended up signing with the Boston Braves. I'd put a good word in for him with the Dodgers, but the Braves must have made Logan the best offer.

In theory, I was to be trained for the infantry. My platoon spent a lot of time in the Alabama woods on what was called "bivouac." This consisted of much stumbling around and getting lost. But a number of times a Lieutenant Smith, the camp baseball coach, would drive up in a jeep and announce he had to take Dobson, Shibe, Logan, and Bragan back to the base for baseball practice. Oddly, I don't remember the other guys resenting us and our good luck. And, of course, we did all the dirty stuff the other guys did except for taking breaks for baseball three or four times a week.

The war was at its height, and in the back of his mind every recruit expected he'd see combat duty. It wasn't a pleasant thought, especially for those of us with families. Even though it was a tough trip for her, twice during my 16-week basic training Gwenn came with our children for weekend visits. Any family time at all was precious. It could have been the last.

While I was in basic training I followed the Dodgers '45 season as closely as I could. A thousand miles or so to the north, Leo was working a miracle. Following that disastrous seventh-place finish in '44, Leo got the team up to third place in 1945, winning 87 games. The Chicago Cubs won the pennant that year—it has been their last one to date.

Mr. Rickey had given Leo the best team he could under the circumstances. Mike Sandlock came up to catch. Bruce Edwards and I ran him off after the war. Eddie Basinski played shortstop that year—and the violin, too. He took my place as team instrumentalist.

In 1946, Leo did even better. The Dodgers finished in a tie for first place, losing in a playoff to St. Louis. What with the team finishing seventh in my last year, then third and tied for first when I was gone, I suppose I should have been worried about my future with the Dodgers when the war was over. Obviously I wasn't indispensable. But I never was concerned about them having a place for me. In a way, the challenge to get through the war and get back to the majors inspired me the same way the initial struggle to get through the minors and up to the big leagues had. My goal in the war was to serve honorably and get the hell out afterwards.

At the end of the 16-week basic training course, the base commander announced anybody interested in Officer Training School should apply and take some tests. With that choice or combat overseas, I chose the test. Fortunately, I passed and was sent on to Fort Benning, Georgia, which was close enough to Birmingham for me to take the bus home on a few weekends.

I had an interesting time at Fort Benning. To start with, I was about 10 years older than most of the other would-be officers in my platoon. For 18 weeks I felt like the father of hundreds. I hung in and earned my commission around mid-summer of 1945. Instead of immediately being sent overseas, I was asked to take myself and my new second lieutenant bars back to Fort McClellan, where I was assigned to teach new recruits how to fire mortars and Browning automatic rifles. It was my first chance to teach. I tried to use humor when I could, and to keep things simple. I told the recruits firing a mortar was easy. You might loft the first shell too far and the second shell too short, then you knew for sure the target was between the two points. I was commended for my brevity of presentation; what my superiors didn't know was I had to keep it simple because I didn't understand the subject too well myself.

It was about this time at Fort McClellan when I first met Tommy Lasorda. I was walking through the headquarters building when I saw him, about as raw a recruit as the Army could possibly have. He asked, "Sir, where do I go for sick call? I've got pains in my chest." I told Tommy to go to a red brick building on his left—the dispensary. He went in and saw a sign which ordered him to sign in and enter a door on the right. Lasorda did, and found a new notice reading "Examination and Diagnosis—sign in and enter the door on the right." He did again, to find a third sign reading, "X-Ray: sign in, enter door on the right." He did that and found himself back outside on the sidewalk.

I was waiting to have a good laugh on him. "Did you see the medic?" I asked. "No, sir," Lasorda replied, "But they've sure got that dispensary organized!"

Even then, Tom Lasorda was full of pepper and ginger—what is now called enthusiasm. He always liked to laugh, and never minded if the joke being laughed at concerned him. These days at banquets when we're both on the program I tell the audience I first met Tom at Fort McClellan when he was carrying a pig under his arm. "Where did you get that?" I asked. "I won him in a raffle," the pig replied. It always gets a laugh, and Lasorda laughs loudest of all.

Shortly after our real first meeting, Lasorda and I were buddies on the regimental baseball team. He had a good curve and decent control, but no fastball to speak of. He was, however, always a holler guy.

We had a good team at Fort McClellan. Rocky Colavito's cousin was on the roster, and there were other decent players. Since we were so close to Birmingham, sometimes I arranged for us to play an all-Bragan team—six brothers and myself and a couple of cousins. We played several games. The Bragans had fun, but never won.

In February 1946 my luck seemed to change. Fort McClellan's commander, a Colonel Wallace Cheeves, gave me orders to report to Korea by way of Fort Lawton in Seattle, Washington. Korea was a mess, with the Japanese occupying it and mostly Russian forces trying to drive them out. I also understood Korea was a very, very cold country—somehow the thought of playing in Boston against the Braves during a snowstorm didn't seem as bad to me as it had a few years earlier.

When I got to Fort Lawton, its commander, Major Tufte, called me and two other stopover officers into his office and said, "You fellows are on orders to Korea, but I really think the war is going to be over soon. I don't advocate sending Category Five soldiers (those who would be mustered out after the war at the earliest convenience to the Army) overseas when they'll just be brought right back. So you're going to go to work for me."

It sounded great. What I didn't know was that Fort Lawton had become famous for its inefficiency. Top officers flying over to the western front often came through there, and one too many generals hadn't enjoyed the accomodations. Major Tufte had to get the base cleaned up, and I was one of the low echelon officers he expected to do it for him.

I was given a detachment of 20 soldiers and orders to restore the base's crumbling barracks. We rebuilt some of them and repainted all of them, meaning I ended my army career the same way I started out in baseball. I'd run my detail all day, then change to workout clothes and throw batting practice for the Seattle Raniers of the Pacific Coast League. It helped me keep my arm in shape.

As the war wound down I couldn't wait to get discharged and back to the Dodgers. In late January 1947 I got my discharge and took the train from Seattle to Birmingham. Gwenn and the kids had come up to meet me, and we had to change trains in Chicago. The north wind was blowing in my life, and I had no doubt it was still 50 degrees warmer than in Korea.

After three weeks in Birmingham I headed to Havana, where the Dodgers were holding spring training. I had notified the club I'd be back just as soon as I'd gotten my discharge papers in Seattle. I got another form letter welcoming me back and giving the dates spring training would get underway.

This was the first time I'd seen the Dodgers at full strength. There seemed to be stars at every position. I remember having special appreciation for Bruce Edwards, a catcher. Mickey Owen had signed with the Mexican League, and I had every hope of getting most of the time behind the plate. Well, Bruce Edwards was a great catcher with superb mechanics. However, at this particular spring training Leo was especially excited about having a full ballclub again and he was a little too anxious to see what kind of players were now available to him. He scheduled our first hard workouts for the fourth day of camp. Edwards, like most players in those days, hadn't worked out much in the off season. Leo put him behind the plate for infield, got all worked up about how powerful Edwards's arm was, and the upshot was that by the end of spring training Edwards left his once-powerful arm in the red infield dirt of Havana. Today a ballplayer would gripe to the manager if he had the tiniest twinge in his throwing arm. Edwards knew if he bitched his arm hurt he'd get laughed at, and that Bobby Bragan would happily take over while Bruce tried to heal. So he kept throwing and his arm went dead, permanently. Yet Bruce Edwards caught 130 games for Brooklyn in 1947 despite the fact he could no longer throw the ball to second base on the fly. Edwards never took infield before regular season games, and if somebody tried to steal on him he'd be so quick to get the ball on the way to second or third that he often bounced it in ahead of the runner.

I couldn't even beat out a guy who couldn't throw. Edwards hit .295 that season, too. I was in just 25 games with a .194 average. Thirty-six at-bats, seven hits. I wasn't fooling anybody. Though I managed to stay around for '47 and part of '48. I wasn't going to be a major leaguer much longer because of physical skills. My brain would have to keep me in baseball.

Though my own performance in 1947 was lousy, I still am grateful to have been part of a very special team. Of course, that was Jackie Robinson's first year. But as great as he was, Jackie Robinson was just one part of a unique bunch of players who made up the post-war Brooklyn Dodgers.

B	E	T	W	E	E	N
I	N	N	I	N	G	S

LEO DUROCHER: I can't even remember half the players we ran through the club during the last war years. There were so many. Most of 'em weren't any good. We finished up there, we finished near the bottom, you played who you had and it was all very frustrating.

I almost won one year in spite of everything. I can't remember the number (the season). But I used what I had and that time I did pretty good. We lost a playoff.

I guess Bragan was gone that year, in the service like the rest of them. What hurt me more, though, was losing Camilli and Whitlow Wyatt. Billy Herman, too. Herman was a hell of a player.

Everybody in baseball just wanted the damned war to be over so we could get back to playing the best against the best.

I wouldn't say Bobby lost a step or two while he was in the Army. He was slow when he left and slow when he came back.

1947

IN SOME WAYS, THE 1947 BROOKLYN DODGERS became the first team of the modern baseball era. Season statistics don't entirely reflect this. We won 94 games, which was good but by no means record-setting. No Dodger hitters were among National League leaders in the traditional "important" hitting categories—batting average, home runs, runs batted in. We played for an interim manager and, for most baseball fans, our '47 team is memorable only for Jackie Robinson's rookie year. We even lost the World Series to the Yankees —a World Series now remembered only because it was the first to be nationally televised.

Yet we did change baseball, and Jackie was only the most obvious part of that.

Originally baseball was a game of speed and daring. Teams strung together singles in the dead ball era. Pitching often dominated. The first renowned major league slugger, Frank "Home Run" Baker, hit 12 in his best season (1913) and just 96 total in his 13-year career. Ty Cobb began stealing bases in bunches and glorified the running game for almost a decade. Few people remember Cobb was a major league star for nine years before Babe Ruth broke in with the Red Sox as a rookie pitcher.

Ruth changed everything, starting in 1920 when he hit a then-unbelievable 29 homers for the Yankees. For seven more years the Babe belted the ball out of every American League ballpark, then set what would be a decades-long benchmark with 60 homers in 1927. Lou Gehrig hit homers in bunches, too. Jimmy Foxx did the same. Baseball fans were swept up in a new phenomenon: power. Team owners, most interested in what would put fans in the stadium seats, built their teams accordingly. Fans wanted home runs and 10-8 games where before a 3-2 contest was the order of the day.

In 1947, exactly 20 years after Ruth's 60-home run season, the Brooklyn Dodgers as built by Branch Rickey went back to smart, speed-defense-pitching oriented baseball. It was the type of play which would typify Dodger teams for a long time. On offense, Brooklyn hitters led the league in just two categories—stolen bases and bases on balls. We also had several players high up in the runs scored category. We'd get our four or five runs a game the same way Cobb's Tigers used to do it—a couple of singles, a stolen base, a sacrifice bunt, a sacrifice fly. We then let our pitching staff, led by Ralph Branca and his 21 wins, hold the lead. And since 1947 was also one of the first years teams recognized the value of a bullpen stopper, it should be no surprise that Mr. Rickey gave the Dodgers one of the best —Hugh Casey.

We played smart baseball. We never beat ourselves with mental errors. It's no accident so many players from that team and the Brooklyn farm system at the time went on to manage in the majors. They included Gil Hodges, Eddie Stanky, Norm Sherry, Gene Mauch, Roger Craig, Sparky Anderson, Dick Williams, Clyde King, and me.

Jackie had much to do with our success. This was the first season baseball writers elected rookies of the year, and Jackie easily won that honor in the National League. He led the league in stolen bases with 29, which doesn't sound like much today after Lou Brock and Rickey Henderson. But bear in mind Jackie's closest pursuer in 1947 had just 14 stolen bases, and that was Pete Reiser, our center fielder. Stolen bases had simply been ignored as part of team offense for 20 years.

Jackie was also second in the league in runs scored with 125, and tied with Pee Wee Reese, that famous slugger, for the Dodger team lead in home runs with 12. Nobody else had more than nine, and this in a season when Ralph Kiner and Johnny Mize tied for the league lead with 51.

For a season that started in chaos with Jackie breaking the so-called "color barrier" and Leo being suspended by Happy Chandler, we ended up doing pretty well, don't you think?

After Mr. Rickey announced Chandler's edict at our season-opening luncheon, coach Clyde Sukeforth managed us in the opening game, which we won. Then Mr. Rickey turned the team over to Burt Shotton, who'd managed some for Mr. Rickey in the St. Louis Cardinal farm system. Shotton was in his '60s, a lovable old man. He was soft-spoken and fatherly where Leo had been much more outgoing and abrasive. The thing I remember most about Burt is that, after we'd lose a close game, the kind that hurt so much, he'd come back into the clubhouse and say, "There's always tomorrow." That was it. No shouting, no finger-pointing. It was just impossible to dislike Burt Shotton. He was the type of manager Walter Alston would be for the Dodgers later on.

If Burt Shotton is remembered at all today, it's for being the second—and last—man to manage in street clothes. Only Connie Mack had done it before. Burt wore a Dodger cap and jacket over his suit or dress shirt and slacks. Clyde Sukeforth would sit on the bench next to Burt during games, and would be the one to change pitchers or run out on the field to argue with the umpires. Burt wasn't allowed on the field during games because he was out of full uniform. I guess it might have made more sense for him to suit out, but he never did and I can't remember anyone asking him why or suggesting he should.

All of the players liked Burt, but we remained loyal to Leo. That loyalty was proven after the '47 Series when we voted Leo a full share of the Series money. Chandler stepped in and negated that vote, saying it wasn't in the best interests of baseball. We really resented that—we'd earned that Series pot and it should have been our right to divide it up the way we pleased.

Burt realized he was only the interim manager. I know that different players kept in touch with Leo during the '47 season. Chandler's suspension barred Leo from the ballpark during the regular season, but I know that during the World Series he sat right behind the Dodger dugout. Whether Leo was in touch with Burt during the season, though, I couldn't tell you. I doubt it, though. Leo had class, and he respected Burt Shotton enough to let Burt manage in his own way.

We had two future Hall of Famers on the '47 club, Jackie and Pee Wee Reese. A third, Duke Snider, joined us halfway through the season. But we were strong up and down the order with players who, even if they didn't rack up the most impressive statistics, played smart and worked well together as a team.

At first base, of course, was Jackie Robinson. Just to see Jackie warming up was to possibly get the impression he wasn't much of a player. He swung the bat kind of awkwardly, and when he ran he looked a little off-balance. That was because he was pigeon-toed. But Jackie was a tremendous athlete, an all-around star in college, and, later on, an All-Star whether he played first, second, or third base for the Dodgers. Jackie was one of only two or three players ever who had a 50-50 chance of being safe after getting caught in a rundown. He was absolutely fearless running the bases and at bat. Frank Robinson is the only other player I know of who never, never bailed out on an inside pitch. Stealing home was one of Jackie's most famous traits, but he never was particularly impressed by his ability to do it. To Jackie, it was almost the same as stealing second.

During the '47 season Jackie occasionally led off. Mostly he hit second or fifth. He had just 48 runs batted in for the season. His job was to get on base and make something happen from there.

Eddie Stanky was the second baseman. He often led off, and was the ideal No. 1 hitter in that he knew the strike zone perfectly. Eddie ended up second in the league in drawing walks with 103 for the year. Often if the count got to 3-2, Eddie would begin fouling off pitch after pitch—sometimes as many as half a dozen. Finally the pitcher would get frustrated or tired and throw ball four. Eddie would take his base, setting the table for the rest of our hitters. He scored 97 runs in 1947. I'll bet he was on base because of a walk 60-75 of those times. He only batted .252 and stole just three bases. Stanky excelled at the part of the game where quick intellect could overcome average physical ability.

Pee Wee Reese, a deserved Hall of Famer, held down shortstop. Pee Wee covered a tremendous amount of ground. Had he played during the national television era, he'd have been considered the fielding equal of Brooks Robinson. Pee Wee was the best No. 2 hitter I think I ever saw. He was an excellent bunter and willing to sacrifice himself at any time to move a runner up a base. The funny thing about Pee Wee as a hitter was that he could never make himself swing at the first pitch. Everybody knew this. Opposing pitchers could assure themselves of at least one strike by just tossing that first offering straight down the middle. In the dugout before many at-bats, Pee Wee would promise us, "I'm going to hit that first pitch this time." But he rarely did.

Spider Jorgenson played third, a frail-looking 155-pound guy who was very consistent at bat, though not a long ball hitter. Spider got five home runs and 67 runs batted in during the season and played a very solid third base. No successful major league team is composed entirely of stars. You've got to have solid, steady players too. In recent years players like Greg Gagne of the Twins and Mike Scioscia of the Dodgers have started getting their due. Spider wasn't flashy, just an honest pro who was greatly appreciated by his teammates.

My roomie Dixie Walker played right field at Ebbetts Field as well as anyone. The brick wall behind him was slanted and went up 18 feet, and then there was a wire fence for 10 feet above that. Caroms were tricky, and Dixie became known as "the People's Cherce" as much for his fielding as for his hitting, which was always excellent. Dixie hit .306 in '47 and led us with 94 runs batted in.

Carl Furillo was the Dodger center fielder. Later on he became famous as a right fielder and led the league in hitting in 1953, but what I remember most about this guy is he wasn't very smart. Mr. Rickey once told him to his face, "You're the dumbest player I ever signed." It was odd. You'd see the guy play and over a whole season he wouldn't pull one bone-headed mistake. On the field he had maybe the best throwing arm ever, certainly in a class with Rocky Colavito and, later, Reggie Smith. But if you tried to talk to him off the field, his lack of intelligence was obvious. He had deeply held racial prejudices and often said insulting things about teammates as well as opponents. Yet I don't think he intentionally acted like a horse's ass. This was just his nature.

Pete Reiser, one of the best pure athletes I ever saw, played right field for us that year. Poor Pete; if he'd stayed healthy he'd be remembered as an all-time great. He established himself as a star in 1941 when he led the National League in hitting, at 21 the youngest player ever to do so up to that point. A left-handed hitter, he also was a jackrabbit getting from home to first. To show what tremendous athletic ability he had, during batting practice he'd turn around, hit right-handed, and pound balls into the left field bleachers.

But Pete was all heart, and on defense all he cared about was catching the ball. He chased one ball hit by Stan Musial, hit the wall and damn near killed himself. Really. After that Mr. Rickey put foam rubber cushions on the Ebbetts Field walls, but there was no fence padding in other parks and Pete regularly caromed off hard surfaces. After a few serious injuries, Pete was never the same player and had to retire too early. But in '47 his body was still holding up somewhat. He led the league in walks with 104 (tying with Hank Greenberg) and he led us in hitting at .309.

Pete Reiser was the one player who moved Mr. Rickey to financial generosity. It was about this time that a fellow named Pascual was trying to sign players away from the majors to the Mexican League. He had lots of money and bought up Sal Maglie and Mickey Owen, among others. American owners couldn't compete financially. Pascual followed the Dodgers on a road trip to Chicago and came up to Pete's room with a suitcase full of money. He showed Pete $250,000 in the suitcase just as a signing bonus, and if Pete would come to Mexico there'd be a lot more waiting for him there. Remember Pete probably wasn't making much more than $15,000 or so a season with the Dodgers. Pete told Pascual not to open the suitcase, that he was loyal to Brooklyn. When we got back home Mr. Rickey called Pete in and said, "I'm aware of what happened in Chicago." Then, and I'm absolutely sure this was the only time in his entire career Branch Rickey did this, he tore up Pete's old contract in front of him, put down a new, blank contract and said, "You fill it in." I'd give a lot to know what figure Pete decided on, but in those days we never discussed terms of our contracts with anyone, be they teammates or members of the media.

Bruce Edwards was our catcher. Every opposing player in the league knew about his bad arm, and every opposing player who tried to run on Bruce usually paid the price. Bruce's quickness in releasing the ball was phenomenal, and our pitchers excelled at keeping runners close to first. Bruce's skills as a catcher were never fully appreciated because he had just this year and 1946 as a fulltime Dodger starter at that position before a fellow named Roy Campanella showed up. That's just the way baseball is. No matter how well you play or how much courage you demonstrate, you're on the bench as soon as somebody better comes along.

Our pitching in 1947 was much better than anyone had expected. Kirby Higbe had been our big winner in '46, but after just a few games in '47 he was shipped to Pittsburgh in a deal that brought us Al Gionfriddo. The new Dodger ace was 21-year-old Ralph Branca, who went 21-12 with a 2.67 earned run average. Ralph forced the rest of us to respect him with some standout performances. Maybe Ralph is best remembered for giving up Bobby Thomson's home run in 1951, but his Dodger teammates remember him as a hardnosed competitor who contributed to several championship teams.

Our other main starters were Joe Hatten (17-8), a left-hander with a very good curveball, and left-handed Vic Lombardi(12-11), who was a smallish control pitcher. They were both better than average pitchers, but truly besides Branca we didn't have a starter who would automatically join the rotation of any other team in the league.

But what we did have was a bullpen closer. Three teams had one in 1947, the Dodgers and the Yankees and the Cleveland Indians. It's no coincidence we met the Yankees in the World Series. For the Yankees, it was Joe Page, for the Dodgers, Hugh Casey.

Now, in the '40s, starting pitchers still took pride in going nine innings. If you failed to complete the game, even if your team got the win and you got credit for a victory, you didn't feel as happy. But for the Dodgers in1947, it was understood that Hugh Casey was always going to be on hand when needed, and it was no discredit to admit in the ninth inning that you were tired, losing your stuff, and the team would be better off with Casey's fresh arm. Hugh recorded 18 saves in '47, peanuts now but an astounding figure then. No other

National League reliever had more than 10, and Page tied for the American League lead with 17.

Casey was the coolest customer I ever met. It seemed that nothing ever bothered him. I recall one time he came into the Ebbetts Field clubhouse before a game and said, "I just ran over a man. He was coming from behind a trolley, and I'm sure the impact killed him." Casey wasn't joking. Any other player would have been too upset to even put on a uniform. Casey suited up, played, and dealt with the situation afterwards.

With that kind of outlook, it was no wonder the game situation didn't exist where Casey was scared about coming in to pitch. In one key game in Pittsburgh, Casey came on with the bases loaded and promptly threw three straight balls to Hank Greenberg, a feared slugger. Casey called time, went into the Dodger dugout, got a wet towel, wiped his face, took a drink of water from the fountain, and strolled back onto the field. Then he threw three straight strikes past Greenberg to earn a save.

Casey also liked to play mind games on the hitter. He'd shake off signs one after another just to make the batter wonder what the hell he was finally going to throw. Often Casey would be shaking his head before his catcher put the first sign down. I know there were times when I was catching that I had no idea what Casey was going to throw. All you could do was hang in there and try to get your glove in front of the pitch, whatever it turned out to be.

Hugh Casey was not a fine physical specimen. He was always overweight, and not what we used to call "hard" fat, either. He had no muscle tone, yet could move quickly and fielded his position as well as any pitcher in the National League. Though uncommon, this kind of athletic ability by an apparent slob isn't unique—Rick Reuschel is the best recent example in the major leagues.

We never thought anything could bother Hugh Casey. He owned a bar and restaurant on Flatbush Avenue, and this became the favorite spot for Dodger players and their wives to congregate after games for meals or drinks. Casey liked a drink, too, and maybe this was a factor in what happened to him just a few years later. He never had another good season after 1947 and soon was traded. Marital problems ensued, and in 1951 he put a gun to his head, called his wife, told her he was going to shoot himself, and did. Rest in peace.

But during 1947 there was a tremendous spirit on the Dodgers. Winning really is contagious. We had the attitude that we'd win any game we played. Jackie was accepted by most players after proving he belonged in the majors, and after the '47 season Mr. Rickey got rid of Dixie Walker and Eddie Stanky as he'd promised he would do. Kirby Higbe went to the Pirates during '47, possibly because of his opposition to Jackie. But mostly, winning made everything beautiful. We pretty much were in front throughout the season. The Cardinals gave us a good run and finished second, five games back. The Boston Braves ended up in third with an 86-68 record. Otherwise, no other team was close enough to threaten us.

I enjoyed the season as a spectator—and that mostly was my contribution. I played in 25 games, mostly as a pinch-hitter or late-inning replacement for Bruce Edwards. My seven hits drove in three runs. I was a very small cog in the Dodger machine, but no one was prouder to be part of that special team.

But I remained positive, helped along by my plan to try to become a manager. I spent a lot of games in the bullpen. When I wasn't warming up pitchers I'd watch what was happening and think to myself what I'd do in each situation if I were managing the Dodgers. I was pleased to find Burt Shotton and I usually were thinking the same way.

My salary for the season was $9,000. I've joked that Mr. Rickey felt sorry for me when I came back from the war and gave me a nice raise, but the real reason must have been Edwards and his sore arm. If Bruce had gone down, I'd have been an experienced back-up. $9,000 was quite a good salary, and I was overjoyed after the '47 season when Mr. Rickey announced he was so proud of the club that we'd all get raises for 1948. Well, during the off-season when I got my contract it was for the same $9,000. I wrote to Mr. Rickey, sending the contract back and noting "with respect" I'd read where he'd promised a raise for everyone. He immediately replied. Mr. Rickey's letter is forever burned into my memory. It went, "Dear Bobby: I sense you are unhappy with the contract offered to you for 1948. For your information, the Brooklyn Dodger club stands ready and willing to make a trade for your services with any other team. If you can assist us in any way, please do so. Respectfully, Branch

Rickey." Enclosed was a contract for the same $9,000, which was more than any other major league team was likely to pay a backup catcher with a .194 batting average from the previous season. I signed the contract and sent it back.

In 1947 we clinched the pennant in a road game at Pittsburgh. There was a big celebration in the clubhouse with champagne for everybody to pour over everybody else. I was truly excited about playing in a World Series. Having recognized my limitations as a player, I knew that this would undoubtedly be the highlight of my active career. I called Birmingham and insisted that George and Corinne fly to New York at my expense to attend the Series with Gwenn and our children.

We had the toughest possible opponent. Joe DiMaggio was the biggest star on Bucky Harris's team, but he was joined by other great players like Phil Rizzuto, Tommy Henrich, Allie Reynolds, and Vic Raschi. Yogi Berra was on the team but hadn't yet dislodged Aaron Robinson as starting catcher. The Yankees had won 97 games, beating second-place Detroit by twelve.

The Series got off to a rough start for Brooklyn. Playing at Yankee Stadium to open up we lost the first two games by scores of 5-3 and 10-3. Branca got knocked out in the first game, with Page throwing four shutout innings for the save. In the second game Allie Reynolds treated our hitters like Little Leaguers, striking out 12 and never really being in danger.

We switched to Ebbetts Field for the next three games. Needless to say, I hadn't seen any action yet beyond warming up relief pitchers in the bullpen. I wasn't unhappy, just glad to be part of a team playing in the World Series. George and Corinne were enjoying themselves anyway. We'd taken the subway to Yankee Stadium for the first two games, and George was so fascinated by the denizens of the New York underground that he said, "Let's just stand here and watch for a while," when I was hurrying to get to the stadium for the game. Just getting my mother and father on the subway was difficult.

If this World Series had ended in five games I'd never have been able to say I played in one. The Dodgers came back on our home field to win Game Three 9-8 and Game Four 3-2. Hugh Casey saved both. Game Four is famous because Yankee pitcher Bill Bevins was one out away from the first no-hitter in Series history when Cookie Lavagetto doubled home two runs to give Brooklyn the win. (We'd scored another run in the fifth inning without benefit of a base hit, proof again that the 1947 Brooklyn club gleaned the benefits of smart, speed-oriented baseball.)

But the Yankees won Game Five 2-1 on Joe DiMaggio's homer and the Series returned to Yankee Stadium with the home club needing just one more win to cinch the world championship. The Yankee march was interrupted in Game Six, though, and this remains my most priceless baseball memory.

Things didn't look good as Brooklyn came to bat in the top of the sixth inning. Vic Lombardi had been shelled by Yankee hitters, and though Ralph Branca had come on to hold New York, Joe Page took over on the mound for the Yankees in the fifth obviously able to protect a 5-4 lead into eternity.

In New Jersey, my father-in-law was watching the game on television. He was astonished in the top of the sixth when it was announced Bobby Bragan would be pinch-hitting for Ralph Branca. "I watched you run in from the bullpen, go to the dugout, select a bat, and walk to the plate," he told me later. "The closer you got to home plate, the tighter the muscles in your face became."

It was no optical illusion. We had two runners on against Page. The left-hander had handcuffed us throughout the Series, and it was obvious if we didn't get to him now he'd hold us off the rest of the way and the Yankees would be champions.

In my mind, the game is still being played. I can see the sky, smell the grass, hear the crowd. I can also feel my knees shaking. They were, hard. Major leaguers get nervous in the same way anyone else would. The difference is we can perform anyway.

With a count of one ball and two strikes, I hit a line drive down the left field line. It might have been five feet fair, and I pulled into second base with a double. My RBI tied the score, Immediately, Burt Shotton sent in Dan Bankhead to run for me. I trotted off the field into our dugout, to be met there by teammates who pounded me on the back. It was wonderful. Euphoria. I learned later that George and Corinne, having long since given up ever seeing their son play in the World Series, both were in the restroom during my time at bat. Well, nothing is perfect, but this moment came close.

Pee Wee Reese followed my double with another hit. The Dodgers took the lead and held it, making Joe Page the losing pitcher. I couldn't celebrate much. After we were finally retired in the top of the sixth I got my catcher's mitt and ran back to the Yankee Stadium visiting bullpen. Tommy Henrich, the Yankee right fielder, told me later he'd always admired how I'd gotten to run in across the field to get to bat, got my double, and then got to run back to the bullpen amid the cheers of Brooklyn fans in the crowd. God, I felt 10 feet tall.

When I got home to Brooklyn after the game, eight kids ranging in age from six to fourteen who lived in the same apartment building were lined up on the sidewalk with cardboard signs saying, "Our Hero." It added to my joy.

But the Series still had a seventh and deciding game to be played. The next day when I got to Yankee Stadium, Burt Shotton met me in the clubhouse and showed me a telegram he'd received from my sister Sue and her husband Dick Whitlow. The gist of the message was that Shotton should let Bobby Bragan catch the seventh game. Shotton let me read the telegram and then just stood looking at me, obviously waiting for me to give some sort of reply. Well, I sure didn't insist on catching. I spent all nine innings in the bullpen. I doubt I could have made much difference. Page came back from losing the previous game to win the seventh for the Yankees with five innings of one-hit relief. I think he retired the last 17 batters in a row.

In the clubhouse after the game, Burt Shotton simply said, "There's always next year." In a sense that was true, and it also wasn't. The Jackie Robinson-related trades would be made, and Leo would be back. I took my $4,500 losing Series share back to Birmingham and spent the next months wondering what 1948 might hold. Surprises proved to be in store.

B	E	T	W	E	E	N
I	N	N	I	N	G	S

LOU BROCK: In the '20s, Ty Cobb was probably the last of the base stealers in an era when base stealing was glorified. That got wiped out by Babe Ruth and the long ball. As far as many clubs were concerned from a standpoint of selling tickets, the stolen base and the hit and run became a liability to the home run. People who paid to get in wanted to see home runs. That simple.

That went on until 1947. Branch Rickey and the Dodgers changed it. The Dodgers suffered some from a lack of hitting ability, certainly a shortage of power. They compensated with team speed and guile. The stolen base became alive again—and by showing that method could be successful again, winning games and getting fans in the ballpark—the Dodgers paved the way for other clubs to designate players to run.

There are still ballclubs who don't run, who still see the single as a setup for the home run. Organizational policy maybe in some cases still stuck in pre-1947. The Cubs didn't run after '47, they still don't run now. I got traded from the Cubs to St. Louis in '64, and when I got there I was told I was designated as the team base stealer. I said, "Get somebody else." I figured the Cardinals could already score runs, a bunch of 'em, but they had Dick Groat at the time, maybe the best hit-and-run man ever, and they figured a runner who could steal being on base in front of Groat would intimidate opponents. Mr. Rickey and the '47 Dodgers created that, see— the stolen base as intimidation.

LEO DUROCHER: I don't talk about (the '47 season). I wasn't there. Rickey took all the credit anyway. He had somebody, Shotton, in there.

BUZZIE BAVASI: Leo was suspended because of our decision to have spring training in Havana. Leo took the heat for something he didn't do. Connie Innimen, who owned and operated the Cotton Club in Harlem, and Memphis Englebert showed up in Cuba. Englebert was a handicapper, not a bookmaker like people said he was. He'd figure out odds and make his own bets on what he'd worked out. But Happy Chandler, the commissioner, heard those two were in Havana with the Dodgers and Chandler figured Leo must have invited them.

Well, I happen to know it was Larry McPhail who asked Innimen and Englebert to come down. He supplied them with game tickets through his press secretary, and even paid their bill to stay at the Hotel Nacional. Red Patterson, the press secretary, told me this. But Chandler thought it was Leo's doing and suspended him. We told Chandler exactly what happened, but he'd already suspended Leo and he would not rescind that suspension. So Leo was suspended wrongly, and I want to make certain everyone everywhere knows this.

DUKE SNIDER: In '47 Burt Shotton had to take over from Leo. I was just a rookie and had no idea who he was. I asked other players and nobody seemed to know much about him. Shotton didn't put a uniform on. He'd sit on the bench and Clyde Sukeforth would have to go out to the umpires and ask them to come into the dugout to talk to Shotton if necessary. Dick Young, the New York sportswriter, labeled him "kindly old Burt Shotton," and it stuck. He was a solid baseball person.

RALPH BRANCA: After Jackie got accepted by most everybody we had a real good spirit. Jackie in, Leo gone, whatever. We were the Brooklyn Dodgers. We just knew we could beat anybody we played.

STAN MUSIAL: They were a great team that season. We finished second to them, I guess four or five games back. They ran the bases like nobody's business. It was Mr. Rickey's idea, you know, that speed could make up for lots of other things.

AL GIONFRIDDO: It was such a thrill, first to win the pennant and then on to the World Series. My only World Series. Against the Yankees, no less. Joe DiMaggio and all of them. Well, it was in that World Series I made that catch off of Joe. So many people still come up to me today and congratulate me on that catch. Everybody remembers it like it was yesterday.

JOE DIMAGGIO: Did he make that catch in that World Series? I played in nine of them, you know (10, actually) and sometimes it's kind of hard to remember exactly what happened in which one.

I do remember how, in that Series, Robby stole bases off of Yogi Berra. We had another catcher on the Yankees named Aaron Robinson whom we felt should play against the Dodgers because of Robinson's baserunning. Robinson played and stopped the Dodgers from stealing so many bases. He was better behind the plate at that time than Yogi, who was very wild with his throws. He'd try to throw someone out and there was a good chance the ball would come on one hop to me in center field. Bill Dickey was eventually hired by George Weiss (Yankee general manager) just for the purpose of teaching Yogi to catch better.

Of course, Yogi soon did improve immensely. We did win that 1947 World Series, didn't we?

BRANCA: It was hard to go home. But we believed we were going to be a good team for a long time. That made the winter pass easier.

MANAGER

TOWARDS THE END OF THE 1947 SEASON, I had a preliminary contract meeting with Branch Rickey Jr. This was an informal kind of visit all players would have with someone from management before heading home for the winter, just to get an idea of what kind of contract the player wanted for the next year and for the player to get an idea where he was supposed to fit into the team.

The big stars —Reiser, Reese, Robinson—would have this talk with Mr. Rickey himself. I was a scrub player. I got the son.

Anyway, I told Branch Jr. that if any managerial opportunity came up in the Dodger organization I'd be interested. Brooklyn had, at that time, 21 farm teams. There were two Triple A clubs, St. Paul and Montreal; two Double A teams, Fort Worth and Mobile; and a bunch of A, B, C, and D League teams all across the country. If I got a chance to manage one of those teams, it wouldn't be important anymore if I could run fast or hit curveballs from right-handed pitchers.

Branch Jr. said, "I'll tell my father," and when I next saw Mr. Rickey at spring training I gave him the same message. He said, "We'll keep you in mind."

With that, I went to spring training in Vero Beach to prepare for a seventh year in the major leagues. After my poor 1947 showing, maybe I should have spent the spring worrying about whether I'd make the club in '48, but I honestly didn't. I was confident that if something happened and I was replaced on the Dodger roster, I'd be given a managing job somewhere. And I never gave any thought to someday having to leave baseball and make my living from some other profession. I knew I was in baseball to stay.

The 1948 season was nowhere near as happy for the Dodgers as 1947 had been. Teams change every year, and the '48 Dodgers had a change at the top when Leo finished his suspension and came back as manager. Burt Shotton became a special assistant to Mr. Rickey, a troubleshooter who would travel around looking at our farm teams and make recommendations about players and managers on them. Mr. Rickey trusted him implicitly.

Meanwhile, Leo came back with the same swagger he'd left with. He didn't call any meeting to apologize for being suspended. Leo didn't think he had anything to apologize for. I'm certain it was around this time he married Larraine Day, the glamorous actress. She was around the camp and provided an extra kind of sparkle.

There were roster changes. Our starting lineup had a different look. Gil Hodges took over at first base, while Jackie moved to second base. Eddie Stanky was gone, and this was part of a growing problem between Leo and Mr. Rickey. Mr. Rickey traded Stanky to Boston during spring training, keeping his promise to get rid of all the players who'd loudly objected to Jackie joining the team. Leo loved Stanky—he was Leo's kind of player. Trading Eddie Stanky, no matter how he might have felt about Jackie in early '47, was not Leo's idea. He made this known, loudly, in the clubhouse all spring. And Mr. Rickey, I'm sure, was not amused.

I don't like discussing whatever estrangement took place between Leo and Mr. Rickey. I truly admired both of them, the best baseball mind and the best baseball manager who ever lived. But all they'd ever had in common was baseball; Leo's lifestyle was the antithesis of Branch Rickey's. Now, I think, Leo believed Mr. Rickey hadn't done enough to defend him against the Chandler suspension, and that afterwards Mr. Rickey didn't show enough interest in trying to get Leo vindicated. In any case, the relationship between them wasn't strong anymore. They were both very strongminded individuals. Neither one liked losing an argument. By the middle of the 1948 season, the Dodgers were a mediocre 37-38 under Leo and the unthinkable happened.

Horace Stoneham, the owner of the New York Giants, wasn't pleased with the way his team was performing under the management of Mel Ott. The Giant record was the same 37-38. Stoneham approached Mr. Rickey, I believe to ask permission to talk to Burt Shotton about managing the Giants. "You can have Shotton or Durocher," Mr. Rickey told him. That had to be a great surprise to Stoneham, and of course he wanted Leo.

Benedict Arnold never got more notoriety for switching from the Americans to the British. Among New York baseball fans, the Giants and the Dodgers were a rivalry to match any world war. Players and managers belonged to one side or the other for life. The two teams very rarely traded with each other. And here was Leo, the brashest Dodger of them all, going over to the Polo Grounds!

Afterwards one story went that Mr. Rickey threatened to fire Leo, and Leo responded, "You don't have the guts to fire me." I'm sure Leo said something like that to everybody he ever worked for. Hell, Larry McPhail, the Dodger general manager before Mr. Rickey, must have fired Leo half a dozen times. He'd fire him one day and re-hire him the next, all before the press, team, or fans ever got wind of it. This time, though, Leo left the Dodgers for good. Taking over for Ott, he guided the Giants to a 41-38 mark the rest of the way, getting his first chance to work with the player nucleus of the team that would break Dodger fan hearts in 1951.

Burt Shotton, Mr. Rickey's old reliable, took over Brooklyn again. The Dodger record for the remainder of '48 was 47-32, an improvement over what the team had done for Leo. I think it had to be a relief for the players to know that the problems between Mr. Rickey and Leo had been settled for better or worse.

I need to jump ahead just a little to show how much Leo was envied or resented by other managers, including one who followed him with the Dodgers. Not Burt Shotton, of course, who was the nicest man you ever met. The Dodger manager who begrudged Leo the spotlight was Charlie Dressen.

Dressen had served Leo on the Dodgers as his third-base coach. I heard Dressen say on many occasions that he was smarter than Leo, that he knew the game better. It got old to listen to. And when Leo left the club in the middle of the '48 season, maybe Charlie expected Mr. Rickey would choose him to take over at the Brooklyn helm.

But Mr. Rickey went with Burt Shotton again. Shotton guided the team to a third place finish that season, going 47-32 and doing a very fine job. In 1949 Shotton managed the Dodgers to the National League pennant with a 97-57 record, one game better than St. Louis. This certainly proves Burt Shotton was qualified in every way to be a major league manager.

Shotton ran the team for one more season, bringing the Dodgers in second to the Phillies in 1950. Then he chose to step down, and Charlie Dressen got his shot at managing the Dodgers in 1951.

Now, in 1952 and 1953 Brooklyn won the National League pennants. Dressen, though not overly modest, certainly knew his baseball. But the 1951 season matched Dressen and Leo head-to-head, culminating in the famous three-game playoff for the National League title. And this is where Leo Durocher proved who the best manager was.

Think about the last of the ninth in the third game. Most people remember only this, that Dressen brought Ralph Branca in to relieve Don Newcombe and Bobby Thomson deposited a Branca pitch into the left field stands. Well, a case could be made that if Charlie Dressen had kept his head in the game the Dodgers would have won instead of the Giants.

In the bottom of the ninth at the Polo Grounds, the Giants came to bat trailing 4-1. Newcombe, who'd finished the regular season with a 20-9 record, appeared to be in control. Shortstop Alvin Dark led off for the Giants and hit a solid single, putting a runner on first. And then Charlie Dressen had Gil Hodges hold Dark on at first base. The next hitter, Don Mueller, scratched a grounder towards right that caromed off Hodges's glove for another hit.

Think about it: If Hodges is playing back the way I'm positive Leo would have handled it, he probably fields Mueller's grounder and at least forces Dark at second, probably gets the ball to Pee Wee and

140

back for a 3-6-3 double play. There would have been nobody on and two outs instead of two on and nobody out. But Mueller got a hit. Monte Irvin followed with a foul pop fly out. It was the first out of the inning. It should have been the third. And then Whitey Lockman doubled, Dressen brought in Branca to pitch to Thomson, and Bobby hit his way into the history books.

It shouldn't have been that way. With Leo, it wouldn't have been that way. Charlie Dressen fell asleep. The great managers, Leo among them, are never caught napping.

Sure, Dressen went on to win two pennants with the Dodgers. He should have won those. The Dodgers were the best team in the league, flat out better than the New York Giants and anyone else. In the big game, the crucial situation, Dressen wasn't up to the challenge.

Dressen's ego really got in his way. After 1953 he tried to force the Dodgers into giving him a multi-year contract, feeling, I guess, he was essential to team success. He got turned down, quit, and turned up in 1955 managing the sad-sack Washington Senators, where he finished dead last in the American League. Dressen later managed in Milwaukee and Detroit, never having all that much success and alienating many of his players along the way. One time somebody asked Rocky Bridges, one of Dressen's infielders, where Rocky thought the team would finish the season. "About six games behind the manager," Rocky replied, a very sarcastic baseball way of saying Dressen thought he was better than the rest of the team.

Incidentally, Walter Alston succeeded Dressen as Dodger manager and won himself a pennant or two before retiring after the 1976 season. Mild-mannered Walter was quite a change from Charlie Dressen. Some Dodger players felt Alston couldn't make up his mind fast enough, but whatever Walter did it must have been right to accumulate a 2,040-1,613 won-lost record over 23 years. I coached a season under Walter and had nothing but the utmost respect for him. Of course, I didn't believe he was quite as good as Leo, but Walter never claimed to be, either. His ego was so much under control that he even had Leo coaching for him in Los Angeles. Rumors always went around that Leo was about to take over the team again, but that never bothered Alston. He just kept on winning.

But before Leo departed another momentous change was made on the Dodger ballclub by Mr. Rickey. This one had repercussions for baseball in general and Bobby Bragan in particular. Burt Shotton was a key participant in this change, too.

During spring training in 1948, a catcher named Roy Campanella played with the St. Paul club. At 27, Campanella was not young for a Triple A player. He'd been a star for years with the Kansas City Monarchs of the old Negro League. When Mr. Rickey signed him, it wasn't with the intention of bringing him straight to the major leagues. There were minor league systems to be integrated, and Mr. Rickey correctly believed the even-tempered, talented Campanella was the perfect black man to do so. So Campanella had a couple of years in the Dodger farm system before he had a chance to join the big club.

I've heard Campanella remembers that the Dodger catchers in '48 were Edwards, Hodges, and Bragan, and that after he arrived Edwards was moved to third, Hodges to first, and Bragan clean off the roster. I don't remember it quite that way. Hodges had been a catcher, but it was always the team plan for him to move to first base. Edwards already was playing some at third, though when the team acquired Billy Cox from the Pirates Edwards became a utility player. Campanella was great, a Hall of Fame player, but nobody got run off.

When we broke camp in 1948, Campanella remained on the St. Paul roster. Edwards did most of the catching for the first months of the season. I caught just five games. Then in June, about a month before Leo left for the Giants, Burt Shotton made a fact-finding trip for Mr. Rickey that greatly affected my career.

Burt travelled from Brooklyn to Fort Worth, Texas, and spent a few days watching the Double A Cats play under Les Burge. Burt ended up calling Mr. Rickey and said, "I'm going to recommend a change at Fort Worth, and the man I'd recommend is in your bullpen." (Most of my season had been spent warming up relief pitchers.)

Mr. Rickey called me about 3 P.M. one afternoon. I was home in my Brooklyn apartment, enjoying time with the family before I left for Ebbets Field and the game that night. "There's an opening for a manager in the Texas League, in Double A," he told me. "Would you be interested?"

Of course I was. This was a tremendous break. Just as it took most players years to work their way up through the farm system, most managers had to take the same route. By starting in Double A, I would get a leg up on my eventual goal of managing in the majors.

"It'll take 48 hours to get waivers on you," Mr. Rickey said. "I'll be back in touch. You keep quiet about it." And I did. I told Gwenn, though. She and I had often discussed my plan of becoming a manager. As a veteran baseball wife, she knew that job would mean lots of travel and uprooting of the family, but she was accustomed to this.

I went to the ballpark that night and the next, suited out and did everything as usual. I don't believe I played in either game. For the whole part of '48 I spent with the Dodgers I was up just 12 times and got only two hits. The move to Fort Worth wouldn't mean the end of my playing days—it was a given Mr. Rickey would expect me to be a player-manager, saving the Dodgers the cost of adding an extra player to the Fort Worth roster. Roy Campanella moved from St. Paul to Brooklyn, a good catcher named Toby Atwell went from Fort Worth to St. Paul, and I took Atwell's spot with the Cats. Making room for Campanella was probably my greatest contribution to the Dodgers.

I didn't spend much time regretting my decision to end my career as an active major league player. I'd achieved my childhood goal as well as my abilities would allow. Most big league baseball players, when they come to the end, have a few special moments to recall. Only the big stars find they have too many high points to recall each clearly. For me, there was the double in the sixth game of the '47 Series, my two home runs in one game off Bucky Walters, catching Dixie Walker off second base with the hidden-ball trick in front of 35,000 fans. Like hundreds of thousands of young boys, I dreamed of being a major leaguer. Like one in a hundred thousand, I'd done it. I couldn't have tried any harder, or being stuck in Bobby Bragan's body, done any better. Now it was time for new challenges.

As Mr. Rickey had promised, he was back on the phone to me two days later. "We have cleared you through waivers," he said. "Come by the office tomorrow morning and we'll visit about it and make the necessary transportation arrangements."

When I went to Mr. Rickey's office I learned I was getting the job on Burt Shotton's recommendation, and that I had to report to Tulsa, where the Cats would play that night, right away. A veteran left-handed pitcher named George Dockins was acting manager until I arrived. I gulped a little when I learned Fort Worth's record under him was 11-0.

Mr. Rickey wished me luck, saying, "You're starting a new career. I hope you'll do well. You never know who's going to be the best manager. We have 21 in the Dodger system, and there's no way to estimate which will become major league managers. But this is an opportunity for you. Burt Shotton will meet you in Tulsa."

I flew from New York to Tulsa. Air travel was becoming more common. During the trip I had plenty of time to think about the kind of manager I wanted to be, how I'd approach the Fort Worth players and fans.

I have always believed major league managers lead; minor league managers teach first, then lead. This was especially true in 1948. By the time a player reached Double A ball he'd probably been in a farm system for anywhere from two to five years. He'd have many of the basics mastered. Double A and Triple A were for honing these skills, teaching all the little extras necessary to succeed at the highest level. I don't think this philosophy is entirely true today; players get to the major leagues shortly after collegiate competition and have to learn basic skills there. Now big league managers have to be psychologists, and know how to deal with balky agents. But in my era, you could pretty much count on how much a player knew as evidenced by the minor league level he'd attained.

I also wanted Fort Worth fans to feel I would become a part of their community. Mr. Rickey often told a story about a newly appointed minor league manager arriving in town and asked an older resident what kind of place it was. The gist was that it was up to the new manager, not the townspeople, to make adjustments. Mr. Rickey carefully pointed out that fans would have more patience with a manager they liked than with one they didn't. I hadn't been to Fort Worth before, but I was going to do whatever it took to become a part of the community.

Because the Dodgers had all their farm teams participate in spring training, I knew a lot of the Cats' players. Big Dee Fondy, the first baseman, was a future major leaguer, as was center fielder Irv Noren. Other team standouts included pitchers George Dockins and Eddie Chandler, second baseman Wally Fiala and right fielder George Schmees.

The Texas League had eight teams: Fort Worth, Oklahoma City, Tulsa, Shreveport, Houston, Dallas, San Antonio, and Beaumont. Some future major league stars were performing in the league— Ken Boyer, Solly Hemus, Gil McDougald, and Vinegar Ben Mizell among them.

One thing puzzled me: I knew the Cats were contending for first place in the Texas League. So why was the manager being replaced?

Burt Shotton supplied the answer when he met my plane. "The man you're replacing did not schedule morning workouts," he told me. "He was only interested in what happened during the game." The clear message was that, in Shotton's opinion, Les Burge had been lazy.

Shotton had another piece of advice. I was wearing a Shriner pin on the lapel of my coat, a Masonic pin. Burt was a Shriner, too, and he said, "Bobby, you don't need to advertise." I took the pin off.

Fort Worth had a doubleheader scheduled with Tulsa that night. I got to the clubhouse and called a team meeting, really just to get acquainted. During spring training the Dodgers always had organizational meetings to determine signs, work on fundamentals, and so forth. Every team in the organization did these things the same way, so since the Brooklyn system was intact I wouldn't have anything new to pick up with the Cats. "You've won 11 straight games," I said. "Obviously you're doing something right."

I told my players I wouldn't have a lot of rules, but whatever rules I set out would be adhered to. They'd report on time for games, obey curfew, and be in no later than two hours after night games. That was about it, except a warning I wouldn't tolerate players breaking helmets or damaging team equipment that didn't belong to them. I assigned myself uniform #10, finally getting the numeral I'd wanted for so long, and wrote myself in as starting catcher, batting sixth, for both games. The Cats won the first to extend our winning streak to 12, then lost the second. I was 1-1 after my first day as a manager.

In 1948, the Fort Worth Cats won the championship of the Texas League. As a result, we played in the Dixie Series at the end of the season, opposing the champions of the Southern League. They turned out to be Birmingham, the same team I'd idolized as a kid. Birmingham's star was a big first baseman named Walt Dropo, who went on to a solid career in the big leagues. The Dixie Series went five games. Fort Worth won the first game, which was played in Birmingham. I hit a home run off a pitcher named Harry Dorish. But from then on Dropo's hitting dominated and Birmingham won the series in five games, sweeping the last four.

Oh, I enjoyed that season. The Texas League schedule ran through Labor Day. The Cats played our home games in La Grave Field, one of the most beautiful minor league facilities in all of baseball. The staduim was out on North Main Street in Fort Worth, eight blocks north of the Courthouse. The Trinity River ran along one side of the stadium. I remember Walt Dropo hit a couple of balls into the water during the Dixie Series. La Grave Field just didn't look like any other ballpark. Even the dirt was unique. Around home plate and the pitcher's mound it was red clay, but the infield surface was Fuller's Earth, an almost black kind of dirt. Ezra Bland, the groundskeeper, did a fabulous job.

The general manager of the Cats, and my immediate boss, was John Reeves. Mr. Reeves co-owned the Cats when they were an independent minor league team. The Dodgers purchased the Fort Worth club after the war, either in 1945 or 1946. Mr. Reeves stayed on after the sale. I liked him very much, and remember him as being very meticulous. The La Grave Field grandstand was always sparkling clean.

One of the most important duties of a minor league manager is to prepare reports after every game and send them to his farm director. I had to learn when to keep my sense of humor in check. A couple of years after I took over in Fort Worth, I thought the Dodgers needed to send me some outfielders who could hit instead of the bunch I had. To get that message across to Fresco Thompson, the Brooklyn farm director, in one game I let my pitcher bat sixth and had my trio of outfielders hit seventh, eighth, and ninth in the order. Thompson immediately sent me a hot letter saying, "If you were trying to embarrass the Brooklyn organization, you succeeded." It was a sharp reprimand to let me know Fresco was unhappy with what I'd done, and I guess the three outfielders didn't appreciate it either. But sometimes in a bureaucracy, which any baseball farm system must be, you can't spend too much time being subtle.

In 1949 all farm team managers were notified by Mr. Rickey that expenses needed to be trimmed and we should no longer send telegrams when special delivery letters might do, and that air mail would be preferred to special delivery. On the few occasions when telegrams must be sent, he ordered, the fewer words used, the better.

Maybe 10 days after that I got a telegram from Mr. Rickey inquiring, "Can you go with your present infield?" That was the whole message. Trying to comply with his new rule regarding brevity, I wired back "Yes." Now, Mr. Rickey had 21 different farm clubs to attend to, and he obviously forgot what he'd asked me about in the first place. The next day I received an additional wire from him asking, "Yes, what?" So I wired back, "Yes, sir."

Though I loved managing in the minor leagues, it wasn't always an easy or pleasant job. The toughest day for me came when I'd been managing my brother Jimmy, whose baseball skills were better than most non-professionals but who still didn't belong at the Double A competitive level. I knew what I had to do, but that didn't make it easier. On the fateful day in 1950, I called Jimmy into my hotel room in Shreveport and cut my own brother—sent him to Newport News in A ball. Jimmy and I both cried. I felt so guilty and wondered whether Jimmy would ever forgive me. A week later the Dodgers demoted catcher Ken Staples to Fort Worth from St. Paul, meaning I had one catcher too many on my roster. The player I moved down a league rung was Norm Sherry, who later went on to make it to the major leagues briefly as a player and return there for a longer stay as a coach and then manager. Before that night's game I was visiting with some fans near home plate at La Grave Field. When Sherry came out of the dugout, I called him over. Norm had a nice smile on his face, obviously thinking I was going to introduce him to the people I was talking to. Instead, when he was maybe 15 feet away, I called out, "Norm—when you see Jimmy, tell him hello for me." Sherry got the message.

Besides being lucky to get a Double A team for my first managing assignment, I was also fortunate to find myself in Fort Worth. I stayed in a motel until Gwenn and the children drove down. We then rented a place Toby Atwell had lived in before he moved up to St. Paul to replace Roy Campanella. It wasn't the best place. Once I found two tarantulas in the bathroom. When it was time for school to start around Labor Day, Gwenn and I decided Fort Worth was where we wanted to live, so we gave up the house in Birmingham and settled in Texas. Besides settling the Bragan family in what we considered the finest city in the country, I think our moving to town permanently sent a message to fans of the Fort Worth Cats that the team's manager appreciated the club's location and traditions.

This is where many minor league managers come up short. They are obsessed with the idea of winning big for a season, two at the most, and then moving up the organizational ladder to coach or manage in the major leagues. They forget that for fans of a minor league team, that team is the focus of baseball interest. Fort Worth Cats fans cared more about whether we got to the Dixie Series than if the Dodgers made the World Series. They were proud of Dee Fondy in the same way Brooklyn fans had idolized Dixie Walker. So when a new manager for a minor league team gets to town and makes it clear right away he considers his job just a stepping-stone to something better, that's insulting to the fans supporting his present team. And whether it's played at a minor league or major league level, the whole purpose of baseball is to give the fans in the stands the best time you can for the price of their tickets.

I soon learned the Fort Worth Cats had a great baseball tradition, more distinguished and varied than that of some major league franchises. As soon as I got to town, people started telling me all about Jake Atz, a former Cats manager. In the '20s, his Fort Worth teams won six consecutive Texas League titles. According to the Atz legend, when he joined the service his name was Zimmerman. But he got tired of always being last in line, so he changed his name to Atz. Maybe it's true. And while Yankee fans might rhapsodize about team legends Babe Ruth, Lou Gehrig, and Tony Lazzeri, Fort Worth fans waxed nostalgic over the Panther Park exploits of Paul Wachtel, Jack Calvo, and Big Boy Kraft. Panther Park was the original Cats' home diamond before the team moved a few blocks east to La Grave Field.

I especially learned about a one-time Cats player named John King, a left-handed hitter from nearby Cleburne, Texas. John King never possessed major league playing skills, but in terms of meanness the man belonged in some Hall of Fame. As oldtimers who had followed the Cats for decades would tell it, King hated hitting against left-handed pitchers and before stepping into the batters box would actually take his bat, point it at the pitcher, and snarl, "Don't throw me any curveballs if you want to live."

I'd already heard a little bit about John King. Wally Dashiell, my manager in Pensacola, had played against King in the Texas League. One time when King was on second, Dashiell got between him and the base on the hidden ball play and made the mistake of crowing, "Hey, John, look what I've got!" King growled, "You son of a bitch, don't touch me with that ball," and actually chased Dashiell through the bleachers, under the stands and into the clubhouse. Dashiell wanted to stop running and swear to King that he'd never, ever even think of tagging him out, but he was afraid to pause because King kept screaming, "I'll kill you, boy!"

When the day came that the Fort Worth Cats had to release John King, the manager feared for his life since King was certain to take offense. Now it happened that on road games King enjoyed sitting out on the porch in front of whichever hotel the team stayed at. So the manager leaned out a window a couple of stories above the porch, attached the release form to a string, and lowered it down in front of King's face.

The John King story had a happy ending, Though he never made it to the major leagues, legend has it he made a lot of money in the oil business after he got out of baseball.

My stint in Fort Worth was also the beginning of Bobby Bragan tales, many of which centered around my sometimes precipitous relationships with umpires. I want to make it clear I never hated any umpires. I just thought some could do their jobs a little better and tried to offer friendly criticism to help them be all that they could be.

During my playing days, both in the minor and major leagues, I was never tossed out of a game. I did not keep this record intact long as a manager. But what most fans and members of the media don't realize is that umpires often have colorful personalities themselves. When I first got to the Texas League, there was one umpire working there named Frenchy Arceneaux. He was black-haired and skinny, just a colorful sort of guy. In one game we had Dee Fondy at the plate. The first pitch to Fondy was low and outside, but Frenchy called it a strike. Dee kind of glared at Frenchy, but he didn't say anything. The next pitch was in the same spot except an inch or two lower. Frenchy called that one a strike, too. With that, Fondy stepped out of the batter's box and roared, "I wasn't going to say anything about the first one, Frenchy, but now you've blown two!" And Frenchy replied, "In that case, Dee, let me apologize for both of 'em."

But when umpires apologize for bad calls, they still don't change them. At least Frenchy wasn't one of the ones who got mad at one player or manager and took it out on everybody else associated with the team. One night at La Grave Field I was catching and Frenchy and I disagreed on some calls. After the third out of the inning, he said to me harshly, "I don't want to hear any more of that. That's the last gripe you've got tonight. One more and you're out of here!" Frenchy didn't leave it at that either. As I walked to the dugout he walked right alongside me, giving me more of the same. But as we got to the dugout Frenchy noticed Gwenn in her usual seat. He took off his mask, bowed, and said pleasantly, "Good evening, Mrs. Bragan, how are you tonight?" before putting his mask back on and continuing to give Mrs. Bragan's husband hell.

I was often tossed out of games for getting sarcastic. Umpires usually will put up with some complaining, but they draw the line when they think you're trying to humiliate them. Unfortunately, I had inherited my mother Corinne's barbed tongue, so I ended up in some situations saying more than I should have and getting an early shower as a result. Later on, Dick Williams would say he learned this from me.

But I will say I learned how umpires think from some of the best during my major league career. The greatest umpire story I was ever part of took place in 1940 when I was still with the Phillies. At that time Bill Klem was the dean of National League umpires, so much the top dog that for many years he only umpired behind home plate, a position on the bases not being dignified enough for him. The other umpires never objected because everyone knew Bill Klem was the best there ever was or would be, except perhaps for Jocko Conlan and Al Barlick.

Klem's method of handling complaints was simple. When he'd heard enough he'd draw a line in the dirt with his baseball shoe and tell whoever was disputing with him, "If you cross that line, you're gone."

In a game at Philadelphia in 1940, the Pirates had us beaten 6-2 in the bottom of the ninth with two out. I came to bat for the Phillies. Danny McFayden, a sidearming right-hander, was on the mound. With a count of one ball and two strikes, McFayden threw me a superb sidearm curve that started at my belt and broke right over the heart of the plate. It was one of the plainest strikes in history, but Klem called it a ball. Al Lopez, who was catching for Pittsburgh, immediately started yelling. Klem drew his famous line. Lopez jumped across it and Klem threw him out of the game. McFayden came running in, crossed the line, and was ejected. Frankie Frisch, the Pirate manager, came racing toward Klem, crossed the line, and found himself tossed, too. Well, when things calmed down Bill Baker came in to replace Lopez behind the plate and Pirate reliever Bob Klinger was taking his warmup tosses when Bill Klem sidled up to me and whispered very softly, so nobody else could hear him, "How in the hell could you take such a beautiful pitch?"

It was a long way from Bill Klem to Frenchy Arceneaux, but the Texas League and managing the Fort Worth Cats were much to my liking. I felt just great at the end of the 1948 season. We had won the league championship and then participated in the Dixie Series. The Dodgers felt I had done well; Mr. Reeves engineered a $1,000 raise for me, so for the first time my salary would be $10,000. Even so, I found a winter job in Fort Worth selling real estate. I could hardly wait for spring training to begin.

LEO DUROCHER: I've got nothing to say about leaving the Dodgers. Rickey didn't like me. He liked getting the attention. Stoneham was an owner who let the manager be in charge. But don't bother asking me about leaving the Dodgers, because I won't talk about it.

BUZZIE BAVASI: Mr. Rickey didn't think Leo was the type of person to run his ballclub. Larry McPhail had hired Leo, too, and Mr. Rickey wanted his own man in the manager's job. That's why he preferred to have Burt Shotton running the team. Mr. Rickey had great admiration for Leo's abilities as a manager, but less regard for many of Leo's personal habits.

DUKE SNIDER: Leo did some things I sure didn't agree with, especially when he went with the Giants and would play against us. Once from the New York dugout he yelled out to Ruben Gomez on the mound to stick one in Carl Furillo's ear, and Gomez hit Furillo in the back. Furillo started toward the mound, but then thought better of it because he didn't want to get run out of the game. He trotted towards first and glared at Durocher. Durocher gestured at him with a finger— you know, "Come on,"— and Furillo lost his temper, charged Leo in the dugout, and there was a big fight. Of course, Furillo got run and that's exactly what Leo intended all along. He got what he wanted, but I had to think it was going too far.

While I played for him I never hated Leo, but I got to the point where I didn't like him that much. But he was a great, great manager. Look at what he did with the Giants in '51—everybody thinks the Giants faded that August and September, but we played over .500 ball. I don't care about his suspension for a season—Durocher belongs in the Hall of Fame. In the late '40s and early '50s, why, Durocher was baseball at that time, the one the fans talked about most.

ROY CAMPANELLA: I thought Durocher was a good manager. He was interesting to play against. Some of the other Dodgers told me he wasn't always good to play for. Shotton was knowledgeable. Dressen was smart, very smart. Jackie always said Dressen was the manager he most enjoyed playing for.

SNIDER: Shotton came back again for a couple of years after Leo was fired or quit, whichever it really was. Charlie Dressen followed Shotton. I think Charlie did everything he could possibly do to get along with his players. He was from the same mold as Leo in that he had the burning desire to win at all costs. Dressen was a very astute man. Whenever we'd play the Giants while Leo was the New York manager, Dressen would make the statement to some of our players that he knew more than Leo about baseball. It was a very interesting comparison, especially since Dressen had been Leo's third base coach on the Dodgers.

Alston came after Dressen. I remember Walter Alston needed someone to ask questions. In 1954 he'd sit next to Jackie in the dugout and say things like, "Do you think I ought to sacrifice, Jackie?" And Jackie would bark back, "Don't ask me. You're the manager— do what you damn want." Jackie never did get along with Walter. Later on Jackie'd say Charlie Dressen was the best manager he ever played for, but I think Jackie only said that because he resented the way Leo would ride him after Leo went over to the Giants from the Dodgers.

Anyway, the team turned it around after Leo left, and when Campy got there during '48.

CAMPANELLA: People forget this, but I went through pretty much the same things Jackie had. Jackie was just up in '47 and I came in '48. At that time Bruce Edwards, Gil Hodges, and Bobby Bragan were the Brooklyn catchers. When they called me up they moved Edwards to third, Hodges to first, and sent Bragan to manage Fort Worth, the farm club. He went down to make room for me.

SNIDER: Bobby got a good deal starting out his managerial career in Fort Worth. Fort Worth was always a good baseball town, and most of us who played there enjoyed it.

When I played for the Cats at La Grave Field the wind always blew in from right like a son of a gun. But one night I hit a ball out over a clock tower they had there, and for that reason I moved up fast in the Dodger chain, only two and a half years in the minors. 'Cause Branch Rickey happened to be visiting Fort Worth that night I hit the homer; it made him believe I could move up quickly. I remember that home run like it was yesterday. Funny how you remember things early in your career much more than things that happened later on.

DICK WILLIAMS: I joined the Fort Worth Cats in July 1948, 10 days after Bobby Bragan got there for his first managing job in the Dodger farm chain. Oh, Bobby was a great disciplinarian. I'd say for that year on that team, players either loved Bobby or hated him. But I know that most of them who learned from him went on every year in their careers to say, "Thank God for Bobby Bragan."

Minor league managers should be teachers first. Now they're all too busy trying to win every game to take the time and teach the way they should. Bobby was a teacher with the Cats and we still won. I've always believed you should learn something from every manager you played for, even if it was somthing negative like what not to do. But Bobby got me believing in team play, in fundamentals, and he was so influential on my thinking. In my own autobiography I say he has a piece of every game won by every team I ever managed. It's true.

What Bobby had to share with his players wasn't limited to baseball. On Sundays some of us would go to church with him, and enjoy breakfast together afterwards. And then there was the way he thought we ought to act, well...

One time the Cats were in a train station. Gwenn, Bobby's wife, used to serve as our traveling secretary sometimes. She'd arrange box lunches for us. This time I think we had in them a couple of apples each, and I started juggling the apples. Preston Ward, one of our players, had eaten one of his apples and he flipped the core at me while I was juggling and hit me on the nose. I took one of the apples I'd been juggling and fired it at him. I missed Preston and just about hit Gwenn. Now, this incident had nothing to do with the game that day, but Bobby would not put me in the lineup. I thought it was for nearly hitting his wife with an apple, but he told me it was because you shouldn't throw things meant for you to eat. See, besides teaching you baseball he taught you how to act like a gentleman.

BLACKIE SHERROD: When Bobby came to Fort Worth to manage the Cats, I was writing for the old Fort Worth Press. He succeeded Les Burge. I don't know why Burge was fired.

Bobby was popular with the fans right away. He was colorful. They liked that. And fans back then weren't as belligerent as they are today. Now they look for faults quicker. But when Bobby took over the Cats he was quickly appreciated as a hard worker and a colorful guy.

As a Press sportswriter, I traveled with the Cats on their road trips. Usually these were made by train, and on that first trip I got to know Bobby. It was his smile that first struck me. When he smiles at you or talks to you, he looks right at you. Most people don't. But he gave the impression to me, and to everybody, that talking to you was absolutely the most important thing in the world to him right at that moment.

I don't know enough about baseball, maybe, to really rate Bobby as a manager. He was probably the best PR man I knew; he sold his team every chance he got. Players who played for him tell me he was a lot like Durocher, thinking games or days ahead of anybody else.

From a sportswriter's point of view, though, he was great. I remember that in San Antonio they had newspapers, one morning and one evening. So the guy from the morning paper would come interview Bobby before a game, and Bobby would have a story angle for him, maybe that the Cats' third baseman had hit in 20 straight games. Then the guy from the P.M. paper would come by and Bobby would have a completely different story angle to offer, maybe that the For Worth pitcher in that game was close to a Texas League record of some sort. I thought that was remarkable. What he'd tell each reporter was never duplicated. Bobby was very popular with the writers.

With the players, well, if he was unpopular with them it was because he was inclined to be a perfectionist. He wouldn't tolerate lack of effort. He was inclined to be caustic, and to people above him in team management as well as to the players below.

Hey, I can't speak objectively about Bobby because he's one of the best people I know in or out of sports. I don't think he ever did anything to be ashamed of. On the road with the Cats, Bobby roomed with Tommy Tatum, his coach. Tatum would say, "Bragan must have the cleanest conscience in the world." Now, Tatum liked beer, he would feel bad when he got up in the morning on road trips like all the rest of us did, and there in the same room with him Bragan would be singing while he was shaving. Tatum just couldn't believe it.

THE '49 CATS

WE ALL REMEMBER OUR FIRST LOVES. EVERY MANAGER, at least the lucky ones, always remembers his first championship team. The Fort Worth Cats won the Texas League in 1948, but I only managed that club for half a season. The 1949 Cats were mine all year.

When I remember that season, the one when I was a young manager who only knew the joys and not the pitfalls (yet) of that precarious profession, I think back to a road trip we took to Houston in late May. Del Wilbur was the Houston manager, and when I arrived at Busch Stadium, the Houston ballpark, I went over to Del and said, "I just won the championship. The Dodgers sent me Chico Carresquel to play shortstop and Carl Erskine to pitch. We've got it locked up." As it turned out, we did.

The season began in mid-February when everyone in theDodger organization reported to Vero Beach for spring training. Though I'd spent my share of springs with the Dodgers, this was the first time I moved up into management circles. It was eye-opening how decisions were made.

Each spring, every player in the organization had the potential to be switched from team to team. Mr. Rickey had a big say in this during his regular weeknight meetings. These evaluation sessions were also attended by the manager and coaching staff of the major league Dodgers, the manager from each of 21 farm teams and several organization scouts. Mr.Rickey's method was if even one manager or coach or scout liked a player, that player would stay in camp. If nobody was interested in a player, he was released. Every player, all 500 or so, would be discussed at length. If you felt a player belonged in a higher classification than he'd played in previously, you said so. Decisions were generally arrived at by consensus, though Mr. Rickey was occasionally known to make a personnel decision all by himself.

Sometimes, Mr. Rickey allowed visitors to sit in on these meetings. This practice paid big dividends for me when Julio D'Areos, who owned the Almendares team in the Cuban winter league, met me and afterwards asked me to manage his club during my off seasons.

At times during the spring, as a manager you'd find yourself being asked to choose between two players. For example, in 1950 both Billy Hunter and Don Zimmer were considered advanced enough to move up to Double A ball as the Fort Worth shortstop. I was asked to pick the one I wanted, and I chose Hunter. Billy had a solid season; when the year was over, Mr. Rickey sold him to the St. Louis Browns, later to move to Baltimore and rename themselves the Orioles. When word got to Zimmer that I'd picked Hunter over him, Zim sent me an autographed 8x10 glossy photograph of himself and a note chiding me for making the wrong decision. And Zim, of course, went on to a fine career as a player, coach, and manager at the major league level.

Hunter, though he never became a star, was one of the best shortstops I ever saw. During the time he played for the Cats, if we had a 4-1 or 5-1 lead in a late inning with a runner at third and one out, I'd play the infield back. But two or three times in that situation the batter hit a hard grounder to Hunter and Billy threw the runner at third out at home plate. This just doesn't happen very often; to do it, a shortstop not only has to have an outstanding arm, he has to have the proper instincts. I loved seeing Billy pull off this rare play.

Later on the Browns/Orioles traded Billy to the Yankees,where Casey Stengel was running things. In a game at Yankee Stadium, at least as Billy Hunter still tells it, there was the same runner on third/ one out situation with Yogi Berra behind the plate. The batter hit a grounder to Billy, who fired home. Yogi Berra had never come up out of his crouch. Yogi almost ate the baseball, and the runner was safe. When the inning was over, Billy Hunter was infuriated when he came into the dugout. He expected Berra to be reprimanded, but Stengel cornered Hunter instead. "If I want you to throw the ball home, I'll play the infield in!" Casey yelled. Different strokes for different folks.

Spring training, Dodger-style, was always a pleasant, learning experience. In 1949 Brooklyn was still several steps ahead of other major league organizations, and the way we did things at Vero Beach was proof of that. The Dodgers used four regulation-sized diamonds, meaning our players got in more game time. We had extra pitching mounds, and string targets to help our pitchers concentrate on throwing strikes. These were innovations of Mr. Rickey. Best of all, everyone's schedule for the next day was posted each night in the lobby of Dodgertown. You knew exactly what you'd be working on—rundown plays, pickoff plays, double steals, ways to stop double steals. All the players were subject to this routine. From major league stars to Class D scrubs, you went over and over the basics until the right moves became natural.

After players were properly conditioned, intrasquad exhibition games began. Fort Worth might play Montreal or St. Paul or Mobile or even the major league club. For organizational unity, Mr. Rickey insisted that during the spring each squad wear regulation Brooklyn Dodger uniforms. The only difference between teams was the color of the uniform numbers. Red belonged to the big club, green to St. Paul, orange to St. Paul, purple to Fort Worth, and so on.

During this spring I would play and manage. Playing in the exhibition games gave me real insights into which players could really do what. From the dugout, angles can sometimes skew vision, but from behind the plate you see everything in perspective. I found out first-hand exactly how much range fielders had or how well individual hitters really got around or didn't on the fastball. And one thing was always prevalent about being player-manager: You were less inclined to degrade opposing pitchers' stuff to your hitters when you had to bat against him yourself. If I told my guys, "This fella couldn't break a pane of glass," I'd be very embarrassed if he then struck me out three times in a row.

Looking back on the five seasons I managed in the Texas League, the '49 Cats were the best of those teams. The way the players on that squad could hit was just phenomenal. Five of our eight regulars hit over .300—Cal Abrams, Bob Bundy, Preston Ward, Chico Carresquel, and Dick Williams.

Williams was a character. He joined the Cats in 1948 maybe 10 days after I did, coming to us as a heralded 19-year-old phenom from California. There were many good things you could say about the young Dick Williams as a player, and if you talked to Dick long enough he'd say all of them. Excessive modesty was not a problem for him. Personality-wise he was very aggressive, a very independent thinker. Most 19-year-olds would be scared or at least shy around older ballplayers. From the day he arrived in Fort Worth, Dick Williams expected to be a team leader.

Williams obviously had the tools to go on to a fine career in the majors. I knew my job would be to harness his personality a little bit. He was so brassy, but if that was channeled in the right way I knew it would simply mean he would become a hard-nosed, aggressive ballplayer. And once the smart aleck portion of Williams' character was tempered, he was as fine a player as there ever was in the Texas League. This wasn't just my opinion. The Tigers had a scout, Red Barkley, whose assignment it was to monitor the Texas League and turn in reports only on can't miss prospects, real stars of the major league near future. In 1949, the only card he turned into the Detroit front office was on Dick Williams.

I enjoyed Dick's company, and got a lot of it. I had a policy while managing Fort Worth that if any of my players wanted to meet me on Sunday mornings for Bible class and church, I'd buy him his breakfast. Dick Williams, Carl Erskine, Eddie Chandler, and Jack Lindsay became my Sunday School regulars. They came for the religion and the free meal both. Williams was usually receptive to my counsel and turned out to be a real leader on the field and off. I was amazed to find that, at age 19, Dick enjoyed going to talk to kids at schools and to men's clubs, public relations sorts of chores for the Cats. He was very good at these functions.

I was lucky to get Dick on my '49 ballclub, but at first he wasn't happy to be there. In a half season at Fort Worth in 1948 he'd played very well. I know he expected to be promoted to Montreal or St. Paul in Triple A ball during '49 spring training, but the concensus at Mr. Rickey's night meetings had him down for one more year of Double A seasoning. Dick started the year sulking. I impressed upon him that he was damned lucky to be a professional ballplayer and that throwing a fit was a sure way not to get to Triple A eventually, let alone the majors. He understood.

While playing for the Cats, Williams met a girl named Norma Massato, whom he eventually married. In spring training of '49 I'd referred to some Italian-surnamed players like Al Gionfriddo and Ted Del Guercio as"foreigners," just making light of their names in good fun. And maybe I made a few joking references to a Dodger Mafia—this was just my natural sarcasm coming forth. One day in Fort Worth during the season, Dick Williams came to me and said, "I'm going to marry one of those foreigners you're always talking about." In that case, it all took on a new perspective. I congratulated him and knew right off the marriage would be successful, which it has been to this day.

What I remember most about Dick Williams, though, is how he always had questions. "Why'd you hit-and-run here?" "Shouldn't we have pitched out there?" We spent great amounts of time at the ballpark, in the lobbies of hotels, and on trains during road trips just talking baseball. There were two others on the team later on, Billy Hunter and Carroll Beringer, who were just the same. This bone-deep interest in the game is always the hallmark of the best managers and coaches of the future. Williams, of course, will be in the Hall of Fame some day. Billy Hunter had a stint managing the Texas Rangers after a long career as a major league coach, and Beringer, who never had the talent to pitch even an inning in the majors, ended up as pitching coach for the Dodgers and the Philadelphia Phillies. Among the young pitchers who learned much of their art from Beringer were Sandy Koufax, Don Drysdale, Tug McGraw, and Steve Carlton.

I was glad to have Williams back in '49 because Irv Noren, my center fielder in '48, was sold by Mr. Rickey to the Washington

Senators after that season was concluded. This is always the danger in managing a minor league team. If you nurture players and get them to the top of their games, it's inevitable they'll move up the organizational ladder or be sold to other clubs. Remember, at this time the Dodgers had 21 farm teams. So they'd keep only the very best for themselves and be well compensated for the contracts of players like Noren, Hunter, and Carresquel.

So when Noren was sold to Washington, I went to Vero Beach the next spring determined to keep Williams as my center fielder. Dick stayed, played well, made the majors 18 months later, and helped win us a Texas League title in the meantime.

The Cats squad stayed in Vero Beach until the Texas League season opened on the first of April. When we arrived in Fort Worth, the Chamber of Commerce threw us a welcoming luncheon with all the local business big shots invited. It was a ritzy affair. At this time Bob Jones, Mr. Rickey's son-in-law, was business manager of the Cats. During the welcome luncheon, the master of ceremonies stood up and said, "Bob Jones will now give the invocation." As our business manager turned pale, another Bob Jones, this one the minister at Fort Worth's First Presbyterian Church, rose from his place at the head table and delivered the blessing. After the luncheon was over, the Cats' Bob Jones grasped the hand of God's Bob Jones and said, "I was never so happy in my life as when I saw you walk to the podium. All I could think of at that moment was, 'Now I lay me down to sleep!' "

The Cats got off to a solid start, and then in May we got Erskine and Carrasquel. That was it. I had the horses, and if we didn't win I knew I'd feel Mr. Rickey's wrath. Fortunately, it didn't come to that. Carresquel made his mark as a ballplayer.

He was a smooth fielder and pretty good hitter. 1949 was his first year in American professional ball. He started the season with Montreal but moved down a notch to us when the transition proved a little tough. Chico spoke little or no English. The first two weeks he was with Fort Worth, all Chico ate was cottage cheese because that was the only food name he knew.

On the field that season, Carresquel made only four or five errors, and three of those were on throws to first base. I don't believe he booted a ground ball all year. And right after the '49 season was over

Mr. Rickey sent Chico to the Chicago White Sox. It was obvious Chico would soon be a major league shortstop, and I hated to see him leave the organization. But at that same time Hunter and Zimmer were the top farm system prospects laboring in the shadow of Pee Wee Reese. Mr. Rickey thought it made more sense to get some return for other prospects instead of letting them wither away in the minors. During the years I managed the Cats, my first basemen were Preston Ward, Dee Fondy, Chuck Connors, and Wayne Belardi. All of them coveted Gil Hodges's job, and all of them ended up being made available by the Dodgers to other organizations. Today with each major league team only having a half-dozen farm teams, let one prospect stand out at any position and he's officially designated the heir apparent to that job on the major league club.

Carl Erskine was a pleasure to manage. He had a good fastball, a sharp curveball and a changeup Dodger pitching coaches described as "pulling the shade down." That's how he moved his arm when he let the pitch go—like he was reaching out and tugging down a windowshade. I knew right away Erskine was special—he had the right aggressive attitude as well as excellent stuff. Eddie Chandler, by contrast, had the attitude but not the stuff. He ended up as a quality minor league pitcher who never quite could make the next step. Chandler, though, went on to a lucrative career as a stockbroker in Los Angeles.

In 1949 Erskine went 15-4, leading the Texas League in strikeouts and winning percentage. In August the Dodgers found themselves in a tight National League pennant race and they promoted him from the Cats. He went right on winning for them; I think he was 8-1 for the Dodgers during the rest of the season.

Minor league fans have to be a special breed who understand the players they love watching most will probably be the ones they end up watching for the shortest time. I used to admire a sign in the Tulsa ballpark. It read, "Home of the Tulsa Oilers," and, underneath in block letters, "Proving Ground for Major League Stars." As long as minor league fans kept that in mind, they could handle the shock when their teams' best players were taken away from them.

The Cats were interesting for fans to watch—and as manager I found the players interesting, too. For awhile in '49 I had Ben Taylor playing first base. He was strong and could hit the long ball, but his manner of thinking was different from normal individuals. We were playing a game in Tulsa when Johnny Temple, the Oiler second baseman, came up with a runner on first in a close game and laid down a sacrifice bunt. Taylor ran in, fielded the bunt, and reached out to tag Temple. All minor leaguers in those days were anxious to show they played the game hard, and Temple was no exception. He tried to jar the ball from Taylor's grasp by punching him on his glove arm. Taylor held the ball, so Temple was out, but he didn't leave it at that. I watched aghast as my first baseman carefully set his glove on the infield grass and chased after Temple as the Oiler trotted back toward his dugout. Taylor caught up with Temple and planted one on his chin, decking him. Meanwhile, of course, the Tulsa runner went around second base and made it all the way to third. If it had taken Taylor longer to cold-cock Temple, the runner would have scored.

A month later we were playing in Shreveport when a scout from the St. Louis Browns came down to the field just before game time to tell me his club had just purchased Ben Taylor's contract. I quickly called Mr. Reeves in Fort Worth for confirmation, and asked him if I could go ahead and tell Taylor the good news. This, after all, was what every minor leaguer dreamed of—being told a major league club wanted him to pack his bags and report for duty. So I was happy for Taylor as I delivered the glad tidings, and dumfounded when he responded, "Well, I sent out my shirts to the cleaners on Sunday, and today's Monday, and they won't be ready until Wednesday—so tell St. Louis I'll be a little late reporting." The whole object of playing in the minors was supposed to be getting to the major leagues, and he was more concerned with his laundry. He ended up playing parts of three years in the majors, for the Browns, Tigers, and Braves. I hope he didn't lose too many more shirts along the way.

I suppose I enjoyed ballplayers who were such difficult characters. Managing, at least in Fort Worth in 1949, was simply fun. I enjoyed filling out game reports at home each night, monitoring in writing how much the players were improving. Morning workouts were fine, too; each day we'd work on teaching this batter to hit to the opposite field or that pitcher to perfect his pickoff move. Little things many fans miss are the things that win or lose most baseball games. I was always thrilled to impart all the inside stuff.

As a former major leaguer managing a minor league club, I enjoyed some built-in respect from most players. I had accomplished what they still hoped to achieve. I had been good enough; they had to prove they were. This usually makes discipline easy. Ballplayers of this era thought primarily about the game and how to make themselves better at it. There were few bonus babies. Nobody had any money, so there were far fewer temptations than kids on the way up face today. As Mr. Rickey suggested, I stressed the importance of self-discipline: Players needed to do the right things because they were right, not because they were forced to follow the manager's orders.

Six players from the '49 Cats went on to relatively successful major league careers—Williams, Abrams, Carrasquel, Erskine, Preston Ward, and Bob Millikin. Considering the competition they faced with so many other quality players on so many other farm teams, it should be easy to see why I could win with that ballclub. Six players from one team eventually becoming major leaguers was just phenomenal. I went on to have championship minor league clubs where no players at all went on to the the majors. The '50 Cats were also fine, and just two of those players went on to the big leagues — Billy Hunter and Don Hoak.

We ended up winning the 1949 Texas League championship by six or eight games. Along the way I picked up the nickname "Black Fox" for the color of my hair and my way of scheming to win games. But I wasn't the only guy nicknamed "Fox" managing in the Texas League that year. Al Vincent, the Tulsa skipper who'd been a minor league manager for 30 years, was the Silver Fox. Tommy Tatum, with his brick-colored hair at Oklahoma City, was the Red Fox.

Catching most games, I hit .298. Jack Lindsey, an infielder, hit .275. Everybody else in the regular lineup hit better than I. Even if I'd hit .400, I wasn't going anywhere. I loved being a manager, and I had no ambition to return as an active player to the major leagues.

After the regular season, the Texas League entered into a four-team playoff. Fort Worth easily beat Shreveport, the fourth-place finisher, and second-place Tulsa whipped whatever team finished third. So we had to play Tulsa in a best-of-seven playoff for the final league title.

It was then I learned about real, lasting pain as a manager. We were tied with Tulsa at three games each. In the final game Milliken pitched for the Cats, Walker Cress for Tulsa. It was 0-0 going into the bottom of the ninth at La Grave Field. Dick Williams led off with a triple down the right field line. The relay throw came within an inch of bouncing into our dugout, and Williams would have scored the winning run right there.

Chico Carrasquel was the next hitter. Al Vincent, the Gray Fox, ordered him walked intentionally. Then I came up, and Vincent had me walked intentionally, too, loading the bases with nobody out.

I trotted to first base. The umpire there, Billy Wilson, said, "It looks like you've got it wrapped up, Bobby." I called time to think things through. I was sorely tempted to put in a pinch runner for myself so I could go and coach third base in case I wanted to put on the squeeze play. I walked to the dugout, maybe meaning to do just that, and as I walked I looked right at Andy Skurski, a former Triple-A player who'd become a Cats' utility infielder. Skurski could hit pretty damn well—he'd been our best pinch-hitter all year—and I could see from his eyes he wanted very badly to get up and win the game for us.

But Jack Lindsey was due to be our next hitter. I had an easy call; Skurski was a better hitter. But somehow I let Andy stay on the bench. I went back to run at first and let Lindsey bat. He grounded to the shortstop, who forced Dick Williams at home. One out.

Then I ignored Andy Skurski again. Walt Sessi, a left handed hitter with major league experience, was my choice to bat for Milliken. Sessi grounded to the Oiler second baseman and Carrasquel was forced at home. Two out.

Cal Abrams, our leadoff hitter, came up. He hit a long fly ball to left, which would have easily scored the winning run with less than two outs. But that wasn't the situation. We went into the 10th having squandered an excellent opportunity to win the game.

With Milliken gone, I brought in a curveball pitcher named Joe Landrum. (His son Billy is currently an ace reliever with the Pittsburgh Pirates.) Landrum gave up a single to Tulsa's leadoff hitter. The next batter sacrificed him to second. Russ Burns, the most dangerous Oiler hitter, was next, and I ordered him walked intentionally to set up a double play. The hitter I wanted Landrum to face was Tulsa's first baseman, a hulking guy named Joe Adcock. Adcock promptly belted a ball over the left field wall into the Trinity River. The Cats were eliminated, and there was no one to blame but myself. That game is still so vivid in my mind. I still wish I had the chance to go back and make different decisions. I'll never forget it, and never stop hurting because of it. It was a sad end to a great season.

CARROLL BERINGER: I spent 1949 and 1950 pitching for Bobby. He caught almost every game. He was a good catcher, better than he now lets on. The Dodgers trusted him with their top pitching prospects. Carl Erskine got moved down to Fort Worth in '49 just because Mr. Rickey wanted this young man with so much talent to have his final grooming from BobbyBragan.

DON ZIMMER: I'd heard a lot about Bobby Bragan as I came up through the Dodger organization, about what a great teacher he was, and I wanted to play for him myself when the time came. By that I mean when I was ready—I had my year in D ball, moved up to C and B and A and then when it was my turn in Double-A I wanted to play for Bobby in Fort Worth.

I also knew that Billy Hunter had been Bobby's shortstop for the Cats, but when I got to Vero Beach for spring training I was on the Cats roster and Billy was with Montreal at Triple-A level. I thought, "It looks like I'm going to get to play for Bragan."

At the end of spring training I was told I'd made the Cats' roster. At this time my wife was very pregnant and back at our home in Cincinnati. She couldn't fly. I went to one of the Dodger executives,

Fresco Thompson maybe, and asked if I could please drive home to Cincinnati, pick up my wife and drive down to Fort Worth to start the season. I got permission. When I got to Cincinnati, there was a phone message for me. Plans had been changed. Bobby had wanted Billy Hunter back and I was going to play in Mobile instead. Bobby always says I sent him a picture of myself with a note he made the wrong choice. Hell, maybe I did. And he *did* make the wrong choice.

DICK WILLIAMS: After the 1948 season I was sure the Dodgers would send me up to Triple-A. I ended up coming back to Fort Worth and at first I didn't like it. I was heavy. I admit I let myself get fat. Bobby used to run me every day with the pitchers even though it was so hot in Texas and I had to play nine innings every night. It was hotter than blazes. But you did what Bobby told you or your name wasn't in the lineup.

BERINGER: I have to say Bobby was a disciplinarian. He didn't tolerate foolishness. He wanted players who knew their roles and were satisfied to fill them. As one example, well, anyone in the bullpen always hankers deep down to be a starter. I pitched out of the pen all of the '49 season, and my complaint to Bobby all season long was, "Let me start a game." "No," he'd reply, "You're doing a good job for me there in the bullpen. Just keep doing it." But I kept on asking for a start.

Well, in that '49 season we clinched the Texas League pennant against Tulsa in the first game of a doubleheader. We were celebrating in the clubhouse between games when all of a sudden Bobby comes up to me with this grin on his face and hands me a ball. "I listened to you bitch about starting all year," he told me. "Now go get 'em." I hardly got anybody out. I went in with a great ERA, certainly under two runs a game, and by the time Bobby came to get me that ERA had skyrocketed past three and was on the way to four. I just got my brains beat out. On the train ride back to Fort Worth Bobby kept coming over to me and laughing. "Did you enjoy your start?" he asked, real sarcastically. "Did you have fun out there?" Bobby laughs at me about this yet.

He took it hard when we lost that 1949 playoff, the one where we had the bases loaded and couldn't get the winning run in. I remember his face after Adcock hit that homer. Bobby looked like a man who was dying.

DUKE SNIDER: It's tough being a minor league manager. Everyone who's ever had that job carries with him the memory of an especially painful loss. Mine came when I was managing the Dodgers' Albuquerque farm club. We had a great club, and after we won our league we went on to play Birmingham for the Dixie championship. This was when Birmingham had Reggie Jackson and Rollie Fingers, the guys who went on to play for that dynasty Oakland had with Charlie Finley in the '70s. Anyway, we won the first two games of the best-of-seven series and I figured we about had it wrapped up, especially because I had this pitcher, Ray Lamb, who could throw hard and who was going to pitch the fourth game for me.

But in the third game we were two runs ahead late and Birmingham had runners on second and third. The pitcher I had on the mound looked like he was looking through Coke bottles—his eyes were that big. I had Lamb warming up; we had a travel date the next day, so I felt he could maybe get one or two hitters and still be ready to go in Game Four. I knew in my gut I should bring Lamb in.

But earlier that year I'd caught hell from Fresco Thompson for using a starting pitcher in short relief. Fresco really got on me about it; he had a tongue that could cut you, that guy. So I wanted to bring Lamb in against Birmingham, but I kept thinking back to Fresco and I just didn't do it.

So the pitcher I left in hit the next batter to load the bases. Dave Duncan was up next for Birmingham. I knew Ray Lamb could strike Duncan out. I got ready to walk to the mound and in my mind I heard Fresco yelling. He was so mad when I brought in Bill Singer that one time in short relief. So I left this guy in again, and Duncan hits the next pitch over the fence to beat us, and we're only up 2-1 in games. I blew that game for us. The loss was mine.

But I told myself I at least had Lamb set to pitch in Game Four. Except it turned out I didn't.

That night two of my players, Willie Crawford and Ted Sizemore, had birthdays. Their teammates threw 'em a party at a local club, and while there my guys got into a huge fight with the University of

New Mexico football team. All my players got beat up, every one of 'em. Bill Sudakis had broken ribs. When we got on the plane for Birmingham the next day, walking up the ramp my players looked like those bandaged guys in the "Spirit of '76" painting. Everybody was hurt. And Ray Lamb, who was going to pitch Game Four for me, had 22 stitches in his mouth. Because he got beat up, he never did get to pitch in that series and we ended up losing it.

I will never, ever forget about this. It still hurts and always will.

CHANGE

I MANAGED THE FORT WORTH CATS FOR FIVE SEASONS, through the end of the 1952 schedule. Just after our great year in 1949 there was what I guess you'd call a power struggle at the top of the Brooklyn Dodger organization. The team's ownership was comprised of four parties: Walter O'Malley and Mr. Rickey each owned 25 percent, as did John L. Smith and Jim Mulvey. Both O'Malley and Mr. Rickey wanted control of the team, but O'Malley got the upper hand when Smith gave him control of his voting rights.

That made it obvious to Mr. Rickey he was out, so he asked O'Malley how much a quarter-share of the Dodgers might be worth. O'Malley said approximately $300,000. Mr. Rickey thought he could get more and reached a tentative sales agreement with a real estate developer named William Zeckendorf. O'Malley didn't want to let Mr. Rickey's share of the ownership get away, so he was forced to buy that 25 percent at the amount Zeckendorf would have paid— $1.3 million. Of that, $1 million went to Mr. Rickey and $300,000 to Zeckendorf to reimburse a down payment he had made.

The immediate result was that Mr. Rickey moved on to Pittsburgh as general manager of the Pirates. As the smartest man in baseball, he didn't have to worry about lining up another job. I'm sure teams came to him. What Mr. Rickey had pulled off was simply a business deal. He made a good profit. I didn't begrudge it to him, especially since his legacy remained with the Dodgers after he left —remains to this day, really. Top-of-the-line spring training facilities, organized fitness programs, an emphasis on speed and sound fundamentals - other teams since have copied this strategy, but Mr. Rickey was the innovator.

I have heard in the years since that while Mr. Rickey ran the Dodgers I was called "Mr. Rickey's boy." I would be complimented if that were true, but the fact was Mr. Rickey had 21 teams to watch over and I was just the manager of one of them. When he went to Pittsburgh, for the Dodger organization it was business as usual. Walter O'Malley greeted everyone at Vero Beach. I remember how when I'd tell him hello he'd always ask, "How's your beautiful wife?" I had great respect for Buzzie Bavasi, who succeeded Mr. Rickey as Brooklyn's general manager, and for farm system director Fresco Thompson. My initial goal—managing the Dodgers under Mr. Rickey—was modified to simply managing the Dodgers.

This wasn't a pipe dream. The Dodger way of doing things was to train a manager in the Brooklyn farm system and gradually move him up until he ran the big club. Walter Alston and Tommy Lasorda are classic examples. They came up through the farm system. Leo was an exception.

From a personal standpoint, sure, I missed Mr. Rickey. I thought then and still think now he was the smartest baseball man who ever lived. I learned a great deal listening to him. But it was not by any means a father-son relationship; when he left Brooklyn for Pittsburgh, for instance, we didn't exchange notes wishing each other well. He'd moved along and life for both of us went on.

And life with the Fort Worth Cats went on, smoothly for the most part. In 1950 we had a fast team, and stole 225 bases while finishing third in the Texas League. Rogers Hornsby, the manager at Beaumont, got his team in ahead of everyone else that season. In 1951 we finished second; my best outfielders were Ted Del Guercio and Al Gionfriddo. John Simmons was my third starting outfielder. These were the three whose hitting was so weak that I hit them 7th, 8th, and 9th, eliciting the nasty note from Fresco Thompson. In 1952 we were second again, led by first baseman Wayne Belardi and short-stop Al Brancato. There were maybe two real major league prospects on that club.

I was very happy in Fort Worth, with my team and the city and with the Dodger organization. I had a fine relationship with Fort Worth general manager John Reeves. In my mind, Fort Worth would be the permanent home of the Bragan family, though my managerial ambition meant I'd hopefully run other teams in higher leagues. My ability, even as I reached my mid-30s, to be a player-manager was a real plus for me. The Dodgers valued that, both for the extra insights into players it gave me and the money it saved them.

If I had stayed with the Dodgers, I think I might have replaced Walter Alston when he moved from running Montreal up to the big club. Then I would have been positioned as Walter's heir apparent.

While I bided my time in Fort Worth, I began earning my niche in Texas League history books by finding new and interesting ways to irritate umpires. I consider umpire-baiting a challenge and an art, especially since I didn't believe in resorting to name-calling and profanity. In retrospect I have to admit I even stayed up a few nights thinking up ways to get even with umpires I believed weren't giving a fair shake to the Cats.

Subtlety was not part of my art. In a game against Oklahoma City in 1950, our team of fast base-stealers was stymied by the home team's grounds crew. They had piled up inches upon inches of soft dirt in the infield to slow us down if we tried to run. I objected before the game began, but to no avail. During the game I mentioned my unhappiness once or twice. Eventually I drew a warning from the umpires that they'd heard enough complaints—I was to shut up or get out. Well, I didn't choose to shut up, and I was ejected. As soon as it was official I'd been tossed, I grabbed a nearby shovel, dug up part of the field, and deposited that new load of dirt on the pile already in the infield. I made a few more trips and added on a few more shovelsful. At that point the umpires told me I had to leave. I said I didn't feel like going quite yet. The umps called on a short, stocky fellow, maybe 65 years old and in a police uniform, to tell me to get off the field. As soon as the officer got 10 feet from me, I hollered to him that I needed to talk to my pitcher. I walked to the mound, chatted a little, and as the cop arrived I took off to visit with my third baseman. The officer ended up following me all over the field; I talked to all nine of my position players before I turned, nodded to the cop, and walked off the field with him. By that time, the Oklahoma fans were cheering for me. The umpires weren't, but I'd had my vengeance and my satisfaction.

Another time in Shreveport, my old friend Frenchy Arceneaux got into it with Walt Sessi, my quiet outfielder who never had an unkind word to say to anyone. How Frenchy could even get Walt mad I never knew, but they were nose-to-nose and Frenchy warned Walt that if he said anything else he'd be out of the game. Our whole bench yelled at Frenchy for that, and he turned and warned everybody in there that he'd run them, too. Well, Walt smiled when he heard that, and Frenchy threw him out of the game for smiling sarcastically. This got me mad. I suggested a few ways Frenchy might improve his job performance and he tossed me, too. Now, in the Shreveport ballpark there were padded light standards inside the field fences, maybe 30 feet from the foul lines. To let Frenchy know how deficient I considered his vision, I mimicked a blind man staggering around the ballpark, walking into the light poles.

Then and in many other instances I got a $25 fine from the league president. He'd also send along letters telling me to clean up my act. I didn't. Often, Mr. Reeves would see to it that the ballclub reimbursed me, and the Dodger executives never said a word about any of it. My players seemed to appreciate what I was doing on their behalf. There is nothing wrong in wanting to win badly, and part of that is wanting each umpire to call each play correctly. If I thought they didn't, well, it was my job to tell them they weren't doing their jobs.

And I took great pains not to pick on umpires indiscriminately. Andy Andrews was the most popular Texas League umpire at the time, and he deserved to be. Andy was always smiling and chatting; he loved everybody and sincerely wished both clubs in any contest could win the game. Then one night in San Antonio he blew a call against us during a close contest in a late inning. I objected vehemently from my catching position, and he turned to me with such a pleasant expression on his face I just couldn't bring myself to say anything that might hurt his feelings. Instead, I simply heaved the ball out of the ballpark, way over the grandstand behind home plate. And Andy said very politely, "Bobby, that's enough for you tonight."

Every game was fun in its way. I was enjoying myself even if I wasn't making much money. After my raise to a $10,000 salary in 1949 I didn't get a penny more the whole time I was with Fort Worth. Well, money wasn't everything. Even the physical wear and tear of catching almost every game didn't dampen my enthusiasm. As I got older there were many games where I would have been pleased to sit out in favor of our second-string catcher, but I always felt we had a better chance to win if I was handling the pitching staff from behind the plate.

I had no plans to leave the Dodger organization. Oh, maybe if some other club had offered me a major league managing job I'd have considered it, but I sure wouldn't have left just to move up to Triple A. In those days, players and managers were much more stabilized in an organization. There was a sense of unity. You were proud to be part of the Cardinals or the Yankees or the Dodgers. These days, any sense of unity is rare. Players can't wait to get six professional years in so they can become free agents. The prevailing color of the game is now green, my friends. And in a way it's a pity.

But what Tommy Lasorda says today about bleeding Dodger blue is just extending the feeling all of us had 40 years ago. You were part of a ballclub, part of an organization. This emphasizes what serious problems Leo must have had with Mr. Rickey to jump from the Dodgers to the Giants. That sort of thing just wasn't usually done.

So Buzzie Bavasi couldn't believe what he was hearing in the winter of 1952 when I told him I'd just as soon leave the Dodger organization. "You can't mean it, Bobby," he kept saying. But I did.

After the '52 Cats season ended, I went to Cuba to manage Almendares in the Cuban league. While I was in Cuba I always read the Havana *post*, the English-language newspaper. To my dismay one morning, I read a short article in the sports section reporting the Brooklyn Dodgers had fired Fort Worth Cats General Manager John Reeves. Stunned, I immediately called Buzzie Bavasi to ask if this was true.

What happened was this: A new Brooklyn Dodger business manager assigned to Fort Worth had told Buzzie at an organizational meeting that Mr. Reeves's main interest was oil, not baseball, adding Mr. Reeves used one of his Cat's secretaries to plot daily maps of where holes were being drilled. Buzzie resented this, and fired Mr. Reeves.

Well, I knew firsthand Mr. Reeves had oil interests, but these never detracted from his ability to run his ballclub. And Mr. Reeves had always, always been good to me. So I informed Buzzie that if it were true Mr. Reeves wouldn't be returning, then I had no interest in coming back to the Cats, either. For the first time, Mr. Rickey's absence really meant something to me. It's unlikely he would have fired a loyal subordinate in the manner Bavasi disposed of Mr. Reeves.

I had no fear of finding new baseball employment. I'd done a good job managing the Cats; baseball is a small society and word had gotten around. As a player-manager, hiring me would save a team one salary. And at no time did I consider leaving baseball to try to support my family in some other business. Baseball was always what I wanted to do. There was no room in my mind to consider other forms of employment.

Well, Buzzie tried to talk me out of it. "I know you think more of the Dodgers than of Mr. Reeves," he said at one point. "No," I told him, "Mr. Reeves has been wonderful to me and my family, and I want to leave. I'll put this in writing if you wish." Buzzie eventually got the message. He knew I'd still have trade or sale value to the Dodger organization, so he told me he'd go to work on moving me and get back to me on it within a few days.

Sure enough, Bavasi called me a week later and said, "We've made a deal with Pittsburgh for a catcher named Joe Rossi," a fellow who played just part of one major league season with the Reds. Buzzie told me the Pirates would be in touch and wished me luck.

I just knew who'd be calling me next, and I was right. Mr. Rickey's voice boomed over the telephone wires. "The Hollywood Stars, our Triple A club, needs a manager," he said. "We'd like you to go there."

Triple A and Mr. Rickey, too! I was thrilled, and immediately agreed to make Hollywood my next assignment. I knew Fred Haney was leaving the Stars to manage the major league Pirates. My replacing him at Hollywood was a clear signal I was next in line to take over at Pittsburgh.

What I failed to consider at the time, though I'd have ample opportunity to think about it later, was that the Pittsburgh Pirates in 1952 were about as far opposite the Brooklyn Dodgers as a major league team could get. In that season, for instance, Brooklyn won the National League pennant with a 96-57 record and the Pirates finished dead last at 42-112. Joe Garagiola was the Pirate catcher then. It's fair to say Joe did not have a distinguished season. Billy Meyer managed Pittsburgh in 1952, and in one game Joe made three errors behind the plate. Mr. Rickey came to Forbes Field the next day and sarcastically told Meyer, "I got a new glove for Garagiola." Meyer replied, quite seriously, "Mr. Rickey, that's the best trade you ever made!"

The Pirates continued their sad sack ways while I was at Hollywood. Haney, who went on to manage the Milwaukee Braves to two pennants and one world championship, couldn't get anything accomplished in Pittsburgh. His clubs went 50-104 in 1953, 53-101 in 1954, and 60-94 in 1955. Mr. Rickey was trying to continue his St. Louis and Brooklyn tradition of building from the farm system up, and poor Haney didn't have much major league material to work with.

Bob Cobb, owner of the Stars franchise, also owned Hollywood's famous Brown Derby restaurant. When I reported to Hollywood, Mr. Cobb hosted a "Welcome Bobby Bragan" luncheon at his famous restaurant. You should remember that in 1953 there were still only 16 major league teams, none on the West Coast. For Los Angeles area baseball fans, the Stars were the absolute peak of available baseball entertainment.

My coming to town was a big event. Dan Dailey, the famous actor-dancer, served as the luncheon's master of ceremonies. At the appropriate moment he stood up at the podium and told the crowd, "I take great pleasure in introducing the new manager of the Stars, *Billy* Bragan." I responded, "Thank you, *Don*." Everybody laughed, and I knew I'd enjoy my time in Hollywood.

CARROLL BERINGER: It was shocking news when Bobby left the Dodger organization. He'd become a legend with Fort Worth, and it was obvious to everybody he would stay with the Brooklyn organization and gradually move up the ladder until he managed the Dodgers.

But knowing Bobby as I did, I wasn't surprised he would give up that kind of secure future over a matter of principle. Put the risk he took into perspective—just 16 major league teams, meaning just 16 major league managing jobs. And of those, the one with the most chance of being long term was the Dodgers.

DUKE SNIDER: When word of Bobby's leaving reached the Dodger clubhouse, a lot of us were amazed. It would certainly have been thought at that time Bobby would be finished with the Brooklyn organization forever. It didn't work out that way, of course.

HOLLYWOOD

I MANAGED THE HOLLYWOOD STARS FOR THREE VERY ENJOYABLE YEARS. Fred Haney, who'd gone on to manage the Pirates, left me a turnkey job. The Stars were a ready-made winner. Many of the players already had or would one day have stints in the major leagues—first baseman Chuck Stevens (Browns), second baseman Monty Basgall (Dodgers), outfielders Tom Saffell and Ted Beard (both with Pittsburgh), and pitcher Mel Queen (Reds), among others. A smart, hard-nosed bunch is what the Stars were, and a pleasure to manage. And after spring training in 1953, the Pirates sent us first baseman Dale Long and outfielder Lee Walls, two fine players. There was no question in my mind— or, I'm sure, in Mr. Rickey's—that with this club I should be expected to win the Pacific Coast League title. Just as the Stars were a step up from the Cats in terms of playing quality, so was the whole Pacific Coast League a jump up from the Texas League.

There were three umpires instead of two for each game, which made a big difference in the quality of officiating. And there were also very long road trips—we might leave Hollywood for a week in Seattle and a week in Portland, two weeks of games with just Mondays off, before coming home. Same thing for San Francisco and Oakland, or Sacramento and San Diego. More convenient were games against our cross-town rivals, the Los Angeles Angels, because we could commute to Wrigley Field from home.

Every Sunday we would play doubleheaders. When you're young, either playing in a doubleheader or going to see one is extra fun. The older you are, the less fun doubleheaders get to be. And in the Pacific Coast League, I can remember many trips to San Francisco where it would rain on Tuesday, Wednesday, and Thursday, forcing us to play doubleheaders on Friday, Saturday, and Sunday to get in all the games scheduled for the week.

Haney had been both successful with the Stars and popular with his players. He had a good touch. A month into the '53 season, first baseman Stevens came up to me in the clubhouse and said, "Any time after we swept a doubleheader, Fred would have a couple of cases of beer in the clubhouse and tell us, ' This is from The Gambler.' " Well, I didn't pick up on it at first, but after the third time or so we swept two and the players wanted to know about The Gambler. I got the message and started buying them a couple of cases on those special occasions. "The Gambler" bit was just Haney's way of making sure no one could criticize him for giving his players beer to drink.

I never did drink, not even one taste of beer. It went back to my older sister Sue who, after she got out of school, still lived at home with the rest of us. She would come in around 1 A.M. after a date, she and her boyfriend half-gassed, and they'd come over to where my brother and I were out on the sleeping porch, sound asleep. They'd pull the covers back and throw ice water on us. It turned us permanently against drinking.

Even without drinking, Hollywood was a glamorous place to be. Bill Frawley was co-owner of the Stars, and lots of other celebrities were regulars at our games. Jayne Mansfield, who had yet to hit it big, was the pompon girl who stood on the top of our dugout and led the fans in cheers for us. The players liked to cheer for Jayne. Even free beer after doubleheader sweeps ran a poor second to Jayne in the players' affections.

During any given game you'd see George Raft in the stands, or Bing Crosby or Frank Lovejoy or some combination of the Marx brothers. Gilmore Field was in the heart of Hollywood—later on when it was knocked down they built CBS Television Studios on the same site. The park seated 11,000 in a nice wooden grandstand, and of course the weather was usually perfect. Before and after many games I'd do radio interviews with Chuck Connors, who hosted our pre- and post-game shows.

Maybe the most avid fan among the celebrities was Harry Ruby, the man who wrote "Three Little Words" and many other hit songs. Ruby once convinced Washington Senators owner Clark Griffith to let him play in a Senators regular-season game. Ruby put on a Washington uniform and I think they stuck him in right field for one hitter, no doubt while the other team had a right-handed pull hitter at the plate. That one moment meant more to Harry Ruby than all the great songs he composed.

I was still a player-manager, catching the majority of the games. My legs were holding up; I continued to believe remaining on the active roster gave me a better understanding of both my players and our opponents.

The Pirates had their spring training in Bradenton, Florida, but the Stars trained in Anaheim. The facilities we had in California were wonderful, but I was sorry not to have any time with Mr. Rickey. He, of course, spent his spring with the major league club on the opposite coast.

But the Pacific Coast League was about as close as you could get to the major leagues without being there. Most of our players had already spent time in the "show," as we called it, and there was always some feeling the league should get a new classification above Triple A because of the quality of play. We were just better than other Triple A-classified leagues. Salaries on the average were higher, and our seasons were the longest of anyone's —up to 200 games at one point (major league clubs played 154 at this time) and still 180 when I got there. The weather was better than anywhere else in the country and farm system players were expected to improve the more they played—so we played more.

It was an ideal job for me. Of course, a lot of my pleasure had to do with a winning team, but the owners—Frawley and Bob Cobb— were congenial, the Hollywood fans were very knowledgeable, and even the Stars' equipment manager was first-class. Nobe Kawana was his name, and later on when the major leagues moved west he became equipment manager for the Dodgers. Nobe's brother Yosh held the same position with the Cubs for 35 or 40 years.

Gwenn and I found a nice house in Studio City, just a 20-minute drive through the canyon from Hollywood. The place we rented belonged to Arthur Treacher, who achieved fame playing a butler in countless movies. He moved out into a bigger and better home, but the one he left behind was just fine for the Bragans. We paid $200 a month, and Treacher left all his photos and other memorabilia in place.

My salary with the Stars was $12,000, a $2,000 a year raise from the Cats days. Every Christmas I also got a $500 bonus from Mr. Cobb, big money in those days. We lived comfortably.

As I expected and hoped, the Stars won the league championship my first season with the team. The Stars' owners shelled out to get all of us watches to commemorate the title. One extra was ordered and given to actor Michael O'Shea. O'Shea was a ballplayer only in his own mind, who'd wisely given up the sport in favor of show business and evidentally had some regrets. He had his own Stars uniform and Fred Haney had given him permission to work out with the team whenever he wanted. I was glad to continue the practice. O'Shea was a delightful man, married to actress Virginia Mayo.

Thirty-five years after we won that championship, Michael O'Shea died of a heart attack while doing a show in Dallas. Virginia Mayo took the time to get in touch with me to say that, when he died, that Hollywood Stars watch was still on his wrist.

We won the 1953 title easily, clinching it with a week left in the season. Other teams had good players—Nippy Jones was with Sacramento, for instance—but we just had more. I particularly remember Bob Dillinger, the Sacramento third baseman who'd just been sent down to the PCL by the Dodgers. Dillinger always waited to hit the curveball. There were times I'd call for nine or 10 straight fastballs, and he'd foul 'em all off waiting for a breaking pitch to hit. Once after sending four or five consecutive fastball strikes into the stands as harmless fouls, Dillinger turned to me and whispered, "Bobby, Mr. Rickey always said as long as you can foul those fastballs off, your reflexes are okay."

Gene Mauch played for the Los Angeles Angels, and even then he was an intense competitor. He hit second in the Angel order behind leadoff batter Gale Wade. Mauch loved to hit and run; Wade had a habit of getting on base and Gene could handle the bat very well. But Mauch and Wade overdid the hit and run; as catcher, I usually knew it was coming. It got so every time the Angels played the Stars, when Wade was on first I'd call a pitchout and throw him out at second base while Mauch watched helplessly from the batter's box. In Hollywood one afternoon I nailed Wade, and Mauch backed out of the box and stared at his teammate as Wade trotted back to the dugout. "You going to hit or pass?" I asked. Mauch replied, "I don't know whether to go after that guy now or just wait until after the game." Gene Mauch could not stand mental errors.

Steve Bilko, the home run-hitting first baseman, was another Angel star. When we took on the Angels in a playoff in '55, I had a pitcher named Bob Garber going for us in the third game. It was a best two-of-three series, and we were tied at a win each. So in the third game the Stars were a run ahead in the bottom of the ninth at Wrigley Field, the Angels' park. Gale Wade was scheduled to hit with a runner on first and one out. I brought in lefty Roger Bowman, and Wade grounded out to the first baseman. He took the easy out, so now they had a runner at second and two down. Bilko was the next hitter. Bill Hall was catching for us, and I brought right-hander Joe Trimble in to pitch. Out on the mound I told Hall and Trimble, "Bilko can't hit Joe's curve. Get two strikes on him, waste a fastball, and throw him another curve." After two pitches, Trimble was ahead of Bilko 0-2. Bill Hall called time and came over to the dugout. "Bobby," he said, "is there really any sense in wasting a pitch? Bilko really can't hit the curve." I said, "Suit yourself," and Trimble threw a curve for strike three. We won the playoff.

Of course, sometimes all the best strategizing in the world doesn't make any difference if the pitcher can't put the ball where he wants it. In 1953 I had a right-hander named Red Witt who went on to have some good years with Pittsburgh. He had a good fastball and not much of a breaking pitch. In one game we were in Portland, ahead by two runs in the bottom of the ninth inning. Our starting pitcher gave up a couple of hits, and suddenly we were up by just a run with two runners on. I brought in Red Witt, who fired eight perfect 90 MPH warmup tosses. He was hot. I was confident. Then he promptly threw four balls, all very high, to the first hitter he faced. The bases were now loaded. I went to the mound and said, "Red, I'm going to be on my knees giving you a low target. Try to follow through more. If you throw me a ball, make sure it's a low one." Witt nodded. I trotted back to the plate and gave him the fastball sign while crouching as low as I could. A tall guy, Merkowitz, was up for Portland. Witt's first pitch hit him smack in the helmet. He turned around and snarled, "Damn you, Bragan, you called for that pitch." I said, "Yeah, sure I did, and now the score is tied." Nobody would deliberately hit a batter and bring the tying run in. If I'd called for a pitch down the middle, Witt would probably have heaved it over the backstop.

I think our final record in '53 was something like 110-70. It was a good season, but you've really got your hands full as a player-manager at the Triple-A level. You have to play harder, and with players so close to the major leagues the daily game reports are crucial. Getting them just right took hours of my time every night. During my three years with the Stars, after each season was over I walked in the clubhouse and felt like I was now able to take a heavy pack off my shoulders and drop it in the corner somewhere.

After the '53 season, Gwenn and the children and I returned to Fort Worth. Our love affair with the city was to endure. And I was genuinely happy to learn the Cats had enjoyed a good season. Max Macon succeeded me there as manager. Don Demeter hit 40 home runs, Danny Ozark had a good year, and a hustler named Sparky Anderson had done well at second base. Fort Worth obviously continued to be a choice franchise for the Dodgers, but I had no regrets.

For one thing, with Hollywood I was a step closer to managing in the major leagues. The Dodgers fired Charlie Dressen after 1953 and replaced him with Walter Alston, who'd been running Montreal. Had I stayed with the Cats in 1953, the Dodgers most likely would have moved me up to replace Walter at Montreal or to St. Paul, their other Triple-A team. Then I'd have been positioned to succeed Walter, though it would have been a long, long wait —he didn't step down until the end of 1976.

Fred Haney, though, was in immediate trouble with the Pirates. It was in no way Fred's fault, but he'd inherited maybe the worst team in the majors from Billy Meyer. Since I was now part of the Pirate organization I wished Fred well, but he did finish dead last in the National League in 1953 and it wouldn't take many more such finishes to have Mr. Rickey looking for a replacement. If so, I felt it would probably be me.

In no way did I have anything less than complete respect for Fred Haney. Prior to moving from the Stars to the Pirates, he'd won about three Pacific Coast League titles himself. Oh, Fred Haney was smart. He had a sly sense of humor, too. In the home clubhouse for Hollywood, Haney had the urinals raised several inches—"It helps me keep my players on their toes," he laughed.

B	E	T	W	E	E	N
I	N	N	I	N	G	S

CHUCK STEVENS: There's no doubt the Pacific Coast League was the best minor league in operation at that time. We played longer schedules and had far superior ballplayers. Most of us had major league experience. Myself, I'd played first base for three seasons with the St. Louis Browns. Generally speaking, when a fellow was coming down from the major leagues, if he had any leverage at all he tried to end up in the Pacific Coast League. The facilities were better, the travel more under control, the cities bigger and nicer than in other major league situations.

LEE WALLS: Hollywood was rated even higher than Triple A. Most players were 30 or older, and very well-schooled. The league had guys like Suitcase Simpson, Al Rosen—on their way to the big leagues or heading in the opposite direction but still with some skills. Only two of us on the Stars with Bobby were under 30. I was 19 and I played for him at Hollywood for three seasons. I should have been in the big leagues that last year but Fred Haney didn't like me.

STEVENS: Bobby was not in the most pleasant situation in Hollywood. Ballplayers like myself had been playing longer than he had

— if you take a young man like he was then and put him in charge of players as experienced or older, then the players often resent it. It could have been that kind of situation with the Stars, but we never did feel that way. Bob gave us, or at least the older players, a great deal of leeway. He managed us with finesse, so to speak.

WALLS: Bobby was very tough. The older players at Hollywood really didn't like him. He was a damn good catcher. He caught 160 games for the Stars one year. Being a manager and being a catcher is just the best deal ever. You can see what your pitcher's got left.

Even after we won the PCL title in '53 by 12 games there was no excitement in the clubhouse afterwards because most of the players just didn't really like Bobby. I was always a hustler, that was just my nature. Bobby liked that, obviously, and put in lots of extra time working with me. The older guys started calling me "Bobby's little bobo."

But he had his mind made up all his players would know basic fundamentals and stick to them. Runner on second, nobody out, you moved the runner to third or the at-bat was wasted and Bobby got on your ass. Hit the cutoff man, always know what the situation was. And taking called third strikes, that just killed Bobby. God, to this day I can still hear him say it: "You can't hit the ball with the bat on your shoulder." That used to be his biggest peeve. Somebody on our team would get called out (on strikes) at home plate and Bobby would scream, "Goddamn, you look like a big piece of cheese standing there! You can't hit the ball with the bat on your shoulder." He said over and over this was the most fundamental rule in all of baseball.

WAITING FOR THE CHANCE

IN MY THREE SEASONS WITH HOLLYWOOD, the Stars had a great record. We were first in the Pacific Coast League in '53, tied for third with the Angels in '54 and won a one-game playoff, and tied for first in '55 and lost a one-game playoff to San Diego.

My work in Hollywood got national media attention. *The Sporting News* named me Minor League Manager of the Year in '53. I also appeared on Steve Allen's TV show—as manager of the Stars I met lots of celebrities and they were kind enough to mention me often while being interviewed about their interest in baseball.

While the Stars thrived at Triple-A level, the Pittsburgh Pirates floundered in the majors. Haney brought them in last in the National League each season. It truly wasn't Fred's fault the Pirates weren't winning—you just can't get the job done as manager without good players, and Haney wasn't getting them. It had to be frustrating for him. I know it must have been for Mr. Rickey, who wasn't working the same miracles in Pittsburgh he'd pulled off in St. Louis and Brooklyn. I can't be sure why he wasn't turning the Pirate franchise around, because I was on the other side of the country. I do feel sure he hadn't lost any of his unparalleled baseball instincts or overall genius.

During the three years Haney had the Pirates and I had the Stars, Mr. Rickey never once mentioned to me that I might someday succeed Fred. I knew he had to be pleased with the job I was doing in Hollywood. The fact I was still young enough to catch most games, saving the club an extra salary, might have been reason enough by itself to keep me employed indefinitely.

I seemed to spend a lot of my time in Hollywood arguing with umpires. The habit came with me from the Texas League. Hollywood fans cheered me every time I came onto the field to discuss bad calls; fans in other cities booed me. I was the manager they loved to hate. This was fine with me. Saying what I thought was part of my nature. And nobody in the Pirate organization ever called to tell me to tone my act down.

The Pacific Coast League at that time had three particularly outstanding umpires, all of whom went on to careers of their own at the major league level. Ed Runge, Chris Pelekoudas, and Emmitt Ashford were the three fellows in question, and I got to know each of them very, very well.

Pelekoudas was a hard worker, but in my estimation he had a physical flaw that sometimes led to incorrect calls against my team. See, Pelekoudas had a nose like Pinocchio. It was monstrous. Never in the world can there have been one of a size to equal it. So whenever in my estimation he missed a call against the Stars, I'd run out and tactfully say to him, "Chris, the reason you missed that one is because you have to watch the play sideways. You cannot see around your nose!" God, that would get him mad. Other managers would never mention his schnozz for fear of prejudicing Pelekoudas against their teams. Me, I couldn't resist. Eventually Chris did get called up to the majors—but only after surgery to reduce his nose size. Really.

Pelekoudas never forgave or forgot where Bobby Bragan was concerned. As a National League umpire some years later calling a game between the Cardinals and my Milwaukee Braves, Pelekoudas was behind the plate in a close game when Curt Simmons got ready to pitch to Hank Aaron. Simmons was a foxy left-hander who liked to throw Aaron soft changeups. He tossed one Hank's way, and it was so damned slow Hank actually double-clutched—moved his back foot forward, took a second stride, and, with his front foot slightly out of the batter's box, Aaron blasted the pitch over the right field wall. Alert to a chance to get back at me, Pelekoudas immediately yelled, "He's out!" a questionable if legal judgment call since many major league batters stand partly out of the batter's box. Hank and I were both ejected by Pelekoudas, but only after Aaron made his point by trotting around the bases.

One evening in Hollywood, Ed Runge tossed me out of a game. I was catching at the time, and had all the equipment on. As I went toward the dugout I turned and threw my catcher's mitt in his direction, then my mask, then my chest protector, then a shin guard, then the other shin guard. I followed by throwing my shirt. There I stopped, but needless to say it was reported in sports sections all over the country that the Stars' player-manager had performed a striptease after being ejected by Runge.

Throughout his career, Emmitt Ashford had an extra-tough row as a black umpire. Ashford didn't try to blend in with the other umpires. Before each game he had a way of focusing attention on himself; after the umpires and managers gathered at home plate, Ashford would turn and take off running at top speed. If he was calling plays at first, for instance, he'd dash all the way to the right field wall, then trot back and take up his proper position. I didn't care if Ashford showboated a little; he was a good umpire who called an even game.

One night in Salt Lake City, Emmitt was calling a game behind the plate. During the contest, two or three balls were fouled off into the Hollywood dugout. One of my players noticed they were American Association balls. Well, there's a rule in professional baseball that games must be played with balls from the league involved, and these didn't say "Pacific Coast League." Well, I waited until the top of the ninth. We were leading 3-2 but in danger of falling behind when I called time and told Emmitt I was protesting the game over use of improper baseballs, though I'd only officially file the protest with the league office if we lost. Ashford told me, "It doesn't make any difference what kind of balls we use." "Well, then," I asked, "Why can't we use tennis balls?" He threw me out of the game.

One of my protests garnered more national attention. We were playing an exhibition game in Long Beach against our arch-rivals, the Los Angeles Angels. Chuck Stevens was up for us and the plate umpire made a bad ruling, calling a foul ball when the pitch had glanced off Chuck's hand, not his bat. I raced out of the dugout to protest. "Will you ask the first base umpire what he saw?" I requested. The umpire shook his head. "Are you telling me you know everything?" I asked. No answer. "All right, then," I said, "I'll lay down and go to sleep at your feet." And I did. I lay down in the dirt beside the batter's box and pretended to snooze. The umpires got very worked up and loudly told me to leave. I let them sweat a little before I did. Somebody took a picture of the scene and it was subsequently printed in *Life* magazine. I had fun with the umpires and players and fans, but I never lost sight of my main job, which was to groom players for the majors and to win games. The Stars had a couple of young players in particular, Lee Walls and Dale Long, who looked like they'd be good ones. We were a successful, glamorous club, and I can honestly say in the winter of 1955 I wasn't even thinking about managing the Pirates when Branch Rickey phoned me in Fort Worth.

CAL MCLISH: Every once in a while there are managers who become stars themselves. When Bobby was manager of the Hollywood Stars he created excitement. People paid to get in just to see what Bobby Bragan was going to do next.

DON ZIMMER: Guys like Bobby were good for the game. I used to read in *The Sporting News* about some of the crazy, funny things he did in Hollywood with umpires and wish I'd been there to see for myself. I mean in some ways at Hollywood Bobby became a legend within the baseball fraternity.

AL BARLICK: When I was an umpire and he was a manager, my personal relationship with Bobby Bragan was good. He never gave me any problems. Of course, I knew other umpires he gave fits to. He couldn't get along with Frank Dascoli, for instance. Bobby irritated a lot of 'em.

CHUCK STEVENS: Bobby was entertainment itself as our manager. We never knew what he'd be up to. Not long after he took over the Stars, we played an exhibition game against the Angels, I think it was, in my hometown of Long Beach. During the game, I was at the plate when Bobby and the umpires got into it over something, a strike call maybe, I can't remember what. But Bragan roared up to complain to the umpires. I stepped out of the batter's box and kind of turned the other way because I was trying to keep my concentration and the way to deal with the situation was to let the manager vent his spleen at the umpire, then the game would start up again. All of a sudden I heard the fans roaring behind me—I turned around and Bragan was lying flat on his back by the plate, his legs crossed and just looking up and talking to the umpires. He was acting like he was tired of arguing so he'd lay down to continue the discussion. It was the damndest thing I ever saw. Even the umpires were laughing.

BARLICK: I think Bobby was a smart enough manager to pick his spots with umpires. He knew who to go to, what he could get away with and what he couldn't. With me, I had the same rule good umpires have today. A manager could come out to dispute a call as long as he didn't get personal and use too much profanity. If managers will stick to those guidelines, good umpires will listen to them.

But Bobby never gave me a bit of trouble when he was managing or when he was playing. I remember him first as a shortstop with Philadelphia. I'll say this—even then he knew the game. I wouldn't want to talk too much about whether he had much ability as a player. But he was a fine manager.

PITTSBURGH

MR. RICKEY WASTED NO WORDS. "I want you to fly to Pittsburgh," he said. "Do this under an assumed name." I knew what this had to mean. But I was thrown a little when Mr. Rickey added, "Come to see me at my house. Do not go to Forbes Field," which was the Pirates' ballpark. It has always been traditional to announce new managers at their team's field. I dropped everything and got a flight north, using the name Dolan. When I arrived at his house, Mr. Rickey started off with some bad news: "I asked you to meet me here because I have been removed from the job of Pirate general manager. Joe L. Brown will take my place, but in my last official act I named you the new Pirate manager."

I was thrilled and sorely disappointed at the same time. Apparently I'd achieved my dream of becoming a major league manager, but it wouldn't be as part of a team with Mr. Rickey. Further, I didn't know Joe L. Brown. It occurred to me that a new general manager might have his own ideas about who would manage the Pirates. I did tell myself that if the job came through I would do everything I could to utilize Mr. Rickey's vast knowledge.

I went on to Forbes Field. Brown turned out to be the son of comedian Joe E. Brown; I'd known his dad out in Hollywood. Brown told me he had a few applicants for the Pirate manager's job, including veteran skipper Jimmy Dykes. He said he'd have to talk to them before officially giving me the job, but that I did have it. This was comforting to a degree, but it was also clear I would be working for a man who did not really hire me. From the first moment, some uncertainty was there.

I immediately contacted Tommy Tatum, who'd been a teammate on the Dodgers and later a coach for me at Fort Worth. I wanted Tatum on my Pittsburgh staff, but his wife didn't want to make the move north. With Tatum unavailable, I called another old teammate, this one with the Phillies. Danny Murtaugh said he'd be glad to come to Pittsburgh.

After a few days Brown got around to making it official: "You're going to manage the Pirates," he said. I had been making $12,500 in Hollywood, and my salary was immediately jumped to $35,000. That part of it was certainly exciting. I felt rich. But losing Mr. Rickey took the edge off my happiness. Joe Brown knew of my regard for his predecessor. It probably influenced my relationship with the new boss. Certainly Brown and I walked on separate sides of the street from Day One, though we were very polite and did our best to work together.

I knew Pittsburgh would be entirely different from Hollywood, where Haney had left me a ready-made winner. Fred gave a good indication that his poor Pittsburgh record was no reflection on his own managing ability, moving on to Milwaukee and winning the National League pennant in 1957 and 1958. A fine manager hadn't been able to win with Pittsburgh; to succeed in Haney's stead, I'd have to operate at a higher level than ever before.

The team was being rebuilt, using young players mostly. To look at their names now is to get the idea the '56 club I inherited was of championship caliber. I had Roberto Clemente, Dick Groat, Bill Mazeroski, Bob Friend, and Vernon Law, among others. But at this stage of their careers they were not the polished players they eventually became. Soon after I arrived we traded centerfielder Bobby Del Greco to St. Louis for Bill Virdon, and Virdon was a fine player from the day he arrived in Pittsburgh. Center field was one position I never had to worry about as long as I had Virdon.

Otherwise, we were a physically small team. The O'Brien twins, Eddie and Johnny, were both diminutive, as were the Freese brothers, George and Gene. I hoped we wouldn't have too many bench-clearing brawls, because my players would have been massacred.

Unlike the Dodgers, the Pirates didn't have a fancy spring training complex. There was just one full playing field and another partial practice field. As much as possible, I tried to emulate the other Brooklyn programs, such as posting the next day's schedule on the night before so no minutes would be wasted in the morning figuring out who was supposed to be doing what where. But it was simply a different atmosphere. Management and player expectations weren't as high. Neither was the quality of athlete. After a couple of days I realized the Triple-A team I'd left in Hollywood could probably play the pants off the major leaguers I'd inherited in Pittsburgh. At least the Stars knew the game. Except for one or two individuals, all the Pirates needed intensive work on fundamentals. Hell, Dick Groat was straight out of college. He had so much to learn—though of course he learned well and became a fine, fine player whom I very much admired.

Then there was a young fellow named Dick Stuart who'd made something of a name for himself swatting 66 home runs in 1955 in the Class A Western League. Stuart was convinced he ought to jump to the majors and hit cleanup, but it was obvious he needed more polishing. I spent an hour explaining to him that he'd be going to Triple-A Hollywood, a huge promotion by 1956 baseball standards. "I think you'll lead the Pacific Coast League in homers," I told him. "That makes two of us," cocky Dick Stuart replied. I shuddered to think what the Dodger veterans would have done to such a loudmouth bush leaguer, but the Pirates either didn't have enough veterans to put him in his place or else none of them cared enough to do it. With Brooklyn, Stuart could have hit 166 Class A home runs without jumping higher the next season than Class AA.

When the regular season began, it was a thrill to come to Forbes Field and be part of major league life again. In the tradition of those times, Forbes Field was unique, huge in the power alleys. In right field the seats were slanted so sharply inwards that often Clemente would have to throw the ball over part of the stands while trying to gun a runner down at the plate. And then there was our batting cage...

The Forbes Field batting cage was a huge steel thing which didn't fold up at all. After batting practice, the grounds crew would take the cage and roll it out against the left-center field fence, where it would stay on the field during the game. We had a ground rule that any ball hitting the batting cage was in play, and if a ball got caught in the cage netting the batter would get a ground-rule double, runners advancing either two or three bases at the umpire's discretion. I loved umpire-discretion calls. They gave me opportunities to chat with my old friends in blue.

The Pirate fans were knowledgeable and enthusiastic. They didn't expect miracles, which was good because with the club I had they weren't going to get them. I felt welcome in the community. I rented a house in the suburb of Wilkinsburg, and Gwenn, Bobby Jr., and Cissie drove up to join me after the school year in Fort Worth was over.

Bob Prince was an outstanding Pirate radio broadcaster. Les Biederman, Al Abrams, and Chili Doyle were the newspaper beat writers who covered the team. I enjoyed talking with these intelligent fellows very much, which immediately caused me problems. My nature has always been to answer any question honestly. I talked too much rather than too little. Before one game against the Giants in the Polo Grounds, one of the writers asked me to compare Mickey Mantle and Willie Mays. You could read in all the New York papers the next day that Pirate manager Bobby Bragan said on his team Mays would always be in center field and Mantle would have to learn to love playing in right or left. As a result, Mays became a good friend of mine.

Whatever faults my young players had as ballplayers, and these were legion, at least they were enthusiastic. If they'd had the skills to match their desire we wouldn't have lost a game. I was most forcibly reminded of this just before the season opener. We were in Columbus for an exhibition game against that city's Triple-A Pirate farm club. Gene Freese played third for us, and in that contest he had to field three thrown balls —thrown balls, mind you, not ground balls with possible bad hops—and he missed 'em all. We lost to a minor league team. After the game, we walked into the clubhouse past a big trash barrel. I waited there for Freese and said, "Drop your glove in this can. I know you can't be as bad as you looked, so it must be your glove. Throw it away!" And he obliged, too. I think the clubhouse boy waited until later on and retrieved the glove for himself. He probably put it to better use than its previous owner.

Of course, my team included Roberto Clemente. Mr. Rickey had sneaked him away from the Brooklyn organization, and for that coup alone Mr. Rickey should have received a lifetime contract as the Pirate general manager. From the first game he played, Clemente was fast and agile. He could field a ground ball, transfer it to his throwing hand, and get it back on its way toward the infield faster than any outfielder I ever saw. The fractions of seconds he saved here saved games for us.

But Roberto Clemente was a morose character. He was very quiet and, when I had him at least, not self-motivated. Not that Clemente did anything he could be fined for. He was always on time for the team bus. He played well. But he did not approach the level he later achieved. Some of his teammates in '56 thought Clemente dogged it, got a pulled muscle when he otherwise might have to face a tough pitcher. I don't think that's true, but I also think Clemente could have become great much quicker than he did.

Bill Virdon was outstanding, an immediate asset to the Pirates. I never understood why the Cardinals let him go. Bob Skinner could swing the bat. Frank Thomas, though, was the only long ball threat we had until we brought up Dale Long from Hollywood. Dale welcomed himself to the major leagues by hitting home runs in eight straight games, a record. Dick Groat was a solid citizen. He was not possessed of a strong arm or good running speed, but Groat learned to make the most of what he had. I got on him a lot, and on Mazeroski, too.

Lee Walls had a special place in my heart. He had a perfect physique, like Ruben Sierra has today. He could throw, had some power to all fields, and, most of all, he had real dedication to the game. It was wonderful to see a young player so eager to improve. He was one of my favorites, and had what I thought of as a "Dick Williams-type" desire. They'd both do anything to win a game.

Amazingly, we got off to a good start in my first year at the Pirate helm. Bob Friend, Vernon Law, and Ronnie Kline proved to be a good starting rotation. May came, and we were in first place. Suddenly there were visions of a high Pittsburgh finish. Reality hadn't yet set in for the players or for me. We were playing above our heads and none of us knew it. They were young players, I was new as a major league manager. Now I know this feeling was like I had when first breaking in with the Phillies—the thrill of being a big league player when you're 21 or 22 just overshadows reality for a while. Well, Mr. Rickey used to like to quote Voltaire, who said, "I prefer the errors of enthusiasm to the indifference of wisdom." Soon enough, enthusiasm started making errors. The Pirates dropped like a rock in the National League standings.

For a while, I remembered who it was I was managing—kids. I did things to boost their confidence, not tear it down. In spring training, for instance, Bob Friend had trouble holding runners on. So I held an intrasquad game and had a couple of runners get picked off by him on purpose just to give Friend a little extra confidence. I did other things to remind myself the game was supposed to be fun. The O'Briens were identical twins, but Johnny could hit much better than Eddie. In spring training I'd pinch-hit Johnny around the sixth inning, then have him switch jerseys with his brother. In the ninth I'd bring out "Eddie" to pinch-hit and Johnny would get an extra at-bat. I never did have the guts to do it during the regular season, though. Looking back, I sort of wish I had.

Bill Mazeroski posed special problems. He was just 19 when we called him up from Hollywood. He was phenomenal with the glove and could turn the double play better than any other second baseman in baseball history. Maz's gloves never wore out like those of other players. He kept one glove for five full seasons. See, the moment the ball hit his glove he had it out and on its way. The leather of the glove suffered less wear.

In one of the first games he played for us, there was a runner on second and a ball was hit up the middle. Mazeroski watched it roll into center field as the run scored. He made no attempt to dive and stop the grounder, maybe giving the hitter a single but stopping the lead runner at third. After the inning was over I called him aside and said, "Could you have stopped that ball if you dove?" He said, "Yes," and I said, "Well, that'll cost you twenty-five," big money in those days. He gulped then, but later on in his career he never stopped thanking me for teaching him that lesson.

During my first year with the Pirates, Joe Brown kept his hands off. Brown had radio and TV shows to think about, and I felt he was quite astute. Still, there was a tension between us. He hadn't hired me; Branch Rickey did. I made a point of asking Mr. Rickey for advice. I could have handled the situation better, I now realize.

During the 1955 season I formed a close friendship with Myron O'Briskey, who ran the Forbes Field concessions. Every afternoon before I went to the clubhouse, I'd stop by Myron's office for a visit. He'd always warn me I was being too outspoken, particularly with the newspapers. He suggested Joe Brown was probably getting tired of reading which player I'd fined for what. Well, if the writers asked me a direct question I just couldn't avoid answering it. O'Briskey warned me I was jeopardizing my job by not keeping my mouth shut, including with the umpires. I didn't heed his advice.

We finished 1956 seventh in the National League with a 66-88 record. Somehow the Cubs did even worse with a 60-94 mark. As usual, the Dodgers won the pennant.

A few individual Pirates had good years. Dale Long hit 27 home runs. Frank Thomas hit 25. Clemente batted .311, though his power numbers weren't much—seven homers and 60 runs batted in. Lee Walls had an excellent rookie year with a .274 average. Groat batted .273, Maz .243. Friend led the staff with a 17-17 record. Kline finished 14-18 and Law was 8-16.

I felt we'd done as well as could be expected. A nucleus was clearly there—Groat and Mazeroski would be a good double play combination. Clemente, Virdon, and Skinner formed a solid outfield. Long and Walls were up-and-comers. When Joe Brown and I went to the winter league meetings other clubs had lots of interest in several of our players, another good sign. I expected 1957 to be memorable for me, and it was—though not in the way I'd hoped or expected.

I finally made it to the big leagues with the 1940 Philadelphia Phillies–I was happy to be in the big leagues even with a bad team.

Spring training in 1943 was held in Bear Mountain, New York. During the war no one went to Florida for spring training.

The 1947 Dodgers (Front Row: [L-R] Reiser, Rojek, Gionfriddo, Stanky, Lombardi, Pitler, Shotten [MGR], Sukeforth, Blades, Lavagetto, Behrman and Reese. Second Row: [L-R] Miksis, Jorgensen, Bankhead, Hermanski, Hodges, Gregg, Furillo, Barney, Taylor, Branca, Miller and Parrott. Top Row: [L-R] Wendler, Comerford, Robinson, Casey, Hatten, Walker, King, Bragan, Edwards and Vaughan.

Celebrating the National League Championship with the Brooklyn Dodgers in 1947. That's me on the piano with Dodger manager Burt Shotten. The whole team joined in on "Beautiful Day for a Ball Game."

*I could tell by the second day
at Camp Wheeler, Georgia,
that the army infantry was not
going to be as much fun as
baseball. Only my second day
and already on KP!*

*There were more major-leaguers in the military than there were in the major
leagues during the war years–but that doesn't mean we didn't play ball. This is
the 1945 Camp Wheeler, Georgia, team. I really looked forward to the three or
four times a week we got to practice and play instead of drill and KP. That's
Carl Scheib of the Philadelphia Athletics on the front row, fifth from the left. I'm
to Carl's left and was a Brooklyn Dodger at the time, and next to me is John
Logan who went on to sign with the Boston Braves. On the top row, second
from the left is Joe Dobson who pitched for the Boston Red Sox.*

*My assignment to the Fort
Worth Cats in 1948 as
manager and catcher gave me
a new lease on my baseball
life. I enjoyed Fort Worth so
much that I knew it would
always be home.*

*The community and fans of the Fort Worth Cats honored me with "Bobby
Bragan Night" at old LaGrave Field. This was one of my most special
memories of my baseball career.*

Stack Hack, the manager of the minor-league Los Angeles Angels, and I, manager of the Hollywood Stars, came up with an idea to assist umpires (sitting left to right) Gordon Ford, Chris Pelokoudas and Ed Runge.

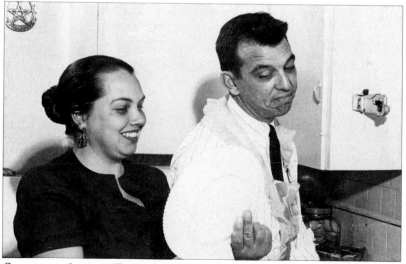

Gwenn was the great "Baseball Wife" and friend. She was always there when I needed her–through the highs and the lows that everyone in baseball experiences. Even folks in Hollywood do dishes.

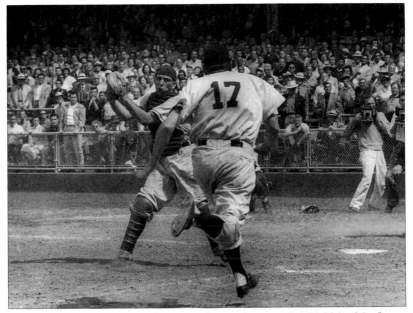

That's me with the Hollywood stars getting ready to tag Cal McLish of the Los Angeles Angels out at home.

Hollywood was a great place to play ball. Until 1958 there were no major league teams on the west coast, so our Pacific Coast League stars were the main attraction.

Since I came from Fort Worth to Hollywood, Ernest Borgnine (right) thought I should wear the cowboy hat as Alan Ladd looks on.

The years in Hollywood gave Gwenn and me a chance to rub elbows with a lot of "stars" other than the Hollywood Stars baseball team. Gwenn and I are visiting with Frank Sinatra and producer Jack Cummings on a Hollywood set.

Here I am with the three blind mice. During a Pittsburgh Pirates game in Milwaukee in 1957 I went out to protest that Braves Pitcher Bob Buhl didn't touch second base when he advanced from first to third on a teammate's hit. These three umpires (L-R) Frank Dascoli, Stan Landes, and Frank Secory threw me out of more games than all the other umpire crews put together. This particular game I decided to straighten things out between me and the umps. I was ejected for arguing, so I strolled back to the dugout and returned to offer my three "friends" a drink of orange juice and discuss the situation. They didn't appreciate the friendly gesture and ordered me to leave again. The National League president Warren Giles didn't see the humor in it either and fined me $100. I probably should not have held my nose on the call.

Chris Pelakoudas and I didn't see eye to eye on a lot of calls. All I wanted to know was the extra point good or not! As a catcher I could see most plays even better than the umps.

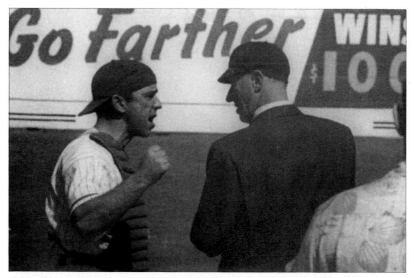

A lot of baseball fans know that Chris Pelakoudas had his nose fixed before he moved to the major leagues to umpire. I was always willing to fix his nose or any other umpire's for free!

Managing in Cuba was always a lot of fun. Rhubarbs were always a lot more interesting when not everyone understood English. I was questioning a call in winter league ball in Cuba in 1951. As manager of the Almendares Blues we were in some really heated games against the Havana Reds.

Even in Spokane umpires and I often had differences of opinion. I think that I am not much different from managers today when it comes to arguing with umpires. Looking back I did get away with a lot, but it's all part of the game. Some of my best friends were umpires, until they made a bad call.

My first major-league manager's job was with the 1956 Pittsburgh Pirates. It was great to be back in the "Big Show." Notice the batting helmet I'm wearing. The Pirates were the first major-league team to wear them.

Gwenn and the kids Bobby Jr. and Cissie called my dismissal a blessing in disguise when the Pirates fired me in 1957.

In 1958 with the Spokane Indians was my first year to be a full-time minor-league manager and not play at the same time. I'll always remember at Spokane I made a 29-year-old into a switch hitter that went on to 14 major-league seasons and a stolen-base record—Maury Wills.

Cleveland was a short tour of duty as manager in 1958. I managed the team from opening day until the first of July. There is a rumor that I put a curse on the Indians when I left that they would never have a winning season. Though the Indians haven't won since I left, I can't take the full credit.

1963 was my first year as manager of the Milwaukee Braves. I managed the last years in Milwaukee before the team was moved to Atlanta.

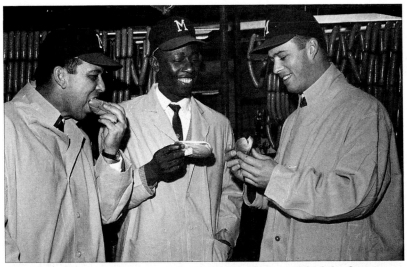

Wisconsin is famous for its meat plants, and in 1963 we visited the Oscar Meyer wiener house. I'm with Hank Aaron whom I consider the most complete player to play the game and a true gentleman and Eddie Mathews whom I consider to have the best swing of any left hander who has ever played the game. Of course, both are members of the Hall of Fame.

I was the first manager of the Atlanta Braves and the first to be fired. The move from Milwaukee was an exciting time for the team.

Starting a major-league franchise in Houston was exciting. Houston's first manager Harry Craft and I toured the state to promote the new ball club—all before the dome.

Roberta and I were married on March 27, 1985, and it has been a "jolly trolley trip into bliss" ever since.

I get a chance each year to get back to the game as the camp supervisor for the Texas Ranger's Fantasy Camp. The camp is held each year in the Ranger's Port Charlotte, Florida, training facilities. It is a lot of fun recruiting both men and women over 30 to fulfill their dreams of being "major-leaguers."

STAN MUSIAL: Those Pirates Bragan managed couldn't play baseball very well, but I'll tell you what I remember most. They were a bunch of midgets. Not one of 'em looked like he was over three feet tall. Shortest team I ever saw.

VERNON LAW: With the Pirates when Bobby took over, there were some young players including myself and we eventually turned out to be the nucleus of a pretty good team—Bob Friend, Roy Face, Maz, Dick Groat—all young players. Bobby did have to deal with some older players who were on the way out.

LEE WALLS: We had some very good young ballplayers - Maz, Groat, Clemente, Dale Long - though Clemente was a big piece of nothing his first years. Virdon and I would get all over Clemente. If a tough righthander was going to face us, Clemente all of a sudden would have a headache or a bad back. I challenged him one day, I said, "You don't want to play tonight because Drysdale's pitching and he might knock you on your ass."

LOU BROCK: If you were a player dogging it or getting out of line in those days, the manager would talk to you tough or, if necessary, your teammates did it.   But back then, hey, your teammates leaned on you whenever it seemed necessary.

DICK GROAT: Because of Bobby I can't really watch baseball anymore, the way these modern guys get out there and do things. If Bobby ever tried to manage today, he'd have a fit. I see games where there's a runner on second, nobody out, and the batter hits a little pop fly or strikes out. Me, I'd die and go to hell if I didn't advance that runner from second to third.

Bobby never had a clubhouse meeting without doing his homework. If you listened to him, you'd always learn something. I remember him telling us once, "Gentlemen, back in 1800-something a guy named Doubleday in Cooperstown, New York, invented the game of baseball. He put three bases and home plate 90 feet apart and said you've got to touch 'em all to make a run, that's the rule. Anyone on my club that forgets this rule, it's a fine, and that'll cost you $50, Walls." He meant Lee Walls, one of our outfielders who'd been called out for missing a base the day before.

WALLS: I never minded Bobby getting on my butt when I made a mistake. It was the way I'd learn. Some of those other guys on the Pirates, though, they took it too personally. All he was trying to do was help them become better ballplayers.

GROAT: Bobby nearly drove me out of baseball. I can remember I used to pick up the newspaper and read where Bobby had said he couldn't win with the Pirates when he had a Triple-A infielder, and I was the infielder he was talking about. At the time I was in the National League top five in hitting. I hit .315 that year. What he said hurt my feelings. Yet now I know he really taught me the game. I really can't emphasize enough how much he taught me. If I'd miss a signal, he'd get on me immediately. He knew how to get your attention after a mistake. After playing for Bobby Bragan, I never really had to look for a signal for the rest of my career. I instinctively knew what to do.

FIRED: PART I

SPRING TRAINING OF 1957 FOUND ME FEELING CAUTIOUSLY OPTIMISTIC. I came to Fort Myers much more familiar with the Pirate players. As soon as the exhibition season opened, Mazeroski started showing just how well he could play second base. I figured he and Groat might end up as the best double-play combination in the National League. I expected Clemente would improve, and Dale Long apparently was going to be a Pirate fixture at first base.

It was a real pleasure to have my parents, George and Corinne, come to Florida for a few days. They had a chance to watch their son manage the Pirates. George seemed to think if Bobby could do it, anybody could. Though he'd played some semi pro ball, my dad was no expert. Still, he arrived at our spring camp at the same time Dale Long went into a mild batting slump. After one game, George took the liberty of pulling Long aside. He told him, "Son, I believe you must be closing your eyes when you swing." Long couldn't wait to tell me about my father nominating himself as Pirate batting coach.

Mr. Rickey also spent some time in Fort Myers. Though not on the official payroll, he had a sort of emeritus status. I conferred with him often. Joe Brown was also around; we didn't talk that much. He certainly never sat down with me to go over the '56 season and point out things he thought I'd done well or areas in which I needed to improve. A polite term for our relationship was "arm's length."

Unfortunately, our early regular season play in 1957 was the exact opposite of the year before. We started out playing poorly and just didn't get better. I let the losing get to me. Never soft-spoken, I talked even more and said many things I shouldn't have. Once when we had a series with the Giants, both teams looked especially inept. I decided at least this club might be worse than mine, and, even though I had great respect for Bill Rigney, who'd succeeded Leo as the New York manager, I ended up making the statement to a reporter that the 1957 New York Giants were the very worst team I'd ever seen. I didn't think much about it until I picked up a paper and saw how those words looked in print. I didn't feel proud of myself, but you can't unring a bell that's been rung. Many of my friends jumped all over me, warning that this kind of mouth-shooting-off was going to cost me dearly. But I kept up my negative comments, to my players and to the umpires, anyone who was around.

The Pirates kept losing; I grew more frustrated. Sometimes when managers feel things are getting out of control, they make changes just to shake things up a little. I decided to try Dick Groat at third base for a couple of games. Groat hated it, and when the team got back to Pittsburgh from the road trip where I'd tried the move even Groat's father came around to rip me.

In the back of my mind I tried to keep Mr. Rickey's favorite admonition handy—when it becomes game time, a major league manager can have only one thought: capital W, capital I, capital N. When you make out a lineup you can't worry that one of your player's parents have traveled 1,000 miles to see him play on the very day you think he needs to be benched. Everything should be secondary to winning, but now as the Pirates lost and lost I started experimenting with ways to boost player confidence instead of focusing on victory above all else.

Hell, there was a game in Wrigley Field when Bob Friend started against the Cubs. Friend had lost a half-dozen games in a row and had no victories at all in his last dozen starts. I left him in the game even though the scoring went back and forth, always up - 3-2, 4-3, 5-4, 6-5. I wanted to get Friend a win and he kept on pitching. We lost the damn game 11-9. I had gotten away from the W-I-N principle, and anytime a manager does that in the major leagues, he's wrong. It's okay in the minors—managers are teachers there. On a big league level managers must be leaders.

I also made mistakes based on personal inexperience. This was my first time performing strictly as a manager. In other places, as a catcher I'd have the best idea of anyone whether my pitcher still had his stuff or had lost it. Now I had to rely on the Pirate catchers for this insight. A manager must have implicit faith in his catcher—if the guy tells you it's time to get a pitcher out, you pull him. But sometimes there are situations where the catcher and pitcher are good buddies, and the catcher doesn't want to make his pal mad. With the Pirates, that was the situation with catcher Jack Shepard and pitcher Vernon Law. Shephard would bamboozle me: "He's got plenty left." Then Law would get his jock knocked off and we'd lose another.

Shepard wasn't the only catcher guilty of this, then or now. Later on with the Braves Joe Torre would try to pull the same stunt on me when his good friend Wade Blasingame was on the mound. I was quicker to catch on by that time.

Then we tried a trade to get the team out of its doldrums. Now, anytime there's an important prospective trade or player purchase, there's a meeting of the minds: the general manager, chief team scout, farm system director, and manager may all be involved. The manager ought to have two votes, since he's the one who's probably going to be blamed if the deal has a bad result for his team.

You constantly talk to other clubs as the season goes along, trying to get a feel for which of their players might be available and who on your roster is especially attractive. You also keep your eyes open if you're involved in winter ball. I recall that between the '56 and '57 seasons I tried to talk the Pirate brass into purchasing the contract of Rocky Nelson, who was in the Dodger farm chain. I saw Nelson playing in Cuba and thought he was the best hitter in that league. But George Sisler, the Pittsburgh scouting director, over-ruled me. He insisted Nelson was a good minor league hitter who'd never amount to anything in the majors. Ironically, two years later the Pirates did buy Nelson and he ended up making a big contribution to their 1960 world championship team.

I loved Rocky Nelson's attitude. Besides Dick Williams, he was the only player I was associated with who, while making an out, would run to first base and not turn right to head directly back into the dugout. Nelson and Williams would turn left so they'd be able to trot by the pitcher's mound and say something friendly like, "Put something on the ball; I can't hit that crap you're throwing."

Anyway, halfway through the '57 season we made the decision we'd try to get Dee Fondy and Gene Baker from the Cubs. I knew Fondy well; he'd played first base for me in Fort Worth. Baker was a veteran shortstop. We were still thinking of Groat as a potential third baseman.

The problem was Chicago's price. They wanted Dale Long and Lee Walls. Long and Walls were both players I valued. They were young, worked hard, and had plenty of potential. But the '57 season was going so badly that we decided a change of faces in the clubhouse might have a positive affect. That didn't prove to be the case. If anything, we were worse off with Fondy and Baker.

Long and Walls both cried when I told them. I cried myself. The three of us sat in the Pirate clubhouse for hours. Both of those players went on to solid careers. Fondy had a couple of decent seasons with the Pirates. Baker never did anything for Pittsburgh as a player, but he did end up working in the organization as a scout.

Though it would have appeared to be impossible, things kept getting worse. When we had well-pitched games, nobody hit. If we scored 10 runs, our pitchers gave up 11. Statistically, we weren't that bad. But statistics don't tell everything. As August rolled around our record was 62-91.

Our next game was in Milwaukee. Stan Landis was the umpire behind the plate, and he was not fond of the Pittsburgh Pirates or Bobby Bragan. In a previous game when Ronnie Kline had pitched for us, Ronnie got mad when he thought Stan kept blowing ball-strike calls. After one such call, Kline hopped off the mound and took a step toward Landis, yelling at him. Landis jumped out from behind the catcher and hollered at Kline to get back on the mound. To protect my player, I ran out of the dugout and snapped, "Ronnie, get back on the mound and do the pitching. Stan, get back behind the plate and do the umpiring." Something about my tone offended

Landis. He pointed at me and screamed, "You, Bragan, take a shower."

I hadn't forgotten and apparently neither had Landis. In Milwaukee that day, Lou Burdette started for the Braves. We suspected— hell, we knew, everybody knew—that Lou often doctored the ball. Before the top of the first inning I told each of my batters to ask Landis, the plate umpire, to examine the ball after Burdette's first pitch. My leadoff hitter did this. So did the second Pirate batter. Clemente came up and followed suit. Landis took off his mask, came toward me in the third base coaching box, and said, "That's the last batter I want to have ask to see the ball." All batters have the right to ask for the ball to be examined. I started toward Landis and Larry Goetz, the third base umpire, yelled at me, "Bobby, get back in the coaching box. We need to keep the game moving. It looks like rain." I replied, "I'm not concerned about the rain, I'm concerned about the spitballs." "You're not concerned about the rain?" Goetz shouted. "Take a hike!"

I was so damned frustrated with the whole season. When I got back to the Pirate dugout I told Danny Murtaugh, my coach, to find me a hot dog and a cold drink. "This is the third ejection I've had from this crew," I told Murtaugh. "I'm going to find out how much sand they've got in their craws, and I'm going to be comfortable while I do it."

Murtaugh couldn't come up with a hot dog, but he brought me a cup of orange soda with a straw. I strolled leisurely out toward the mound. The umpires surrounded me, insisting I leave the field for good. I looked over Landis's shoulder and saw Red Schoendienst, the Milwaukee second baseman, laughing fit to die. I said to my assembled friends in blue, "You're the only crew that keeps throwing me out of games. Let's discuss it. Would anyone like a sip of this drink while we do?" Oh, they got mad. Eventually I did leave the field, but I got my satisfaction. After the game I also got a telegram from the National League office fining me $100 for behavior President Warren Giles described as "farcical."

But we had to leave Milwaukee to continue our road trip in Chicago, and the worst was yet to come. We got to Chicago and I arranged to have dinner in a nice restaurant with Howard Cosell and

Bob Prince, the radio voice of the Pirates. I guess Howard was in town on some sports assignment. The place where we ate was on the famous Chicago Loop, and there was a Dixieland band playing. They were the Asuntos, a famous band from New Orleans. As the Asuntos struck up "Mack the Knife," a waiter came to our table to tell me I had a phone call: Joe Brown had come to Chicago and wanted to see me immediately in his hotel room. "It seems appropriate they're playing Mack the Knife," Cosell commented. Everybody knew what was going to happen.

Any manager who gets fired and says he's surprised is lying. You can always tell when it's coming. I read the Pittsburgh papers every day and knew the writers were blaming me for the Pirate woes.

Brown said on the phone, "I just checked in and I need to talk to you." He could have told me right then, as far as I was concerned.

I knocked on Brown's door about 10 P.M. He answered the knock in his pajamas. Tears rolled down Brown's cheeks as he said in a trembling voice, "Bobby, this is the most difficult thing I've had to do, but we're going to make a change." I exercised my bravado. "No need to cry, Joe," I said. "We've been more or less walking on opposite sides of the street. This is no surprise." And that was it.

Clyde Sukeforth, one of my coaches and a friend from the Brooklyn days, took over the Pirates for one game. His loyalty to me was such that he told Brown he wasn't interested in the fulltime managing job. After Sukeforth declined, Brown offered the position to Danny Murtaugh, who accepted.

I went back to the hotel. Julio D'Arcos happened to be there. He immediately told me he wanted me to come back and manage Almendares during the winter. That helped. Then a Pittsburgh area Dodge dealer, Sam Liberto, hosted a little ceremony at his country club where I was given a new Dodge convertible to drive home to Texas. That also eased the pain.

Being fired wasn't pleasant, but I didn't panic. I knew there'd be another job in baseball for me. I spent some time with my family and then I had to leave for Cuba.

Under Danny Murtaugh, the '57 Pirates turned around and finished the last part of the season at 26-25. Then the very same club which lost consistently with me became a pennant contender, finally winning the World Series over the Yankees in 1960 when Maz hit his famous seventh-game homer.

In all honesty, I doubt the club would have had the same success with me. Murtaugh was an excellent handler of personnel, better at not hurting people's feelings. I was so insistent that each player go all-out every minute on both offense and defense that I became too impatient. I felt if one of the Pirates took a called third strike with two outs and the bases loaded that it was an embarrassment to me personally, proof that somehow I wasn't doing my job right.

I took my frustration out on my players in very public ways. If a Pittsburgh pitcher threw, say, eight straight balls, my demeanor as I approached the mound to take him out made my red-hot anger apparent to everyone in the stands. I wouldn't gently say, "It doesn't look like you've got it today," and pat him on the butt as he walked off the mound. Instead I'd snatch the ball and walk away from him in anger.

I can only say that if I had the Pittsburgh experience to live over again I'd try to be more patient. The talent was there, but my actions to utilize it were all wrong. I do think Joe Brown wasn't enamored of me from the start; had Mr. Rickey remained the general manager he might have been able to reason with me. Working for a general manager who didn't hire you is a manager's nightmare, with only one likely conclusion.

So I headed down to Cuba wondering more which team I'd join next than if I'd ever get another major league job. And within a few weeks, my major league adventures started all over again.

LEE WALLS: Bobby was a Branch Rickey fundamentalist. He loved that old man. It was so obvious. Joe Brown would be hanging around the park in Fort Myers and he'd see Bobby and Mr. Rickey with their heads together. You know how that had to make Joe Brown feel.

VERNON LAW: The players were all surprised when Bobby got fired so soon. I will say that Bobby was a very competitive individual, and it hurt him for us to play like we were. Basically he knew how to handle players. If he had more time, maybe—but he didn't.

WALLS: While Bobby was the manager, Groat couldn't play short-stop worth a damn. Bobby made Vernon Law and Bob Friend into winners. Those two started out nervous as hell on the mound. They didn't understand what Bobby was doing for them, making them toughen up by getting on them so hard. You think it's any coincidence so many of the young players Bobby got with the Pirates eventually turned out to be so good? Murtaugh was a good guy, knew his baseball, but he reaped the benefits of Bobby's work. I don't want any of those guys on the old Pirates knocking Bobby.

Goddamn it, he helped them become successful whether they want to admit it or not.

DICK GROAT: Danny Murtaugh, when he took over after Bobby was fired, well, maybe he knew more about me emotionally and mentally. Two days after he became Pittsburgh's manager he announced his middle infielders were Mazeroski and Groat. Under Bobby, I remember nights walking the streets of St. Louis and Cincinnati trying to decide whether I should retire from baseball or not.

Could Bobby have succeeded with the team the way Murtaugh did? Probably, if he could have toned down his criticism. Bobby in those days lived in a Utopian world. Here he had two of the best players in the game—the best right fielder in Roberto Clemente and the best second baseman in Bill Mazeroski. He did not realize there couldn't be any major league manager who could end up with the nine best guys in the game all on the same field for him at once. You have to end up using the best points of the other less talented players you have to work with.

But Bobby and I eventually became very good friends. Bobby became one of my staunchest supporters when he could make himself look at me objectively. When he was later coaching with the Dodgers he came up to me once and said, "I was 100 percent wrong about you." I've always respected Bobby Bragan since then, and I always respected his knowledge of baseball even before that. He could teach you to play the game right, but he was such a taskmaster at it.

FIRED: PART II

KNOWING I WOULD BE GOING BACK TO CUBA IN THE FALL tempered any worries I might have had spending the summer of 1957 at home in Fort Worth. I filled the days with pleasurable things. Alex Grammas was now managing the Cats, and I often went out to La Grave Field to watch games. I did interviews with the local newspapers, read *The Sporting News* and visited with scouts who'd come out to see the Cats. My ear was to the ground; baseball is such a close-knit fraternity that you can keep track of all the rumors of potential job openings.

If I hadn't believed it before, I now knew for sure managers were hired to be fired. I resolved to learn from my mistakes with the Pirates and take a longer time getting fired from my next major league job.

In October I returned to Cuba. Almendares was, as always, a fine club, and this time around I had a real standout third baseman named Tony Taylor. It was my custom, when I had a native kid with talent, to tout him to the many major league scouts who combed the Cuban winter league for prospects. I resolved to sing Taylor's praises; in my estimation then the youngster belonged in the big leagues, and he proved me correct by going on to a solid 20-year career with the Phillies and the Tigers, among other clubs.

Hank Greenberg, the Cleveland Indian general manager, arrived in Cuba in January 1958. Hank was a warm, likeable individual. I'd known him well for many years and valued his friendship. When Hank arrived in Havana he sent word he wanted me to meet him in his room at the Nacional Hotel. Maybe he just wanted the lowdown on Taylor from me, but I admit that on the way over I entertained hopeful thoughts. The Indians had concluded their 1957 season with a 76-77 record under Kerby Farrell. They had a mostly veteran ballclub with some promising youngsters added to the player mix. Maybe, just maybe...

Hank Greenberg had no baloney about him. As soon as I arrived he said, "Bobby, I didn't like what happened at Pittsburgh. I want to name you manager of Cleveland." Naturally, I accepted immediately. I never even asked about contract terms. There was a wide range of managerial salaries in the majors—even in those days you might command $75,000 or $80,000 annually if your name was Casey Stengel. Lower echelon managers, the unproven ones, made maybe $35,000. I got $35,000 with the Indians.

I was flown to Cleveland for a press conference. Kerby Farrell was also a longtime friend, and when we visited in his hotel room he actually cried while we discussed his dismissal. Any manager losing his job feels regrets about things done or not quite accomplished. I'm sure Kerby believed that if he'd been allowed to keep his job a little longer he could have turned Cleveland around, but he wasn't going to have that chance.

The Indians had been in decline since Al Lopez left the team to manage the Chicago White Sox two seasons earlier. It had been a quick sinking in the standings. Under Lopez in 1954 the Indians stormed to the American League pennant and set a major league record with 111 victories in the process. Though Cleveland lost a shocking 4-0 World Series sweep to the New York Giants (1990's straight games shellacking of the mighty Oakland A's by the lesser-touted Cincinnati Reds is a good recent equivalent), that 1954 Indian club was one of the all-time greats.

But Lopez left and some key players including Vic Wertz, Bobby Avila, and the entire frontline pitching staff of Early Wynn, Mike Garcia, and Bob Lemon appeared to have entered career downslopes. There didn't seem to be much team spirit. I decided once again to try and bring the Dodger way of doing things to another club, and loved having Eddie Stanky as one of my coaches. I knew Greenberg would give me a free hand in spring training to do things the way I wanted them done.

And then in February I picked up a Fort Worth newspaper and read that Greenberg had been fired. Once again, I'd been hired by a general manager I'd never get to work for. My heart sank at the thought, and damn near plunged from sight when I read who Greenberg's successor would be—the notorious Frank Lane.

"Trader Lane," everybody called him. The man who was famous because he made changes just to shake things up, with no plan really in mind. Lane had been general manager of the Cardinals some time after Mr. Rickey. I didn't think it was any accident that St. Louis had quickly dropped from contention in the National League.

Frank Lane sure hadn't hired me, and I had absolutely no doubt his presence would mean my exit, sooner rather than later. Well, you play the hand you're dealt. I decided to see how things went in Tucson, where the Indians held their spring training camp.

The Cleveland training facility was a step down from what the Pirates had in Fort Myers, which itself was a huge step below the Brooklyn camp in Vero Beach. The Indians had just one field—that was it. I asked Emil Bossard, the groundskeeper, to clear an area outside the field so we could at least work on some running routines while hitting and fielding drills were going on.

Frank Lane was a constant presence. He didn't offer advice, or even constructive criticism. All Lane wanted to do was blow his own horn and denigrate everything and everybody else.

God, all the players who bitched about my "can't hit the ball with the bat on your shoulder" saying should have gotten a load of Frank Lane. Lane thought when our hitters took a called third strike it meant everybody secretly mocked the general manager. He was very outspoken in such situations. Lane's habit during spring training was to sit directly beside the dugout, right next to me. This made it easier for him to tell me everything I was doing wrong, and kept him close enough to the players to offer them his insights, too.

During one spring training game, we had Minnie Minoso at bat. Minnie took ball one, and Lane hollered, "Way to watch 'em, Minnie!" Ball two: "Good eye!" Ball three: "One more and you're on first base!" Called strike one: "You're still ahead." Called strike two: "That's enough, Minnie!" Called strike three: "You look like a big bag of shit with a cherry on top!"

Hey, I never went *that* far.

Lane liked to complain about everything. He even found a way to gripe at me about Tony Taylor. All during the winter season at Cuba I'd talked Tony up to the major league scouts, trying my best to get the kid a big league opportunity. I swear the first thing Frank Lane ever said to me in Tucson was, "You touted Tony Taylor to such an extent that the Cubs drafted him before we got our turn."

As the spring progressed, I got a better idea of my personnel. We had some good players, and they seemed to respond to the positive atmosphere I tried to bring to Tucson. Outfielder Gene Woodling, a very plain-spoken individual, told me just before we broke camp that 1958 had been the best spring training camp he'd ever attended. I said, "Well, I just took the ideas from the Dodgers." Maybe the one player who impressed me most was right fielder Rocky Colavito. Colavito made his mark on most fans with his prodigious power, leading the American League a couple of times in home runs over the course of a very fine career. But what got me about this athlete was his throwing arm. Rocky Colavito could have knocked down walls with his throws from the outfield. He threw hard and accurately, one of the all-time great outfield arms along with Clemente, Reggie Smith, and Carl Furillo.

Bobby Avila could still handle second base, but Vic Wertz was practically through at first. Eventually we replaced him with Vic Power, and Power was just maybe the best-fielding first baseman in major league history. Larry Doby was also with the team, and I recall he had a bad neck. Every day when I'd walk into the clubhouse Doby would already be there, his neck stretched out by some strange contraption. The Indian center fielder I inherited didn't impress me at all. Roger Maris had difficulty catching fly balls close to the wall. He was the most wall-shy outfielder I ever saw. In spring training one of my coaches was assigned to spend 30 minutes every day hitting balls over Maris's head so he'd get rid of his fear of colliding with the wall. Excessive effort was not Maris's problem. He didn't look very impressive with the bat, either, and in his own words, "I was born surly." He would not have won any personality contests. I didn't find much playing time for him once the season started.

Any manager would have loved having Minnie Minoso on his team. I'd known Minnie for years. He was the national baseball star of Cuba, and my managing days there had helped us establish a warm friendship. During the winter of '57 the White Sox sold Minnie to Cleveland, and when the sale was announced just before a game about 10 reporters ran up to Minnie in the dugout to ask his opinion of the deal. "You were sold for $250,000; what do you think about that?" Minnie was queried. At that moment the Cuban national anthem was played, so Minnie had time to collect his thoughts. After the music ended, he favored the assembled press with this statement: "Anytime I'd pay that kind of money for a human being, she'd better have blonde hair and blue eyes."

Mickey Vernon was still an active player in '58. He had slowed down in the field but the former American League batting champ still had some hitting skills. Pitcher Mudcat Grant had great velocity on his fastball; overall, he was the team's best athlete. But he loved music as much as baseball. On one road trip the team was taking a bus to the airport. Grant started getting on with this huge radio; the damn thing must have been three feet long. I said, "Mudcat, you can make this trip, but your radio can't." It didn't endear me to him.

I loved Bob Lemon. He was nearing the end of his Hall of Fame career, but he was such a gentleman. As Bob often said, he never took his troubles home with him from the ballpark because he left them at some bar along the way. Ray Narleski and Don Mossi gave Cleveland an adequate one-two, right handed-left handed bullpen punch. And another Indian pitcher was Cal McLish, who I remembered from my Brooklyn Dodger days. Cal was a finesse pitcher, very smooth and smart.

Overall, a veteran group. I felt we could contend but was also aware of a glaring weakness. On paper we were a club with a chance, but Mr. Rickey would have been the first to point out we had absolutely no team speed. Only Gary Geiger, whom I'd chosen to replace Maris in center field, had enough speed to steal 25-35 bases. Minoso could run some, too, but that was it.

I'd hoped Frank Lane might tone down his know-it-all act some when the regular season began, but I was quickly proven wrong. Early on we were playing Baltimore, where Paul Richards was rebuilding the Orioles as their manager. We were getting beat by one run in the ninth and had a runner on first base with two outs. A right hander was on the mound for Baltimore and we had left handed hitting catcher Russ Nixon coming up. Richards brought in left handed pitcher Billy O'Dell, whom I'd later manage in Milwaukee. I called down to our bullpen to summon right handed hitting catcher J.W. Porter to pinch-hit for Nixon.

Up in the press box Frank Lane, whose eyesight wasn't so good, asked, "Who's Bragan bringing in now?" "Porter," Lou Hatter, a Baltimore sportswriter, told him. Lane promptly predicted, "He's an automatic strikeout." The first pitch from O'Dell to Porter was a called strike one. Then Porter swung and missed at a bad pitch for strike two. Up in the press box, my trusted friend Frank Lane was pointing out to one and all how Bragan was blowing the game. O'Dell's third pitch was straight down the pipe, and Porter just stood there. It should have been strike three and out, game over, but somehow plate umpire Bill McGowan called it a ball. Everybody on the Baltimore side of the field complained. Paul Richards was beside himself. And, don't you know it, Porter hit O'Dell's next pitch over the left-center field wall to win the game for us.

Lane leaped to his feet in the press box and screamed, "I signed Porter to his first contract! That's my boy!" Hatter said, "But Frank, you said Porter would strike out." Lane replied pompously, "He did. The damn ump wouldn't call it." After spending my whole baseball career either playing or managing in the National League, I found the American League to be somewhat different. The brand of ball played there was more nonchalant. Even the umpiring was different. The American League umps wore the old-fashioned balloon chest protectors, causing them to look over the top of the catcher rather than to the side as National League umps could with their inside chest protectors. Accordingly, the American League strike zone was higher.

Of course, there were many fine American League players. I was very impressed with Mickey Mantle. Al Kaline could do everything well—field, hit, run if not with speed then with good instincts. Yogi Berra was some kind of a catcher. Someone else whose antics got more public attention than his great skills was Jimmy Piersall. Still, some thought Piersall was the American League equivalent of Willie Mays. A nervous breakdown earlier in his career inspired a book and movie titled "Fear Strikes Out." Fully recovered, Jimmy Piersall didn't strike out that often and he played a shallow center field beautifully. In 1959 the Red Sox made a mistake and traded Piersall to the Indians, but I was already long gone.

Team rivalries weren't as bitter in the American League, maybe because the Yankees had dominated for so long. Fraternization was the rule of the day, and sometimes goodwill extended far beyond that. I remember that as the 1958 season opened, Rocky Colavito began his year in a terrible batting slump, 1-for-23 or something like that. We went into Boston for a series and before the first game at Fenway Park Ted Williams spent 30 minutes working with Colavito to get his swing straightened out. That was a friendly thing for Williams to do, but I don't recall anything like that happening in the National League. This is the best example of why I found the American League so buddy-buddy.

As a team, the Cleveland Indians began the '58 season in the same kind of slump as Rocky Colavito. The potential was clearly there, but the results weren't indicative of the talent. A number of beloved Indian players—Lemon, Garcia, Avila, Narleski— did what they still could on the field, but their age was showing. We had so many guys on the way down, what Mr. Rickey used to call "anesthetic baseball players—they put the manager to sleep." Pitching in particular was supposed to be the backbone of our team, but this was the area where we were hurting worst. Herb Score obviously wasn't going to return to the greatness he'd exhibited two years earlier before a line drive by Gil McDougald almost killed him.

McLish and Mudcat Grant were going to be good ones, but they were struggling. My vaunted bullpen of Narleski and Mossi couldn't get anybody out.

Still, I felt like things would get turned around. Younger players like Colavito and Power would find their batting strokes, and Minoso was a certified All-Star. The players needed time to fuse together as a unit. In the meantime, it was up to the manager to help them reach that point.

I did my best to avoid repeating mistakes I'd made with the Pirates, but I also had high expectations of each man on the club. Respect was my number one requirement. Whether it was Minoso or Lemon, the established stars, or a fringe player like Bill Moran, treatment and discipline were the same. In retrospect I can see this approach means you enjoy the players' respect, but their liking for you suffers.

We muddled our way into the season. A particularly painful memory is of Casey Stengel bringing the Yankees into Cleveland for a doubleheader. I started two left handers, Score and Hal Woodeshick. Damned if in both games Casey didn't send out line-ups loaded with left handed hitters—Tony Kubek, Jerry Lumpe, and Norm Siebern besides Yogi Berra. Four of Casey's first five batters in the lineup swung from the left side. I was really pleased, right up until the umpire yelled "Play ball" and the Yankees started pounding the ball all over Municipal Coliseum. They embarrassed us, 13-1 and 12-2. Casey might have conned sportswriters with his rambling manner of speech, but that old man's mind was crystal clear when it came to figuring out which of his hitters would do best against opposing pitchers. I'd always admired Stengel, but after that doubleheader I respected him even more.

We'd win two, lose three, win two, lose two, always staying just on the underside of .500. Frank Lane was always around, but wavering rather than offering consistent advice. He had been an outstanding referee in the National Basketball Association and was very solid physically, even in his mid-60s. I never felt comfortable with him. This feeling increased rather than lessened the longer I worked with him.

Oh, I knew what had to come eventually. I wasn't Lane's man, and he always liked to live up to his reputation as a colorful sort who'd make wholesale changes. But I thought I'd at least have a chance to find a house to rent in Cleveland.

I was still living in a hotel; the school year in Fort Worth ended and Gwenn and the kids drove north in early July to join me. They'd been in the hotel with me for three days when I left for the ballpark and a game pitting Cleveland against the Boston Red Sox.

It's a game I remember very well. McLish came out on the short end of a 1-0 pitching duel when he gave up a ninth inning home run to Ted Williams, leaving us with a record of 31-36. The team wandered back to our clubhouse, where one of the clubhouse aides told me Mr. Lane wanted to see me in his office.

With anyone else, I would have believed 67 games wouldn't be considered enough opportunity to fail. It wasn't much more than one-third of a season. To anyone who knew baseball it was obvious the Indians would improve as the year went along and the team had time to jell. But this was Frank Lane. I knew what he wanted.

Lane wouldn't have recognized tact if it hit him in the face. As soon as I got to his office he smirked and said, "I don't know how we'll get along without you, Bobby, but starting tomorrow we're going to try." I didn't have much to say. Lane continued, "Would you like us to pay you every two weeks for the balance of the season or would you like a lump sum payment?" I took the lump sum and paid off our mortgage in Fort Worth.

When I was canned by the Pirates I made a point of returning to the clubhouse to meet with the players. I didn't do that this time. But when Minnie Minoso heard about it, he burst into tears and made a point of finding me and presenting me with a gift of 50 Cuban cigars. We've remained close friends.

Lane hired Joe Gordon to replace me, and the Indians did come together as a team and finished the '58 season 46-40 under Gordon. 1959 found the Indians finishing second to the Chicago White Sox with an 89-65 record, and then in 1960 Gordon led the Indians to a 49-46 mark in early going. Trader Frank made baseball history by swapping his manager to the Detroit Tigers for Jimmy Dykes, the Tiger skipper. Cleveland went downhill from there and the team hasn't really had a pennant-contending club since. There's an ongoing rumor I put a curse on the Indians after Lane fired me. To this day I get calls from Cleveland sportswriters and disc jockeys who ask if it's true. No, it isn't. I didn't need to hex the club. Having Frank Lane as its general manager was curse enough.

You can imagine my wife's reaction when I came back to the hotel that day and told her I'd been fired. Gwenn found it hard to believe. "Where to now?" she wondered.

We didn't head back to Fort Worth. Instead, I sat and waited in our Cleveland hotel room for the calls I knew would come. And they did.

First I heard from Jack Kent Cooke, who wanted me to manage his Toronto team in the International League. It was an intriguing offer and I told him I'd consider it. But then I got a call from Dick Walsh, a Dodger administrator, who said he wondered if I'd be interested in taking over Spokane, the Dodgers' new Triple-A farm club in Washington. I told Walsh I'd report there in 48 hours. I was going back to the best organization in baseball.

Frank Lane died in Chicago in 1980 or '81. By then I was working for the Texas Rangers, and baseball commissioner Bowie Kuhn wired to ask if I would represent him at Lane's funeral in Dallas. Had I not received Kuhn's request, I would never have gone to Lane's funeral, but as it turned out I was glad I did.

I drove to the Dallas cemetery and looked around for the large crowd I expected to be in attendance for Lane's services. There wasn't one. I sighted a cemetery employee in a pickup truck and asked if he'd direct me to Frank Lane's funeral. He said I should follow him, and we drove about $1^{1}/_{2}$ miles before he stopped, pointed, and said, "The service will start in about 30 minutes." I looked where he indicated and saw a building. "In the building?" I asked. "No," he replied, "over by that open grave."

There were two people already there. One was the preacher. The other was Lane's Mexican widow. Lane was Catholic and had divorced his first wife to marry her at a time when divorce was not recognized by the Catholic Church. He'd lived with his second wife for 18 years, but because of his church not allowing divorce, after Lane died there was a question over who controlled where he'd be buried, his second wife or his daughter. The daughter won out, so Lane was being laid to rest in Dallas instead of Mexico.

The three of us sat by the graveside for a while. A Dallas city councilman, Bill Milby, arrived. Then came Lane's daughter, her husband, and their two children. That was the entire group.

The preacher whispered to me, "You knew this man well. Would you offer a eulogy?" "I certainly will," was my quick response, and I did.

CAL McLISH: Bobby had some bad luck with the Cleveland Indians. Really when he got there the vaunted pitching staff started to fall apart. Bob Lemon came up with a bad arm. Mike Garcia had a bad arm. The pitching staff fell apart, and one day all of a sudden Bobby's gone and Joe Gordon's taking over.

I guess Bobby got fired in May or June. The general manager who hired him got fired, and the new general manager was going to want to bring in his own man. I hadn't pitched very well for Bobby. I felt badly about that because I liked him. I came to respect Joe Gordon. Joe did a great damn job with our young hitters like Colavito and Woodie Held. He talked to 'em about hitting the ball up the middle and they responded, the team started doing better. That damn Colavito was so strong, he'd hit 10 balls a game 500 feet foul. Gordon got him to hit up the middle and he hit homers to all fields. Pretty soon Colavito led the league in homers or tied with Killebrew, I think.

With the Indians, Bobby might have been too impatient. The pitching staff all got old at once, but it wasn't their fault. Bobby got on them and he wasn't with the club long enough to get what Joe Gordon did, young pitchers up from the minors with great arms.

Gordon got Jim Perry, Gary Bell, guys like that. Bobby couldn't make himself wait to see what would happen. I think that's what the real problem was.

I'm asked many times about who I think were the good managers. I put Bobby right up there with Gene Mauch and Alvin Dark. Those three were kind of alike in that they really got into the game. They saw everything that was going on. Some managers succeed by just seeing one important thing at a time. Bobby and Gene and Dark tried to succeed by controlling everything. Well, if you were a young player willing to learn, those were guys you could sure learn from. But lots of players don't want to learn.

Geez, Bobby knew his baseball. If he'd gotten to stay someplace long enough in the majors, Cleveland or some damn place, he'd have calmed down and been all right and built them a winner. In Cleveland I never really did know the story on why they made the change. Bobby could have gotten those young pitchers to replace the old ones and gone on from there. But Joe Gordon ended up doing it.

I remember the day Bobby got fired. What happened was, I pitched this game against the Red Sox and we lost 1-0 when I gave up a home run to Ted Williams. Bobby kidded me years later that if I hadn't let Williams get the hit, he'd still be Cleveland manager. Maybe so.

RETURN OF THE PRODIGAL

I WAS BACK WITH THE BLUE. DODGER BLUE, of course. In the six-plus seasons I'd been away, the quality of the organization had remained the same, but not the location of its major league club. In 1958, what would have been unthinkable just a few seasons before happened: The Dodgers and Giants took their storied rivalry west, with the Dodgers moving to Los Angeles and the Giants to San Francisco. Putting "Los Angeles" in front of "Dodgers" instead of "Brooklyn" would take some getting used to. Still, it was a tremendous relief to be back with the organization I revered above all others.

It took two days to drive from Cleveland to Spokane. I had time to do some thinking. Spokane was to the Los Angeles big league club what Montreal had been to Brooklyn, the Triple-A club that was, for many players, the last stop before the majors.

This might also be true for the new manager of the Spokane Indians. The 1958 season marked Spokane's first as a Dodger farm club—it only made sense for the Dodgers to keep their Triple-A affiliate reasonably close to the major league franchise. This way, a player called up to the Dodgers could arrive the next day. If the Triple-A team had remained near the East Coast, travel would have been extended at least another day.

I was happy in my new surroundings and content to be a Triple-A manager. I respected Walter Alston tremendously. He'd been at the Dodger helm since 1954, and with spectacular success. But I knew from experience no major league job is completely secure. Even if Walter stayed with the club for many more years, I was still young. I could wait for my turn. After all, there were just 16 major league managing jobs at any one time. Already I'd gone through one-eighth of them!

My being hired to take over the Spokane Indians—it was unique, going from the Indians to the Indians—was a signal of the Dodger organization's faith in me. My predecessor in Spokane was Goldie Holt, a fine, fine baseball man. Holt was an innovator whose ideas are still a vital part of today's game. He invented the "time" play to pick runners off base, with signals being passed from pitcher to catcher or pitcher to infielder, with the pitcher whirling to make a pickoff throw on a certain count instead of a split-second decision based on the position of the infielder. Holt was being moved to another job with the Dodgers to make room for me in Spokane. It felt nice to be wanted. Another plus to the Spokane job was the presence of Spencer Harris as general manager. He'd moved over from the same job in Fort Worth, and also had served for some years as camp supervisor at spring training's Dodgertown in Vero Beach. For a change I was going to a place where I'd be on good terms with my boss.

Of course, moving from a major league to minor league managing job was undeniably a demotion. My salary with the Spokane Indians would be $15,000 a year, a considerable drop in pay. But I also had my lump sum payment from Cleveland and no more mortgage payments to worry about. Besides, in 1958 $15,000 went a lot further than it does now.

When I arrived in Spokane, Spencer Harris met me with open arms. I was delighted with the facilities—the ballpark was brand-new and the fans were excited to have a ballclub. The custom in Spokane when an Indian player hit a home run was to poke paper money through the wire screen behind home plate as a sort of reward. At the time, fans felt ballplayers probably weren't compensated enough. I don't think they feel that way anymore.

Well, the first thing I learned was that my best slugger was out with an injury. Jim Gentile, a massive first baseman, was well-known as a prima donna with an explosive temper. A few days earlier he'd struck out in the clutch and punched a dugout water cooler. The result was 16 stitches in Gentile's hand and a hole in the Spokane lineup until he was healed.

Along with Gentile, left fielder Bob Jenkins provided most of Spokane's long balls. Big Frank Howard was just turning into a home run threat. I had two other outfielders who could handle the bat—Tommy Davis played in center, and Chuck Essegian took his turn in left or right. In another year, Essegian would hit two home runs to help propel the Dodgers past the White Sox in the 1959 World Series.

Steve Bilko, who earlier had been a Pacific Coast League foe, was now on my side. Norm Sherry handled catching duties; Bob Lillis played a good shortstop; Tony Roig was a solid second baseman, and Don Miles had the potential to be a good outfielder. Unfortunately, he never got past Triple A. Miles had married a millionaire's daughter and spent more time phoning her long distance than he did practicing to improve his baseball skills. Miles had the same weakness as Roger Maris, a tendency to shy away from balls hit over his head which might require close communication with an outfield fence.

Jenkins proved to be a colorful type, certainly the most tightfisted ballplayer I ever met. Spencer Harris had arranged some advertisements where, if an Indian player hit a home run, he'd get 10 gallons of gasoline and a dozen hot dogs donated by local merchants. I think there were some other gifts too. Well, anytime Bob Jenkins hit a home run he'd no sooner step on home plate than he'd be sprinting through the dugout to the clubhouse telephone to dial the magic number and ask, "Are you going to have the gas and hot dogs ready for me?"

Soon after I arrived, we lost a close ballgame due completely to some foolish mistakes. Afterwards I called a meeting and emphasized how important it was for every player to go all out all the time —to run hard while chasing every fly ball, to go all out toward first after hitting a routine ground ball. "It's like when a fan comes to the ballpark, buys a ticket, and then goes to the concession stand," I said. "Now, when he asks for a hot dog and a cold drink, he puts his money on the counter and he wants what he's paid for right away. It's the same when he puts down his money to watch you play—he expects and deserves to see your best efforts from the first pitch to the last. So anytime in future games you forget what I've told you and don't go all out, I'm going to take some of your money."

All the players listened open-mouthed. Big Frank Howard, always a little on the sensitive side, growled, "Bobby, are you talking about me?" I replied, "Are you doing your best, Frank?" "Hell, yes," Howard said. "You bet I am." "Well, then, I'm with you, Frankie baby," I concluded.

Four days later in Portland, Bob Jenkins hit a ground ball back to the pitcher and jogged to first base. As he returned to the dugout I yelled from the third base coaching box, "Bob, that cost you $25." By his expression you would have thought I said $2,500. For the next six years, the first Christmas card I received always came from Bob Jenkins. He'd wish me all the best for the holiday season, hoping he could have his money back. Lord, Jenkins was a tightwad! Playing winter ball in Latin America, he'd routinely take his wife and child into a restaurant and order one Coke and three glasses of ice.

I spent my first few games in Spokane watching the team. Tom Saffell, who'd been my center fielder in Hollywood and then again with the Pirates, was the Spokane player-coach. So Saffell took care of business for my first few games and I carefully observed the team. I saw they had potential. I also saw they were sloppy.

I called a clubhouse meeting and set down some rules. Besides the usual admonitions to hustle and play smart, fundamental baseball, I also gave guidelines to basic professional appearance —how jerseys should be tucked into pants, how stirrup socks should be worn and so forth. I also didn't make any bones about how they would have to adhere to what I wanted.

My first move was to make Saffell the roommate of Jim Gentile. Gentile had tremendous potential, but I knew it wouldn't be realized if he didn't calm down some. Saffell, I thought, would be a good influence on the younger player. On the first road trip after that we went into Sacramento. Saffell and I had breakfast the next morning and he told me he'd been awakened at 3 A.M. when Gentile, completely nude, stood in front of a mirror with a bat in his hands taking practice swings and talking out loud. Saffell didn't seem to find this as unusual as I did, and I wondered who was going to influence whom the most.

There was another player on the Spokane roster who would become perhaps more special to me than anyone else I managed. Just a few days into my tenure at Spokane I was standing by the batting cage before a game. Batting practice time was almost over, and the players were taking turns jumping into the cage for one last swing. In his haste to get a final turn, Maury Wills swung left-handed. Sometimes you notice things: he looked natural doing it.

Maury Wills had spent seven years as a Dodger farmhand, failing miserably at the plate because, hitting from the right side, he simply couldn't hit a right-handed pitcher's curveball. I could well relate to this. But where Maury and I shared this batting weakness, his skills far exceeded what mine had been as a fielder and baserunner. In those two areas, Maury was performing at a major league level.

So I asked Maury if he'd try becoming a switch-hitter. He agreed he didn't have anything to lose, and for the next four weeks he came to the park an hour early to practice swinging from the left side. Immediately he showed he could adapt.

But it's one thing to hit in batting practice, and another when fans who paid to see the scheduled game don't show patience for a worthy experiment. "We don't want to start this in games before the home crowd," I told Maury. "We'll give it a try on our next road trip."

We went to Sacramento again. They started right-handed pitcher Joe Stanka, and Maury went 2-for-4. He was a switch hitter thereafter, and finished our Pacific Coast League season batting .300.

For the next part of the Maury Wills Story, the Dodgers owe the Detroit Tigers. During the spring of 1959 the Dodgers sold Maury's contract to the Tigers on a "look-see" basis. Detroit acquired Maury conditionally so they could get a look at him; if they liked him enough to keep him on their ballclub, they'd have to agree on a price with Los Angeles. I hated to see Maury leaving the organization, but I was happy for him, too. There was no doubt in my mind he'd make a fine Detroit shortstop for many, many years.

However, the Tigers didn't agree with that assessment. Towards the end of the spring I sat with Tiger vice-president Rick Farrell and the Dodgers' Buzzie Bavasi as they watched a game between Detroit and Los Angeles at Vero Beach. Rocky Bridges had started at short for the Tigers, but late in the game Maury pinch-ran for him and promptly stole second and third. Buzzie said to Farrell, "Well, you see what he can do. You've got him for $35,000." To which Farrell replied, "That's $25,000 more than I want to pay." Buzzie's response was, "Well, he's worth more than that to us at Spokane," and Maury moved back into the Dodger farm system.

But not for long. Maury rejoined my club full of confidence. He knew he could be a big leaguer—more than that, a valuable big leaguer. As the '59 pennant race heated up, Buzzie called me in Spokane and asked what player I had who might help Los Angeles down the stretch. I unhesitatingly said, "Maury Wills." He ended up taking the shortstop job away from my old pal Don Zimmer, hitting .260 while fielding with his usual brilliance. In 1960, his first full season, Maury led the National League with 50 stolen bases and was on his way to a career that should have landed him in the Hall of Fame. Hopefully, he'll one day be voted into Cooperstown.

I admit I take special pride in the baseball accomplishments of Maury Wills. Hopefully I helped many players, even those who never did make it to the major leagues. But it's special to look at Maury and feel it was my help that boosted him that extra notch necessary. We've remained fast friends, and whenever I reflect on my being fired in '58 by Cleveland, any lingering resentment is offset by the knowledge that getting canned by the Indians gave me the chance to contribute to the career of Maury Wills.

Overall, 1958 wasn't a great season for the Spokane Indians. We finished in the second division of the Pacific Coast League, my lowest standing ever as a minor league manager. Our pitching was the big problem, and there's a story that one of our hurlers named Patterson even denied to a barber during a haircut that he was on the Spokane staff for fear the barber, who might have been an avid but disappointed fan, would slit his throat.

There are lots of barbershop stories in baseball lore. My favorite concerns Pete Gray, who achieved fame after World War II by playing outfield for the St. Louis Browns with only one arm. When I managed Fort Worth, Pete was playing for the Dallas club in the Texas League. Before a game at La Grave Field, Pete went into the barbershop of Fort Worth's Texas Hotel and asked to get a haircut and shave. In shaving him, the fumblefingered barber cut Pete's face in two or three places. When he was finished and let Pete up from the chair, the barber said, "Say, you look familiar. Haven't I shaved you before?" Pete answered, "No, sir, I lost my arm in the war."

I spent the winter of 1958 back home in Fort Worth. Castro had come to power, ending American participation in the Cuban Winter League.

It was wonderful to return to Vero Beach for spring training in 1959. I didn't need to be introduced to anybody. After the relatively primitive conditions of the Pittsburgh and Cleveland spring training facilities, Dodgertown shone like a jewel and I felt like I was back in the real big leagues.

During the spring, my need for pitching at Spokane was tantamount. Alston constantly borrowed the better hurlers on my club as well as outfielders and infielders to supplement his major league roster in exhibition games. The frequency with which players were borrowed was a dead giveaway on who I was apt to have for the Pacific Coast League season. I liked what I saw, and anticipated contending for the PCL title.

To begin with, I had Jim Gentile back through his own fault. During spring training he was sold by the Dodgers to the White Sox, a tremendous career break since Gil Hodges was still firmly entrenched at first for Los Angeles. When Buzzie Bavasi informed Gentile of the deal Jim promptly went around the clubhouse trying to swap his Dodger Blue sweatshirts for the black style worn by the White Sox. Unfortunately for Gentile, he went on celebrating too far into the night. In those days all the players, coaches, managers, and team executives slept in barracks. Gentile showed up much the worse for wear long after curfew. Clay Bryant, the St. Paul manager, was acting as officer-in-charge that night, and he and Gentile got so vocal with each other Buzzie emerged from his room and informed Gentile he was cancelling the White Sox deal because of Gentile's unbecoming conduct. Buzzie did, too, and Gentile opened the season in Spokane instead of Chicago. Eventually the Dodgers sold him to Baltimore, and he had some great seasons with the Orioles. Gentile was likeable but sometimes his own worst enemy. He'll admit that himself.

When spring training was over I'd lost Frank Howard and Steve Bilko, but picked up the ace pitcher I needed in Roger Craig. Art Fowler and Bob Jenkins were back, as was Maury. With the help of other players including Norm Sherry, Tommy Davis, and Bob Lillis we ended up finishing second for the season.

It was a great year for me, one with many happy memories. There was a team spirit that could always rise to the occasion. One night in Sacramento Gentile had little luck with left-handed pitcher Marshall Bridges, striking out his first three times up. After the third strikeout, Gentile came back to sit next to me in the dugout, his head in his hands. When our turn at bat was over, he remained seated. I said, "Are you going to play or pass?" "I'll play," he said, picked up his first baseman's mitt and went back onto the field. Then Gentile struck out for the fourth time in the top of the ninth, but we rallied anyway and won the game. Afterwards in the clubhouse, Gentile sat around visiting with Bill Brenzell, the Dodger scout who had signed him, going on and on about how badly he felt because of the four strikeouts. I tapped him on the shoulder and said, "Be happy, Jim. We won the game." "*You* be happy," Gentile snapped. Later on our clubhouse manager, Nobe Kawana, had T-shirts printed up with "*you* be happy!" emblazoned across the front.

Incidentally, Brenzell worked as a Dodger scout for 20 years or more, and I believe Jim Gentile was the only player he signed who made it to the big leagues.

Oh, I enjoyed being in Spokane. It was much more fun than my experiences with the Pirates and Indians. Teaching is so much more a part of managing in the minor leagues. In the majors, players can complain a manager is doing something *to* them. Everything in the minor leagues is unquestionably done *for* players. The atmosphere is more positive. And any Dodger farm team was run as a first-class operation. It was the Dodger way.

I saw much of my job at Spokane as a responsibility to make the players react positively to any game situation. This included prohibiting any gripes about weather conditions. Once when we played in Phoenix it was so hot, well over 100 degrees, that my players aired constant complaints about not being able to breathe. Several refused to sit in the dugout, preferring to stay in the shade of the tunnel connecting the dugout with the clubhouse. I said loudly enough for all to hear, "It's just as hot for the other team. Concentrate on the game," but the whining went on. After an inning or two I announced, "Any other complaint about the heat and it will cost that man $50." Art Fowler was on the mound for us, and an inning later he came into the dugout after retiring Phoenix, threw his glove on the bench, and moaned, "By God, it's hot." Then, after a brief pause during which he remembered my warning, Fowler added in a hearty tone, "And that's just the way I like it!"

I recall it was on that same trip to Phoenix that Maury wasn't on our bus when it left the hotel for the ballpark. I inquired in the clubhouse, and somebody finally said Maury had some personal problems and had gone back to be with his family in Spokane. This turned out to be true, and Maury rejoined the team the following day. He explained his situation and I understood why he had needed to make a trip home, but he'd done so without asking permission first and I had no choice but to fine him. Poor Maury; $50 in itself was a lot of money for a minor league player in those days, and he'd also spent three times that much on a plane ticket to Spokane and back to Phoenix. But I took that $50 and told him never, never to do something like that again.

Late in the 1959 season, just before Maury went up to join the Dodgers, I wandered into Spencer Harris's office and Maury wandered right in after me. "Did you have something on your mind, Maury?" I inquired. "Yes," he said. "I was wondering if I could get that $50 back." Before I could even say the word, Spencer Harris answered for me in the negative. Well, even today whenever I see Maury he makes reference to that $50. He surely can't entertain thoughts of getting it.

After the Pacific Coast League season ended, I made an enjoyable trip to Los Angeles to watch the Dodgers take on the White Sox in the World Series. This was the Series where Larry Sherry emerged as a real hero in relief, and my former player Chuck Essegian hit two homers for Los Angeles. It's hard to root against former players you enjoyed managing, even if they're opponents: I also remember Al Lopez inserting Minnie Minoso for defensive purposes in one game, and Minnie making a great catch to save a run. I was quietly happy for him.

I went back to Fort Worth for the winter feeling a deep sense of satisfaction. I loved my job in Spokane. I was part of the Dodger organization again. I fully expected to return to Spokane in 1960.

Except I got a call from Buzzie Bavasi. Buzzie said Walter Alston wanted me to serve as his third base coach with Los Angeles. Immediately, thoughts of Spokane vanished. I accepted.

B	E	T	W	E	E	N
I	N	N	I	N	G	S

MAURY WILLS: When Bobby Bragan took over the club at Spokane, I was first of all enthralled, because I didn't think someone who had been a major league manager would be willing to come back down to manage in the minor leagues again. That made me think there was something special about Bobby Bragan.

It was the funniest thing. Bobby was our manager for a week before he said anything. He just observed us. On that club, we were supposed to be in the clubhouse at five, dressed by five-fifteen, so on. So we went about our business as usual and he watched.

After a week Bobby called a team meeting, the best I ever observed in the minors or in the major leagues. And he got on us. Oh, he got on us. He told us we were to be fully dressed by five. "I want you in full uniform," he said, and then went on to tell us precisely how we were going to put that uniform on—blouses tucked in neatly, pants legs folded just so, and we had to fold the tongues of our shoes down. At that time it was considered hip or cool by many of us to leave the tongues of our shoes sticking up. We thought it looked good. And Bobby said we'd fold them down or get fined. I thought, "Jesus Christ! Oh, shit! This guy wants to make us see what being professional is all about!"

I continued to be overwhelmed as he taught us there was a right way, his way, to do everything, where before we'd been sloppy. I mean, we had guys on the team who smoked, almost everybody smoked then, and they'd leave the dugout smoking and just be putting their cigarettes out when they crossed the foul line. Well, you sure didn't do that under Bobby Bragan.

TOMMY DAVIS: Bobby Bragan to me was an unusual manager because he insisted on doing things his way. He was a ballplayers' manager in the sense that once we were in the clubhouse he was in charge and nobody else. I understood that, I came to applaud him for that. And anything that happened in the clubhouse, anything he said or did to come down on a player, that stayed in the clubhouse. That's the way it should be.

WILLS: Without Bobby Bragan, there would have been no Maury Wills in the major leagues. That simple. The mistakes I made during my career were my own; the successes were mine and Bobby Bragan's. I knew from the start I was one of the players he loved best, what he called "my little bobo."

Bobby told me to switch hit, and let me ease into it so I was comfortable. He told me to run the bases, use my God-given speed. He made me believe in myself at a time when it seemed like nobody else did.

DAVIS: Bobby had these great sayings, great ways of putting things. One time—and you should remember I was young and immature, that's the excuse—I was batting third or fourth for him in a close game at Spokane and I bunted and made it to first base with two out in the ninth. We were down one run. Then I immediately got picked off first. End of game.

That night in the clubhouse after the game Bobby just said to everybody in general, "Anybody hitting third, fourth, or fifth on my team does not bunt with two outs in the ninth when we're one run down. The next time anybody does that, it'll cost him $500." Big money, that was.

Well, the next day during batting practice I kind of told Bobby I didn't think my bunt was so bad. Steve Bilko was hitting behind me and he'd been hot. Bobby looked at me and yelled, "See your name in the lineup today? Well, I'm going to erase that son-of-a-bitch right now!" And he did, too. I never talked back to him after that.

WILLS: One time I did a little something, left the team for a few hours to see my family without telling Bobby, and he fined me $50. Bobby told me if I was good, I might get the money back for Christmas. I'm still waiting.

DAVIS: I grew up in Brooklyn and I'd heard all the stories about Bobby opposing Jackie Robinson and not wanting blacks on the Dodgers. But he obviously learned from that. I always felt comfortable with him. He treated me well and I never had a complaint.

LOS ANGELES

WHAT I WANTED MOST WAS TO GET BACK TO THE MAJOR LEAGUES. There's no denying the major league appeal overshadows any responsibility in the minors. I had known Walter Alston when he managed Montreal, Brooklyn's top Triple-A farm club. Alston was a former school teacher, a laid-back type who seldom raised his voice but still had the respect of his players. (All except Jackie Robinson; Jackie never did take to Alston.)

Like me, Alston didn't have much tolerance for complainers. On one road trip, the Dodgers got on a bus at the airport and many players immediately began complaining the bus wasn't good enough —the seats weren't of sufficient width, the aisle was too narrow, the interior smelled bad, and so on. Alston asked the driver to pull to the side of the road and stop. Then he announced to one and all, "Anyone wishing to get off the bus and walk to the hotel can do so at this time." The remainder of the ride was passed in silence.

I took the invitation to be Alston's third base coach as a sign. Now, a manager's most important assistant is his pitching coach. He is entrusted with the most important element of the team. But there is also a key role for the third base coach, or perhaps two. When a third base coach makes a mistake in a game, either sending the runner to home into an easy out or in holding a runner unnecessarily and costing his team a run, it's a major mistake. The very best third base coaches over the years—Charlie Dressen, Alex Grammas, George Myatt—seldom blunder. They have keen vision to constantly keep both the baserunner and ball in sight, along with solid knowledge of the opposing players—who's got a great arm in the outfield? Which second baseman loses a second in pivoting to relay the ball to the plate? Plus, it's often the third base coach who runs the team in the manager's absence, usually after the skipper is tossed from the game by an umpire.

If Alston wanted me as his third base coach, it meant he had considerable faith in me. We'd known each other for some time, and in 1960 I was 43. Alston was 49 and had managed the Dodgers for six seasons. It was not unreasonable to think he soon might want to move into the front office. If so, I would be in position to succeed him. Managing the Dodgers had been my career goal since my playing days under Leo. After my painful detours with Pittsburgh and Cleveland it appeared I was back on track.

I was one of four Los Angeles coaches during the 1960 season. Greg Muleavy coached first and worked with the hitters. Joe Becker was pitching coach and Pete Reiser worked with our outfielders and gave baserunning instruction. My salary was the same $15,000 I'd received in Spokane. Alston was undoubtedly in the $60,000-$75,000 range.

During the Dodgers' winter organizational meeting, Alston came over to me and said, "Glad to have you." It was a simple, direct greeting from a simple, direct man. He did not see me as a threat to his job. The Dodger organization didn't function that way. We all supported each other.

We quickly found a place to live. When I managed in Hollywood we lived in the San Fernando Valley, but with the Dodgers finishing up their brief stint at the Coliseum it made sense to base my home closer to the city of Los Angeles. We settled into an apartment. Soon after we moved in, one of the other tenants saw Gwenn sweeping the front porch and asked if she was Mr. Bragan's cleaning woman. The apartment complex had no appeal to my wife from there on in.

In Vero Beach during spring training, each Dodger coach was given specific daily assignments by Alston. Mine was to run batting practice, with the pitchers hitting first, then the reserves, then the starting lineup, the same order in which they'd take their practice swings during the regular season. I saw a lot of old friends—Hondo Howard, Maury, Essegian, many others—and it was a happy time. I was also asked to supervise the players' bunting drills. Now, bunting is an art lost to most present-day ballplayers. Maybe current Dodger center fielder Brett Butler could have held his own with Maury or Nellie Fox, but I can't really think of anyone else in today's crop. But in spring training 1960 at Dodgertown, players often bunted a couple of hundred balls a day each, and pitchers always did. Roger Craig and Johnny Podres soon demonstrated they could bunt with precision, deadening the ball exactly where they wanted every time. Bunting is like dancing—once you get the hang of it you don't easily forget it. You actually catch the ball on the bat, using the bat as you would a glove. Eventually I gave Podres and Craig the ultimate diploma: I sent 'em back to Alston with the message they didn't have to come to bunting drills anymore. I wasn't able to do this with Sandy Koufax, Don Drysdale, Stan Williams, Larry Sherry, or Ed Roebuck.

Once the regular season started I kept the same duties, and coached third base during the games. The Coliseum was a unique park, with a very short left field fence just 290 feet from home plate. Given the right trajectory on a batted ball, many youth leaguers could have cleared that fence. It caused special dilemmas for a third base coach, though. Because the opposing left fielder would play so shallow, on any single to left the Dodger runner on second had better be Maury or Jim Gilliam or Tommy Davis if I waved him on home, not Wally Moon or Gil Hodges. I recall without being egotistical that not one time in 1960 was I booed by the fans for waving a runner home into an easy out. I also got a couple of tries at running the Dodgers on my own, though not many—Alston was very conservative in his approach to umpires and consequently didn't get thrown out of too many games.

Los Angeles, the defending World Champion, was obviously a club capable of winning every game it played. To find the reason, there was no need to look farther than the starting pitchers. Koufax, Drysdale, Podres, and Stan Williams were an intimidating rotation. They helped me understand the difference between the Dodgers and the two major league teams I'd managed. Give me that Dodger starting rotation in Pittsburgh or Cleveland and I guarantee things would have been different. Well, with the Pirates, anyway.

Watching Don Drysdale warm up 15 minutes before a game was always enjoyable, though not for his catcher. It wasn't unusual for Norm Sherry to perform this task with his mask on. Drysdale would first hold his fastball with the seams; 10 times in a row the ball would scream at the catcher at speeds over 90 MPH and the ball would sink, dip to the right. Then Don might put his fingers across the seams, change the angle of his arm and the eleventh fastball would zoom in at 90-plus and, at the last second, veer to the left and seem to rise. Sherry had to keep his mask on, or eventually he'd have been missing some teeth.

Sandy Koufax had a great fastball, which everyone knows. Not everybody recalls Sandy's curveball was just as wonderful. In all baseball history only Bob Feller and Lefty Grove might have been compatible in that both their fastballs and breaking balls were of equal excellence. Warming Sandy up meant making sure you knew beforehand which pitch he was going to throw next. If he threw you five curveballs in a row and then crossed you up with a fastball, you simply were going to be hit. He threw so hard there was no way a catcher could react in time.

Very few people remember that Stan Williams, the big right-hander, was just about as fast as Don Drysdale. Williams never did have great control though—the most famous evidence of this being in the third and final 1962 National League playoff game against the San Francisco Giants. Williams came on in relief, walked a batter intentionally, walked the next batter unintentionally, and the Dodgers ended up losing. Roger Craig, on the other hand, had pinpoint control. He could throw his slider on the black of the plate—the black outline that rims the white part of the plate—anytime he wanted. Ed Roebuck, who anchored the bullpen, threw a good sinker. Neither Craig nor Roebuck had much velocity, though— warming them up was a pleasure.

Well, the 1960 season kicked off and it turned out to be a pretty mediocre one by Dodger standards. The defending world champs finished fourth in the National League with an 82-72 mark, 13 games behind my successor Danny Murtaugh and Pittsburgh. I admired Danny for the job he'd done with the Pirates. Good for him, I thought. I was glad to see Murtaugh's club go on to nip the Yankees in seven games when Bill Mazeroski hit his famous last-game, ninth inning homer off Ralph Terry.

I had a few instances of special satisfaction in how some of the 1960 Dodgers performed. Maury came through as I'd been sure he would, hitting leadoff, batting .295, and leading the league in stolen bases. Big Frank Howard hit 23 home runs. Tommy Davis took over as the regular Dodger center fielder and hit a solid .276. Roger Craig earned an 8-3 record with spot starts and long relief. My boys from Spokane, at least, had come through for the team.

It wasn't all love and kisses between me and all former Spokane players. Chuck Essegian struggled through a lousy year off the bench, managing just a .215 batting average. Before one game at the Coliseum I was running batting practice, and each scrubeenie, as we called the extra players, knew he was allowed just 10 swings. Essegian got his 10 and then continued to swing. I knew he was going through a rough time and didn't say anything until he'd taken five extra. Then, when he didn't show any sign of stopping, I hollered, "Time to get out of the cage?" He dropped the bat, glared, and snarled, "You wanna make me?" There wasn't much choice—I challenged him. Fortunately he didn't accept and got out of the cage to make way for the next hitter. I understood Chuck's attitude. He understood mine.

I must admit I felt some emptiness in being just a coach instead of a manager overseeing everyone else. To fill some of the spare time I found I had away from the ballpark, I began to host a sports talk show five nights a week on Los Angeles radio station KABC. When necessary I could tape shows in advance or in the mornings before night games. I never had any problem talking, so the show was easy.

I also enjoyed getting to know Dodger players who hadn't crossed my path before. Wally Moon was a real gentleman and student of the game. Though Wally never did become a big, big star, he achieved a certain nationwide notoriety while the Dodgers played in the Coliseum. Even though he batted left-handed, Wally proved adept at slicing the ball over the short, 290-foot left field wall. During all of 1960, whether Wally hit those cheap home runs or some other batter accomplished the same trick, announcers called each such home run a ""Moon shot."

The Coliseum seated 90,000, and even though Los Angeles fans immediately took the Dodgers to their hearts it was rare for all the seats to be sold. Accordingly, players asked for more passes than would have been usual on another club or in another park. Before one game a Dodger exec expressed amazement the players and coaches had requested a total of 190 game passes. We told him we were eventually shooting for 300. Personally, I left passes for young and old.

Another odd memory of 1960—for some reason I can't recall, it became customary after every home game for cupcakes to be served in the clubhouse. Everybody loved eating those cupcakes, so when Koufax or Drysdale would take the mound in the top of the ninth with a lead, we'd holler at 'em, "Remember it's cupcake time!"

Walter Alston handled the fourth place finish pretty well. It wasn't his nature to shout or place blame. I remember being amazed at how the otherwise conservative Alston rode a motorcycle to the park. Alston's nickname was "Smokey" because he chain-smoked during games. He tried to be discreet about this, but he always had one lit up.

Frank Howard provided thrills with his bat and laughs with his unique personality. It was lucky for the world Frank was born with a tolerant streak, because he was so strong he could have broken in half anybody who razzed him. Yet it was impossible to resist riding him about some things.

In one game, Big Frank led off an inning with a single. Pete Reiser was the first base coach and I was at my usual position in the third base coaching box. Alston flashed me the signal to have the runner at first move on the next pitch—the hit and run. I flashed the sign to Frank. Now, as a reinforcement, the first base coach always called the runner's name to assure him the signal to hit and run was really on. So Reiser said, "Heads up, Howard." Big Frank promptly raised both hands in the air and yelled, "Time out." When time was granted by the umpire, Frank walked directly to Reiser and said, "Pete, you managed me in Victoria, Texas, and we've been together for some time. Why don't you start calling me Frank?"

Another time, Howard was hitting third in the order, just ahead of Tommy Davis. For some reason, they were sharing a game bat. As was Frank's frequent custom, he struck out. As he walked toward the dugout, Davis, who was standing in the on-deck circle, stuck out his hand for the bat. Frank shook hands with him, believing he was being congratulated for his strikeout.

My family enjoyed being in Los Angeles, Bobby Jr. especially. The Dodgers were then and have continued to be a ballclub that extended special privileges to the families of its players and coaches. There was a Junior Dodgers baseball team formed, and Bobby Jr. played on it. Lefty Phillips, who eventually managed the California Angels, was hired by the Dodgers to coach this junior team.

When the season was over, we drove back to Fort Worth. I worked out a plan with KABC to spend weekdays in Los Angeles doing my radio show and to fly in to Fort Worth to be with my family on the weekends. That lasted one week. Then Gwenn informed me I needed to tell KABC, "To hell with the radio show." She was right.

After the 1960 season, the National League determined it would expand from eight to 10 teams in 1962, with new expansion franchises going to New York and Houston. The Mets and the Colt .45s, as the Houston club was called then, would hire executive staff and prepare to draft unprotected players from established National League rosters after the 1961 season. Also, those clubs could hire scouts to try to sign amateur talent before the draft.

As an old National Leaguer, I was happy our brand of ball would be coming back to New York and its knowledgeable fans. As a transplanted Texan, it pleased me to see my adopted state get major league baseball. Otherwise, I didn't much consider the expansion process. I was third base coach of the Dodgers.

But during the winter of 1960 I got a phone call from Gabe Paul. Gabe had been general manager at Cincinnati and Judge Roy

Hofheinz, the money behind the Houston expansion club, had hired him as the new franchise's general manager. Paul told me he'd asked Buzzie Bavasi for permission to contact me. Would I like to come work for him in Houston? "You'll be closer to home in Fort Worth, and you'd answer only to me," Paul said. "Help me put together this expansion ballclub."

It went unsaid, but I believed I understood it anyway: If I took the job, Paul would possibly make me manager of the .45s when they began National League play in 1962. I was interested.

I firmly believed I was in position as Alston's heir apparent at Los Angeles. But Walter showed no sign of stepping down soon, and history proved it. He went on for another 16 seasons at the Dodger helm. I wouldn't have had the patience to wait that long.

Still, I didn't accept Paul's offer right away. I tried to call Buzzie several times, only to find he wouldn't take my calls. In Buzzie's mind, I guess, I'd resigned already. His policy was if anybody wanted to leave the Dodgers, fine, but don't expect a warm goodbye. All I wanted to do was explain to Buzzie what the appeal of the Houston job might be, and ask if he could give me a more specific idea of how the Dodgers saw my future with their club. But he wouldn't talk to me.

I ended up calling my brother Jimmy, who'd worked nine years under Paul as a scout for Cincinnati. Jimmy said, "Gabe Paul always was fair with me." It appeared my Los Angeles bridges had been burned for me by Buzzie. I called Paul back and accepted the Houston job.

It hurt to leave the Dodgers again, but I told myself I'd get an expansion team and the chance to instill all Mr. Rickey's principles from the very beginning of the franchise. Gabe Paul and I would build a winner.

Little did I reckon on the possibility of Gabe Paul being relieved of his duties in another six months—but that's exactly what happened.

```
 ┌─────────────────────────┐
 │ B │ E │ T │ W │ E │ E │ N │
 │ I │ N │ N │ I │ N │ G │ S │
 └─────────────────────────┘
```

MAURY WILLS: It was great to be reunited with Bobby in Los Angeles in 1960. We took up right where we left off: I was his bobo again. Bobby really fit in well. Unlike some other organizations, the Dodger way was for players to pay attention to the coaches and learn from them. Bobby had those pitchers bunting like you wouldn't believe. Everything seemed to be going right on schedule for Bobby with the Dodgers, not that Walter Alston wasn't doing a good job. But you just knew who'd be taking over after Alston decided to move on.

JOHNNY PODRES: Old Bobby, man, I'd bunt the ball right in practice and he'd holler at me, "Sacrifice the whole world over!" I worked a lot with him, learned a lot from him. He was a good coach in the sense he knew what he was teaching as well as how to teach it. He commanded respect.

DUKE SNIDER: The news Bobby was going with the new Houston expansion team was a shocker. Bobby Bragan would have fit in perfectly one day as manager of the Dodgers. He could have done what Walter Alston did and Tommy Lasorda is doing, settled in for a long and very successful run as Dodger manager. Well, baseball's like life, I guess—some people get the best chances and others don't. Usually it's just luck or timing. I still wonder, though, why Bobby would have left the Dodgers.

TOM LASORDA: Bobby Bragan taught me a lot of baseball. I looked up to him with admiration and affection. He didn't have the best of luck in some situations. And Bobby has such tremendous knowledge. I mean, if you compare me with Bobby in terms of knowing the game of baseball, there is no comparison. He knows so much more. It could have been Bobby who followed Walter Alston, certainly. Like they say—the breaks of the game.

SHOT DOWN BY THE
COLT .45s

THE NEW NATIONAL LEAGUE EXPANSION FRANCHISE WAS, like many other things in the city of Houston, the brainchild of Judge Roy Hofheinz. In all my years in baseball, the Judge is the only man I met who might have been close to Mr. Rickey's intellectual equal.

Hofheinz graduated from law school at age 20, entered the bar a year later, was elected a judge in Harris County at 26 and mayor of Houston not long after his 30th birthday. Besides the Houston baseball team itself, the Judge's most notorious contribution to the game is the Houston Astrodome, now surpassed in size and architectural majesty by other domed parks but always to be listed in history books as the first.

Roy Hofheinz made his fortune through canny land acquisitions financed by partner Bob Smith. Together they purchased large plots of land just outside Houston city limits; then the Judge, as mayor, saw that this property was annexed into the city, shooting these property values sky-high.

In short, where the Hofheinz/Smith team was concerned, cash flow in 1961 wasn't going to be a problem. The Judge had wanted to bring major league baseball to Texas, long a state understood to be populated with football fans. Hofheinz' plan was to elevate baseball above a sport, to turn the game into "family entertainment." He was often quoted as saying he would give Houston a team and stadium where "mothers and grandmothers" would buy tickets for the spectacle even if they didn't understand the first thing about pitchouts or rundowns.

Where the Judge came up short of Mr. Rickey was in baseball background. He wasn't schooled in the sport and knew it. Accordingly, when he got an expansion franchise for Houston he hired Gabe Paul as its first general manager. The team would be called the Colt .45s, honoring the state's Western tradition. Just a few years later when the space race consumed the public interest, Hofheinz cooly renamed his team the Astros with nary an apology for any cowboys the name change might offend.

But team names and where the club played would be Hofheinz's baliwick. Gabe Paul was to run the baseball side of things for the Houston Sports Authority, as the Judge named the operation.

When Gabe came in, the soon-to-be-major-league Houston club was a Triple-A squad in the American Association managed by Harry Craft. Harry was already the starting center fielder on a great Cincinnati Reds team when I broke into the majors with the Phillies; later he had an unsuccessful try at managing the Kansas City A's. Harry's club played its games in Houston's old Busch Stadium. When Houston's National League squad opened in 1962, the Judge planned for them to play in a hastily rigged field adjacent to the site of the Astrodome, which would take several years to construct. Even if Colt .45 fans couldn't enjoy a magnificent ballpark right away, the Judge reasoned, they at least could be treated to the sight of the world's first domed stadium under construction.

The first people hired by Gabe included Tal Smith as an administrative assistant, Bill Giles in the same capacity, Paul Florence as supervisor of scouting, Charlie Morris as road secretary, and myself as farm director. My job primarily was to scout major league and Triple-A players who might be made available in the expansion draft and make recommendations to Gabe. My salary was $17,500.

I jumped right in. For the first two months on the job I sat in a Houston Sports Authority office answering letters and calls from prospective job seekers. It was my task to hire the scouts; I'm proud to say I immediately got Red Murff on board. Red became a baseball legend; he personally has scouted and signed about 40 major leaguers, his most famous signing being Nolan Ryan when Red scouted for the Mets. But Red did one hell of a job for the Colt .45s; among others he got us catcher Jerry Grote. If Houston had hung on to Grote they wouldn't have had to worry about a catcher for 10 years or more. Eventual front office laxity let Grote slip away to the Mets, where he was a mainstay and occasional All-Star long after his Houston catching successors were back on the farm or wherever else they might have come from.

All of us in the Colt .45s front office worked in the same two-story building as the Judge. He was simply a working machine. No matter how early you arrived during the day, his car was already in its office parking slot. No matter how late you left work, the Judge was still in his office toiling away.

I liked the idea of working for Gabe Paul. Our few months together certainly gave me the idea we made a great team, one that might soon evolve from general manager - farm director to general manager - manager. Unfortunately, this potentially rosy future was torpedoed by some potholes and a crumbling press box.

Gabe's home was and is in Tampa, Florida. Though he'd bought a home in Houston, he still made frequent trips to Tampa during 1961. He returned from one such trip to find that Spec Richardson, general manager of the American Association Houston franchise, had taken it upon himself to spend a few thousand dollars filling pot holes in the Busch Stadium parking lot and dressing up the ballpark's dilapidated press box. As general manager of the major league franchise, Gabe believed any such expenditures should not have been made without his approval. He roared around the Houston Sports Authority offices upon his return asking who had given Richardson permission to make the Busch Stadium improvements. Upon learning Judge Hofheinz had given the okay, Gabe was faced with the problem of whether to let the matter go or insist on some sort of showdown with his boss.

What happened next is vivid in my memory. The night before he discussed the situation with the Judge, Gabe asked me to have dinner with him. We went to a Mexican restaurant. As soon as we were seated Gabe asked, "Bobby, do you know what the duties of a general manager are?" I said, "I have an idea," but Gabe wanted to do the talking. For the next fifteen minutes he related a general manager's job requirements as he saw them, including authorization of any ballpark expenditures. It was obvious Gabe was rehearsing for his meeting with the Judge.

I thought Gabe made some good points, but the Judge obviously didn't. At one point, Gabe told the Judge that "to spend that money unnecessarily will make people wonder about me and my credibility. What Richardson did makes me look foolish. I can't be identified with this because of my reputation." To which the Judge said, "You think you have a reputation? What do you think I have?" And that was the beginning of the end for Gabe in Houston.

The Judge didn't fire Gabe, but I'm sure he made it obvious even a town as big as Houston wasn't big enough for both of them. Within weeks Gabe resigned to join the front office of the Cleveland Indians.

Perhaps there was a spark of hope in my heart the Judge might turn to a former big league player and manager as his second general manager. No successor was immediately named for Gabe. A few weeks later, though, I was making a scouting swing through American League parks and had a chance to chat with Paul Richards, the manager of the Baltimore Orioles. Richards told me, "Bobby, if Judge Hofheinz gives me what I want, I'll be the next boss in Houston." Whatever it was Richards wanted, he evidently got, because the Judge named him general manager. From there on in, I answered to Richards; Judge Hofheinz kept himself completely removed from the baseball end of things.

Of the half-dozen of us hired by Gabe Paul, I can only speak for myself when I say I didn't hear from him after he left, not even a note or call to say, "I'm sorry I got you away from your other job." I don't have anything against Gabe; I still consider him a friend. But when you become a general manager and hire people away from other good, secure jobs you might remember your responsibility to them. Gabe could have let Spec's spending go, maybe by just asking him not to do anything like that again without checking with Gabe first.

So now I worked for Paul Richards. I felt I knew Paul very well. When I was managing in Fort Worth, Paul managed Buffalo in the

International League. Even then he had a fine reputation as a solid baseball man—unafraid, innovative and especially good at handling pitchers. It had always been clear very few people, if any, could claim to be close to Paul, but we certainly seemed to have gotten along. He had a way of getting influence over his higher-ups; even with Buffalo he had enough suction with the team owners to get them to hold spring training in Waxahachie, Texas, Paul's home town. The Fort Worth Cats would play a home-and-home exhibition series with Buffalo each spring, one game at La Grave Field and the other in Waxahachie.

Paul would always be thinking one step ahead of the opposing manager. In one key game while he managed Buffalo, Paul had the opposing pitcher walked with two out so Sam Jethroe, the fastest player in the league, would have to hit with the baserunning disadvantage of having the much slower pitcher on base ahead of him. Paul also insisted on proper execution of fundamentals—it was nothing for him to have the ballpark lights turned on for an hour after a night game for his hitters to take extra batting practice.

While his players may have been put off by Richards's aloof personality, they respected him. Dick Williams, who played for Paul in Baltimore, said for two years Paul never so much as said "Good morning," to him. Once, when they were sitting side-by-side on the Oriole bench, Richards looked past Dick and said to coach Jimmy Adair, "Have Dick Williams pinch-hit."

For the balance of 1961, I worked under Richards in the Houston front office. I travelled the country evaluating players. For the expansion draft, each of the existing clubs would protect 15 players from their 25-man rosters, meaning 10 players from each National League team would be available to us and the New York Mets. When a player was selected from an existing team's roster, that team could then protect three more players, with another rule that no team could lose more than three players total to the expansion draft.

So those of us in Houston would play the same game over and over, one pretending to choose for Houston and the other for New York. "I'll take Al Spangler, outfielder, Milwaukee," the "Houston" representative might say. "I choose Roman Mejias, Pittsburgh," the

"Mets" would reply. In this way we readied a list of the players we wanted in the order we hoped to select them.

Before the draft, we were also allowed to sign any free agents we wanted—that is, players who weren't already under contract to any existing team. The best of that bunch was Rusty Staub, a highly—touted high school player from New Orleans. Rusty commanded a sizeable bonus, and we also had to sign his brother to a contract knowing the brother didn't have the potential to be a good minor league player, let alone a major league prospect. But Rusty Staub was worth just about any price—he was intended to be the crown jewel around which we eventually built a pennant contender in Houston.

All through that year, I wondered what my eventual role would be with the Colt .45s. Certainly I wanted to be manager, but it became clear over the weeks and months that Paul Richards did not consider me a confidante. Finally he scheduled a press conference. Just before the press arrived, Richards pulled me aside and said, "Bobby, I'm going to name Harry Craft manager of the Colt .45 team. I can make you a coach, or if you have a preference to remain in the front office I can handle that." I said I thought I'd rather coach, and it hurt. I had already been a coach with a much better team and organization; it was a comedown to be on the coaching staff of an expansion club. But I had to make the best of a bad situation. Perhaps I spared an unkind thought or two for Gabe Paul.

In the winter of 1961 we had a winter camp in Arizona for the free agents we'd signed, and Craft named the rest of his coaching staff. It was obvious who really was deciding who would be hired—Lum Harris, Jimmy Adair, Clint Courtney, Jim Busby, and Cot Deal were all old cronies of Richards's, either in Baltimore or Chicago, where he'd earlier managed the White Sox. I was odd man out. I guessed then, and was officially notified later in spring training, that I'd be assigned the lowest rung on the ladder—bullpen coach.

The day of the expansion draft provided some diversion. It was an exciting day. The Houston brain trust, in which I was still included, met with members of the commissioner's office and New York Met representatives at a New York hotel. We flipped a coin and began to choose players, with each club having three minutes to make its selection. After all the work we'd put into scouting, there was no need to consult lists to see whom we wanted. The first roster of the Houston Colt .45s was pretty much what we'd hoped—Spangler, Mejias, knuckleballer Ken Johnson from the Reds, Joe Amalfitano from the Giants. I felt I had influenced the choice of three fine young Dodger players—Bob Aspromonte, Norm Larker, and Bob Lillis. Veteran pitchers Turk Farrell and Don McMahon lent some experience to an otherwise young staff. It was as good a club as we could have hoped to draft.

We were helped along by the Mets' apparent decision to draft older players familiar to New York fans—old Brooklyn Dodgers Gil Hodges, Charley Neal, and Roger Craig, as well as grizzled veterans like Frank Thomas and Richie Ashburn. While Houston gained an initial on-field advantage, the Mets swept us away at the box office. Their 1962 squad became the lovable, incompetent Mets whose bumblings entertained the team's fans for a few years until an insurgence of fine young pitchers—Tom Seaver, Jerry Koosman, Nolan Ryan—led the club to an upset World Series win over Baltimore in 1969. As for Houston, well, the team eventually reached a plateau of drab achievement. To date there have been a couple of division titles won for the fans in the Astrodome, but not a World Series appearance.

The first Houston Colt .45 spring training was held in Apache Junction, Arizona. It was a desolate, forbidding spot miles away from any major city. The motel in which the team was housed was within walking distance of the ballpark, but it was a dangerous walk. Clint Courtney killed an average of three rattlesnakes a week on his way to and from the games there. What I recall of the facilities is that they were barely adequate, if that. I hated the whole experience.

I should be honest at this point and say I remember very little about the 1962 season with the Colt .45s. It was an awkward time for me, a bad time. I tried to put it out of my mind as quickly as possible, and apparently I succeeded. I remember bits and pieces of things, nothing more.

I had been accustomed to spring trainings where everything was planned in advance and no moments were wasted. With the Colt

.45s, it was the opposite. Nobody knew what he would be doing until the last minute. I personally never was sure if I was supposed to stay with the "B" squad in Apache Junction or go with the "A" team to play the Cubs in Mesa. Harry Craft would be given all his instructions by Paul Richards on the spot, and then get word to the rest of us as best he could.

So far as I know, there was just one meeting of the full coaching staff all during camp. It came the day before we were to conclude spring training. Paul Richards came into the clubhouse and told Craft, "Be sure all your staff have paper and pencils." Then Richards told us we had 17 pitchers in camp; we were each to write down the names of 11 we thought should make the major league roster. Whether Richards gave a damn about our opinions, I can't say.

That whole spring training was a sloppy operation, run by one man's ego. Paul Richards had his own agenda, and to hell with what anyone else was trying to get done. Why, during daily drills where we'd be practicing rundowns or cutoffs and relays, he'd walk out on the field and announce, "I want Jim Umbricht and Jim Campbell," names of players he wanted to excuse from workouts so they could join him to play golf. Usually he wanted the same players, ones who needed to practice baseball fundamentals instead of putting. And the team manager never, ever, stood up to him. With all due respect to Harry Craft, whom I liked then and consider a friend to this day, he was not allowed to make his own decisions. He simply did what Paul Richards told him to do. Hell, it was Paul Richards who told me I'd be bullpen coach, Paul Richards who named protégé Lum Harris third base coach, and old buddy Jimmy Adair first base coach. This is no knock against Lum or Jimmy, but I never thought Harry Craft was given the option of deciding which coaches he wanted to do what.

It was Paul Richards who was running the club. I thought it was obvious he had eventual plans to get rid of Harry Craft and make Lum Harris manager—it did happen after about three seasons. I never figured in Richards's scheming. A lot of the time I wasn't even in the bullpen; he'd call me in and tell me to go off somewhere to help scout some free agent player of consequence. Tom Paciorek was one of them, I recall. I spent very little time working with the

Colt .45 players—I got so bored I started writing a baseball column, "Bragan Bunts," for the *Houston Chronicle.*

I seethed. I sulked. Mostly, I waited. I knew some other opportunity would come. It had to. For me Houston was a dead end, as long as Paul Richards was around. At least when I travelled with the club I was going to different National League cities, seeing old friends with other teams. I made it known I was available. One thing I didn't do was ask for a position with the Dodgers; I just had too much pride.

Houston was the one big mistake of my baseball career. I made a bad choice, though Gabe Paul and Buzzie Bavasi had a lot to do with it. I guess I wasn't the easiest person to live with during 1962, but thank God Gwenn was an unshakable Bobby Bragan fan. She kept telling me everything was going to be all right. And, even at its worst, 1962 and the Houston Colt .45s meant I was still part of major league baseball.

Funny—as I write this I keep thinking of little quirky things. How Paul Richards, for instance, collected all those little airline liquor bottles—miniatures—he could. Once I met with him at his home in Waxahachie and saw he had cases and cases of them. We took a flight once to the major league winter meetings in Hawaii. During the flight Paul said, "Bobby, I know you don't drink. Get some bottles for me." I put four or five of those little bottles of scotch and bourbon in my suit pocket. As soon as we arrived at our hotel Richards hurried to my room to collect his bounty. No doubt there were other rooms he visited for the same purpose.

And then there was that 1961 Arizona winter camp for prospects and free agents. We had a daily mandatory breakfast at 6 A.M. I'd get up at 5 A.M., go down the sidewalk to the side of the hotel where Cot Deal was sleeping and yell, "COT DEAL!!!" as loud as I could. One morning the woman who managed the complex stuck her head out her window and screeched, "You crazy YAY-hoo, I'll be glad when you're gone!" It was a bright spot, about the only fun I had in that camp.

Then there were those asinine Western outfits. The Judge was determined his team would reflect Texas, and each of us was given $600 to purchase identical outfits of a blue Western-cut suit, blue-

and-white striped cowboy shirt, blue 10-gallon hat, and boots. The order from on high was that we'd be 100 percent represented in these outfits when we travelled from National League city to city. But it never happened. Norm Larker didn't like to wear hats. Turk Farrell just didn't like the idea. Harry Craft threatened and wheedled, but invariably two or three guys would refuse to play dress-up on every road trip.

A few days before the 1962 season was over, I got a message to go to see Paul Richards. Instead of sending me on a scouting assignment, he told me to fly to Chicago's O'Hare Airport and meet John McHale, the general manager of the Milwaukee Braves. "He wants to see you about managing his team," Richards told me.

It wasn't a complete surprise. When the Colt .45s had made our last stop in Milwaukee, Braves' manager Birdie Tebbetts called me aside and whispered, "John McHale's going to be talking to you." Birdie didn't say anything else, but word was already spreading he planned to leave the Braves at the end of the season and take over the Indians for Gabe Paul. So the hoped-for word from Milwaukee had been a bright beacon at the end of a very dark tunnel.

I met McHale at a hotel in the airport. He got right to the point. "Bobby, I want you to be my manager at Milwaukee," he said. "You come highly recommended. (He didn't say by whom, and I didn't ask.) We'll pay you $35, 000."

I didn't waste any time accepting.

B	E	T	W	E	E	N
I	N	N	I	N	G	S

GABE PAUL: I knew Bobby Bragan as a player and as a manager. When I went in to form the Houston organization I went after Bobby as farm director. A farm director has a lot of responsibility—he has to hire scouts and be the ultimate judge of player talent. Bobby knew a lot of people in baseball, which was a big advantage for an expansion team. He could call friends with any major league club and get very candid opinions of players there.

I hated to go from Houston when I did, but the circumstances after I got there were different from what I was led to believe they would be when I was hired. I would like to say I never had problems with Judge Hofheinz, really. These things happen in any baseball organization or any organization, period. I have no hard feelings.

I felt Bobby Bragan would be an asset—and be perceived as an asset—to the organization whether I was part of the Colt .45s or not. I have no idea what might have occurred after I left, and I really can't speculate. But I will say no matter what ever happened to him, Bobby never lost his enthusiasm. This was impressive and unusual.

JERRY GROTE: Red Murff signed me for the Colt .45s. I was just a kid. I went to one of their camps and Lum Harris was pitching batting practice. Paul Richards and Bobby Bragan were watching. Richards told me to get in and catch, told the batter to swing through the pitch and let me throw down to second. Well, Harris had that protective screen in front of him batting practice pitchers use. I said they had to take down the screen. Richards said to shut up and just throw the damn ball. I cut loose and hit the screen. Red Murff, who was there, said to try again. I guess my throw went one inch above the screen and nearly tore the guy covering second in half. Lum Harris said to take down the screen. On the next throw, the second baseman flinched, because my throw went maybe one-half foot over the top of the mound. He thought it would short-hop but it hit his glove dead on. I knew they should have moved the screen right away, but around there if something wasn't Paul Richard's idea, forget it.

Red Murff was the best scout ever. Some guys signed a whole bunch of players but only after other guys did the basic scouting. Red probably saw me play 25-30 times. I knew him from my sophomore year in high school. He could smell talent. I think the best scouts should be in the Hall of Fame—if there's room for broadcasters there, there should be scouts, too, and Red ought to be the first.

Red and Bragan were the class of the Houston organization at that time. I think most kids, myself included, were scared or in awe of Bobby. He had that gruff voice, and on the field he was very hotheaded. Billy Martin probably took lessons from him—Bragan was that wild sometimes. But of all of them, all the baseball people around, he knew as much or more than any of 'em.

HARRY CRAFT: Bobby and I were together as players. I went up to Cincinnati in '37 and I think he must have come up the same year or a year later. Oh, yes, he was a fine man, very capable, just a good man to have around. I was glad to name him to my coaching staff at Houston.

BOB ASPROMONTE: I was 19, a kid with the Dodgers, when Bobby took me under his wing. He taught me to be smart, to keep track of the things on the field I needed to be aware of. He made learning baseball enjoyable.

In that first spring training for the Colts, we were in no man's land, absolutely by ourselves in a desert town. It was 20 miles to

Mesa, 80 miles to Tucson. I think the whole point was to make the players understand we were going to be together all season so we might as well get to know each other right away. We all stayed at the Superstition Ho Hotel. At night Bobby would tell stories and keep us all entertained.

At that time the team management, the whole organization was sort of in disarray. There was no before, so to speak, so everything had to be worked out for the first time. I think this was to be expected for an expansion team. We won the Cactus League that first spring training. We won a whole lot of games in Arizona so something must have been done right. Hey, after we won the Cactus League Judge Hofheinz had World Series tickets printed as souvenirs for each of the players and coaches. We kept those tickets in our locker room. It was a classy gesture.

CRAFT: After that first year, 1962, I would have liked to have kept Bobby. But Paul said we were not going to renew him. I don't know why. As far as I was concerned Bobby had done a good job for me. Paul said, "We'll write Bobby a letter this winter and tell him we won't be having him back." I said, "I'll talk to him. It's right to tell the man to his face." That's just the way I am. I talked to Bobby on a Friday before we left on a last road trip after a Sunday game. I told him, "We're letting you go. Paul says he's not going to renew your contract. I guess it's up to me to tell you. You and Buzzie Bavasi are buddies; come on this last road trip with us to Los Angeles and San Francisco. You can feel out those clubs for a job, and something might come up." He took it well, Bobby's a real gentleman.

Well, it shows how things can happen. He went with Milwaukee as their manager, got that job with a day or two left in the '62 season and it was great. I was happy for him. I just thought the world of Bobby. We still exchange Christmas cards. Sometimes things just don't work out for particular people and teams. That it didn't work is nothing against Bobby or the Houston club.

ASPROMONTE: It was obvious there were differences between Bobby and Paul Richards. Bobby didn't feel he had enough input. He wasn't a longtime Richards' man; Richards had an entourage he brought with him. Bobby was the outsider.

Harry Craft would never say anything bad about anybody. A fine man, Harry. Now, I have fond memories of Paul Richards. I thought he was a most astute baseball man. He upset a lot of people, but he could spot talent and get the best. Still, Richards had an aloof way about him. He was very much reserved, while well, Bobby was fun, good to be around. The team warmed to him, made it obvious he was popular. Paul was more conservative. I swear the man couldn't smile. It was just a case of opposites getting in each other's way, and Paul was the general manager and Bobby was the coach, so Bobby had to go.

Did Bobby tell you about those Western outfits? God, we were supposed to wear those when we travelled, at least on planes and from the airport to the hotel. People would see us and think the rodeo was in town. The hats got old real fast. A lot of us wouldn't wear them. Harry nailed us with fines. He asked nicely if we'd please wear the Western stuff. But it was hit or miss. I guess Farrell never did wear his at all.

CRAFT: Hofheinz gave us $600 apiece for nice Western clothes and asked that all of us wear them on road trips. I said it was fine with me, but I needed to have a club meeting to see if everyone would do it, because it had to be everyone or not at all. The players were happy about it. Even the team trainer got the Western clothes. That's the way it worked. It made for nice team unity to dress alike that way.

DICK WILLIAMS: I've got all the respect in the world for Paul Richards, but he hurt himself with the way he treated Bobby Bragan. Bobby could have done great things with an expansion club. I know Bobby tries to say nice things about everybody, but I doubt he'll ever be able to bring himself to find any good in Paul Richards.

MILWAUKEE

WHEN I WAS HIRED AS MANAGER, the Milwaukee Braves were owned by a 12-member partnership based in Chicago. The group included the owner of the Sara Lee Company, a highly placed executive with Johnson & Johnson, the owner of a pharmaceutical company, and other financially comfortable executive-types. John McHale was the managing partner, in much the same position George W. Bush is today with the Texas Rangers.

I knew quite a bit about the Milwaukee players. Having spent the 1962 season with the Colt .45s, I knew the Braves' roster was one of well-known players, many with All-Star credentials. But I also knew many of those players were on the downside of their careers; in fact, before I took over the team some of the longtime Braves like center fielder Bill Bruton and shortstop Johnny Logan were being let go. In Bruton's case, it happened a few seasons too early. He joined the Detroit Tigers and had another good year or two before he finally slowed down.

From 1962 and earlier, my 1956-57 stint with the Pirates, I considered the Milwaukee baseball fans to be dedicated but naive. The city's love affair with its baseball team had been one of the sport's biggest stories of the 1950s. Major league-starved Milwaukee took the Braves to its collective heart immediately, and with good reason.

The franchise moved to Milwaukee from Boston after the 1952 season. The Boston Braves had been a sad sack bunch, closing out their final year in Massachusetts with a sorry 64-89 record. There were no established stars on that team; a young third baseman named Eddie Mathews did sock 25 homers in '52, and the team's pitching ace, lefty Warren Spahn, struggled to a 14-19 mark.

But the Milwaukee Braves of 1953 were the most improved team in baseball, rising all the way to an incredible 92-62 mark and a second place finish under the leadership of manager Charlie Grimm. Mathews led the National League with 47 homers. Spahn won 23 games. Milwaukee fans went nuts over the club; there was really nothing in town a Braves player could buy for himself. Every man on the roster, from the cleanup hitter to the bullpen coach, got free automobiles from Seelig Ford or Wally Ranke Chrysler. Dairy products were provided; the players just had to tell what they wanted and how much of each item. Dry cleaners clamored for the honor of doing their laundry. The team loved the city, the city loved the team. Baseball heaven. It doesn't happen very often. Charlie Grimm's club kept the Milwaukee fans happy for the next couple of seasons with third- and second-place finishes. A young second-baseman-turned-outfielder named Hank Aaron arrived in 1954, batting .280 and hitting 13 home runs as a rookie. Right-hander Lew Burdette emerged to complement Spahn in the National League's best one-two, left-right starting tandem. By 1956 my old pal Fred Haney took over a young, powerful club obviously on the brink of accomplishing great things, and Fred helped the players deliver. The 1957 Braves won Milwaukee's first National League pennant, then beat the Yankees in a dramatic seven-game World Series to become world champions. In 1958 Milwaukee repeated as NL kingpins, but lost their world championship to New York in another seven-game Series. In 1959 the Braves and Dodgers tied for the National League pennant, and the Dodgers won a playoff. For that three-season stretch, the Milwaukee Braves were as good a team as any in the major leagues. Only the Yankees and Dodgers could offer a comparable number of charismatic, big-name stars.

But it's often the most passionate love affairs which cool quickest and turn nastiest. Haney left the team after the '59 season. He ended up heading the new Los Angeles Angels expansion team that joined the American League in 1961. Charlie Dressen took over the Braves for a season and a half. In 1960 Charlie's record was respectable; the Braves finished second and seemed poised to continue dominance of the National League. But 1961 found the team slipping ever so slightly; Birdie Tebbetts replaced Dressen halfway through the season and Milwaukee slid to fourth place.

Milwaukee fans saw the trend continuing, and they didn't like it. Having enjoyed a contending club from the start, they found even short-term mediocrity unacceptable. In 1952 they cheered every Brave fly ball, certain their heroes could do no wrong. By 1962, when the Braves finished fifth in the National League despite a reasonably good 86-76 mark, County Stadium patrons booed more than they cheered.

Bottom line: When I arrived in Milwaukee for the 1963 season I knew there would be no freebies for me.

But I had other things on my mind, and most of my thoughts were pleasant. I truly liked and respected my new boss, John McHale. He was a Notre Dame graduate, father of six children, a devout Catholic who tended to find the good in people rather than concentrate on their faults. When I was hired, McHale indicated to me that incumbent pitching coach Whitlow Wyatt and bullpen coach Ken Silvestri were already signed to multiyear contracts, as was third base coach JoJo White. I hired Dixie Walker as my hitting coach and felt I had a talented staff.

JoJo White was a funloving character, though not overly bright. He'd had a fine major league career as an outfielder with the Tigers and A's, but for the life of him this man could not remember any of our team's signs. JoJo had to write them on the palm of his hand with a ballpoint pen. His vocabulary was limited, too. One night, John McHale invited the Braves coaching staff to a party following the game. When I finished dressing I walked out to tell my coaches I was ready to leave when they were. JoJo, still in uniform, said, "Go ahead, I've still got to shower and shave." Thinking to hurry him up a bit, I asked, "Do you want to use my Norelco?" "No," JoJo replied, "I'll come in my own car."

I loved the idea of managing the Braves, of getting a team for the first time that had a tradition of winning more than losing. I was going to manage Aaron, Mathews, Spahn, and Burdette. They'd need little instruction from me; I could write their names on my lineup card and let them take care of business from there. The Milwaukee supporting cast was superb, too, better than many of the best players I'd had in Pittsburgh and Cleveland. Del Crandall was the regular starting catcher on National League All-Star teams. Frank Bolling was a wise old pro at second base, and shortstop Roy McMillan was the best fielder at that position I ever saw. At shortstop, Roy was every bit as skilled with the glove as Brooks Robinson was at third base.

I used spring training at West Palm Beach to look over young players and let the veterans work their own way into shape. Almost immediately we let first baseman Joe Adcock go to the Cleveland Indians, and signed a young free agent catcher named Joe Torre. Joe, who went on to a fine career with the Braves and Cardinals, winning the Most Valuable Player award one year in St. Louis, was a real sight in 1963, the fattest kid I'd ever seen in uniform. He weighed 250 pounds, at least, maybe more. All the veterans got on him about his weight, Spahn in particular. Sometimes Joe was practically driven to tears, but when he got mad he took it out with his bat on opposing pitchers. The more I saw of Joe Torre, the more convinced I became Del Crandall wouldn't hold his starting job much longer.

As usual, I tried to run spring training the Dodger way. Each day's workout schedule was posted the night before. Fundamentals were stressed. The Braves' spring training facility had one full diamond and an additional half-field for infield work, so it was tough to get the full squad all working at once.

During spring training I got to know the most unique travelling secretary in baseball history. Donald Davidson was a midget, little but loud. He gloried in his short stature. Bud Seelig furnished Davidson with a flashy car outfitted with special pedal extensions. Donald careened around like a race car driver, often having fender-benders. When that would happen he'd zoom over to Seelig's dealership, casually order repair department personnel to fix the damage, and just as casually tell them to rig the pedal extensions on a loaner car so Davidson wouldn't have to be without transportation while waiting for the repairs to be made.

As travelling secretary, it was Davidson's primary task to have hotel accomodations arranged in advance of the team's arrival in each city. When players didn't like their rooms for some reason—maybe they hadn't been cleaned—they'd raise hell with Davidson and he'd rush to rectify the situation. Usually he'd ask the player involved to pick him up and place him on the top of the registration desk so he could look down at the hapless clerk he was berating.

It was a crueler time for appearance-related practical jokes. Spahn and Burdette often made Davidson's life miserable. Their favorite stunt while the team was on road trips during spring training was to get to the ballpark early and tell the guard at the players' entrance a crazed midget was following the team, and would the guard please have the little fellow detained if he showed up? Of course, Davidson would arrive with the rest of the team and be held in custody, usually red-faced and screaming, while the players filed into the clubhouse and tried hard not to laugh so much they gave the joke away.

During my spring trainings with the Braves, an outfielder named Lee Maye gave me my final lessons in race relations. Maye was a very proud black man who did a good job as Milwaukee's center fielder. The team had added catcher-first baseman Gene Oliver from the Cardinals, and Oliver was one of those guys who just said whatever came into his head. One day I'd been hitting fungoes to the outfielders during an especially hot afternoon,, and afterwards Maye came back into the clubhouse streaming with perspiration. Oliver took one look and hollered, "You're sweating like a Ubangi." Immediately Maye, wet uniform and all, made his way back onto the field to find me. "Bobby," he said, "You're going to have to insist Gene Oliver apologize to me." Oliver, not having meant any harm, did so right away.

Another time I was hitting outfield fungoes again, with Lew Burdette shagging their return throws for me. I recall Lew telling me, "This hasn't happened with the Braves before," meaning the previous managers had relegated the chore to one of their coaches.

Me, I enjoyed it. Anyway, when you hit fungoes, trying to get the flies as close to the outfield fence as possible, inevitably you hit a few too hard and they go out of the park. To retrieve such balls, I'd asked two young blacks to stand on the other side of the fence. I hit two or three over, and neither of the shaggers moved. I hollered, "Throw those balls back in." One of the kids responded, "Which one of us are you talking to?" I yelled back, "The darker one." As soon as I said that, Lee Maye left the outfield and began walking in toward me. Even before he moved, I knew I was wrong. Lee didn't run in, but he walked up purposefully. When he got to where I was standing, he remarked, "Bobby, you shouldn't have said what you did." I responded, "Lee, you're correct. It was wrong and I apologize." It didn't happen again. I made certain of that.

Maye was a tall, pleasant-featured man, but he had very large, protruding front teeth. Because of them, Eddie Mathews gave Maye the nickname of "Shark." Maye waited to get even, and one day late in spring training a ground ball got smashed towards third base and turned Eddie Mathews inside out, with Eddie really just trying to get out of the way of the ball without getting hurt. At the end of the inning, Maye loudly told Mathews, "You looked like a matador trying to field that grounder."

When I visit today with baseball fans, most of them want to know about some of the Dodgers—Mr. Rickey, Leo, Jackie, Maury Wills — or Spahn, Mathews and Aaron, the Braves' Hall of Famers.

My impression of Warren Spahn is that he might have been the best left-handed pitcher who ever lived, certainly from the standpoint of longevity as a dominating hurler. Spahn was a complete ballplayer. He fielded his position well, could hold runners on base as well as anyone, could lay down a sacrifice bunt, and, when needed, deliver the winning hit himself. Spahn was committed to his own excellence—he'd work hard and had high personal expectations. On days when he pitched, you simply had to stay away from the man. He was lost in total concentration; any comment to him would go unheard.

But I soon learned that Spahn might just as well have stayed away from the team on days he wasn't scheduled to be on the mound. Warren Spahn's single interest was Warren Spahn. He wasn't concerned about anyone else. During spring training in 1963 we had Wayne Blasingame, Bob Hendley and Denver Lemaster, three young left-handers who were trying to make our pitching staff. Each was having some problems with his move to first base while trying to hold runners close to the bag. Because of the limited field space, usually I divided the team up for two different workouts. Spahn had had his workout earlier; somehow I envisioned Spahn spending some time with the young pitchers, tutoring them on the finer points of his own excellent pickoff move. Well, he didn't want to. That was for the coaches to do. Spahn only consented to share some tips when I took the workout schedule for the coaches and wrote his name in to work with Lemaster, Hendley, and Blasingame.

Lots of stories have been written about Spahn and Burdette being inseparable pals. Perhaps they were, but to me their personalities couldn't have been more different. Burdette was a fun-lover; I seldom heard Spahn laugh. Where Spahn was physically gifted, Burdette had to resort to cunning; that, and a spitball. Where spitballs were concerned, Lew had one of the best.

Lew Burdette was a team player. I loved him dearly—still do. He'd work with younger players without being asked. During games when he didn't pitch he sat on the bench and pulled for his teammates, and offered suggestions to whichever of our pitchers was on the mound. Lew still recalls I gave him the honor of pitching Opening Day in 1963, choosing him over Spahn. It was the only time this happened during their years together at the top of the Milwaukee pitching staff. I'd like to think I let Lew pitch the first game because he'd been so outstanding during spring training, but the truth is I probably felt he deserved the honor over Spahn because of their difference in attitude.

I'm sure I would have been a better manager if I hadn't been influenced by a ballplayer's personality. Players' attitudes and off-the-field habits sometimes affected my treatment of them. Actually, performance on the field should dictate the manager's decisions.

Even into the early 1960s, drugs weren't a factor in major league baseball. Cocaine, marijuana, whatever—you never even thought about drugs being a problem for any player. In the Braves' locker room, like every other major league locker room I'd been in, there was a big jar of what we called "greenies"—amphetamines, they're better known as today. Some players would take them every once in awhile. I never did. I assumed they were relaxants. Overall, drugs were absolutely of no concern to me as a manager.

Alcohol was. On every team there would always be one or two guys who drank a lot—my old teammates Chuck Klein and Lloyd Waner are good examples. It wasn't considered bad form to drink the night away, so long as you could come to the park the next day able to play. We've learned a lot in the years since about alcohol abuse, but when I managed the Braves I had the same rule other managers had—players couldn't drink at the bars of the hotels where the team stayed on road trips because that's where the coaching staff gathered after games to hoist a few. The players had to congregate and do their drinking somewhere else.

Personally, I had absolutely no interest in drinking. I enjoyed the conviviality of talking baseball and telling stories with my coaching staff in hotel lobbies, dining rooms, or any other convenient spot. I didn't like bars—ever. And I certainly didn't like ballplayers who spent the hours after games slugging down drinks in semidark clubs. My opinion was reinforced when one of my players on the Braves—one of the best third basemen ever, a Hall of Famer - continually made an ass out of himself because of drinking too much.

Until I managed the Braves I wouldn't say I had any player with a drinking problem on one of my teams.

But in my opinion, Eddie Mathews was an alcoholic. He was also one of the very finest third basemen in baseball history, and a player with a picture-perfect swing. Today, maybe, a manager and/or team ownership would talk to someone like Mathews and counsel him to get into a clinic and get off the booze. But in 1963, the philosophy was, "if he plays well, let him alone."

One of my team rules was no drinking by players on plane trips. The flight attendants knew in advance they weren't to serve our players any alcohol. On every flight during my tenure with the Braves, Eddie Mathews found a way to get himself some drinks. He simply wasn't able to get through a few waking hours without it.

Curfew meant nothing to Mathews. He'd have his first drinks and set out to party the rest of the night. After my first season with the Braves I named him team captain, hoping that might convince him to set a good example for his younger teammates. It didn't work. A few months later at the Chase Hotel in St. Louis I got a call from the night manager at 2:30 A.M. He said, "One of your players is on the sixth floor, pounding on the stewardesses' doors." I had to go down and convince my captain it was time for him to let other people get some sleep, and to go to bed himself.

Fining Mathews didn't help. I had a team rule that everybody in the starting lineup had to take fielding practice before games. Mathews missed practice before a game in Forbes Field. I fined him $50 and scheduled a team workout on the next day, which was supposed to be a day off. Mathews showed up on time for the workout. He came over to my locker, pulled out his wallet, and said, very sarcastically, "Here's your fifty—in cash." He smirked and made his way to the field.

I'm sorry to say I never spoke directly to Eddie Mathews about his drinking. At times he was so nice. He was a Mason, same as I. Even when he stayed out late, he played hard and very well. I do believe it's true that as great as Eddie Mathews was, he'd have been even greater if he'd taken better care of himself. God knows what kind of hitting records he could have set with that beautiful, beautiful swing. And Eddie had a keen sense of humor. After we traded Warren Spahn to the Mets, Spahnie came back to County Stadium to pitch against us. Mathews came up with the bases loaded and clobbered a grand slam home run off his former teammate. I can still see Eddie rounding the bases, taking his seat in the dugout, and saying simply, "My cup runneth over."

So far as I know, Eddie never changed. Because he's a member of the Hall of Fame he's always invited to participate in Oldtimers' games. Usually, these games are held in conjunction with baseball card shows, so the former players can get paid to play in the game and then earn additional money signing autographs for card collectors. I arrange the Oldtimers' games for the Texas Rangers, and a few years back I invited Eddie to participate. At the card show held the day after the game, a man with a 13-year-old boy in tow came over to me. "Eddie Mathews was my idol when I was growing up," he said, "but now it sickens me to have him blowing his whiskey breath into my son's face." Mathews hasn't been invited back to a Texas Rangers Oldtimers' game since, joining a small, select company: Willie Mays, who was a no-show once at game time, Willie Davis, who stayed around an extra two days and ran his room service bill sky-high, and Bob Feller, who makes too many demands.

To this day, I don't think major league baseball does enough to educate players on the dangers of drinking. Drinking's still acceptable by baseball standards; the main area of concern is drugs. If I had it to do over again, I'd try something to help Eddie Mathews. As it is, when I think of him it's with a beer bottle in his hand instead of a bat, and that's a sad way to remember an association with one of baseball's all-time greatest hitters.

Mathews wasn't my only discipline problem with the Braves. Eddie's escapades didn't even begin to compare with the shenanigans of Rico Carty.

Rico Carty was one of the best two-strike hitters ever; he'd cut down on his swing and protect the plate. He was an outfielder-catcher, and while his defense was just adequate he more than put up enough offensive numbers to compensate. But Rico had another side, a personality he himself called "Beeg Boy," with a Latin accent. Beeg Boy couldn't get along with anybody else for any length of time. No matter who I assigned to Rico as a roommate, that player would be back within days demanding a different arrangement. Rico simply did whatever he wanted whenever he wanted, and the wishes of others didn't merit his consideration. Once he even got into a fight with Hank Aaron during a flight, and Hank Aaron was the most easygoing man anybody ever met.

If you looked closely at Rico during games, you'd notice a huge bulge in his hip pocket. That was Rico's wallet. He didn't trust the trainer to keep his money in the clubhouse lock box provided for this purpose. Rico used his wallet as an extra sliding pad. It would have afforded more protection during slides if I hadn't fined Rico so much or so continuously. It seemed like I was always taking his money, about $2,000 every season in a time when salaries weren't a tenth of what they are today.

Usually Rico was fined for being late to practices and team buses and, especially, ballgames. Once in San Francisco he showed up at Candlestick Park in the fifth inning. "Meestair Brah-gan," he said, "I thought it was a night game." I replied, "This'll cost you $500, Rico." Instead of keeping his mouth shut, Rico responded, "Why not make it one t'ousand?" I said, "One more word and I will." End of conversation.

Except for his run-in with Rico, Hank Aaron never caused anybody a moment's trouble or worry. He was as great off the field as on, the ultimate ballplayer to manage. I could go to the ballpark every day and write Hank's name in the lineup, confident in the fact he'd be ready to play and play exceptionally well. Only Hank among all the hitters I managed didn't care who took the mound for the other team. He ended up hitting more home runs off Don Drysdale than anyone else, and Drysdale was *the* right-handed pitcher right-handed hitters never wanted to face. Drysdale was truly mean on the mound, in the tradition of Sal Maglie and Early Wynn, two other guys who made opposing hitters shake. Hank liked hitting against Drysdale, enjoyed the challenge, and I think that had some mental effect on Don, who was used to being the intimidator in a hitter/pitcher relationship.

Of all the players I ever managed, Aaron was the best, better even than Roberto Clemente. There was not an ounce of "hooray for me" in Hank Aaron, which made seeing him break Babe Ruth's home run record all the more enjoyable. Hank set his records while playing as part of a team, not as a one-man show.

Hank's been kind enough to say often that I made him a complete player. That's absurd, of course. But we did have a meaningful conversation in 1963. After the first month of that season I called Hank into my office and said, "There's only one reason Willie Mays makes $125, 000 a year and you make $75, 000. Mays runs, steals bases. As of this moment, you've got the green light. Steal a base any time you wish. You don't have to wait for any signal; use your own judgment." Hank ended up stealing 31 bases in 34 attempts, and he finished second in the league that year to my little bobo Maury Wills.

Even though he was one of baseball's biggest stars, Hank never lost the common touch. He was a friend of anybody on the ballclub, with the occasional exception of Rico Carty.

He'd eat dinner with the rawest rookie. Hank also treated the press well, answering every question, and was perhaps the most dedicated autograph-signer on the Braves. During offseasons Hank was always ready to speak to civic groups, schools, or other organizations. One in a million, Hank Aaron.

I can only remember one time Hank didn't cooperate with the media, and it was the only time I didn't either. We were playing the Cubs in Wrigley Field. Jack Brickhouse was the Cubs' radio play-by-play announcer, and one of the best in the business. He'd have a postgame show, and had to ask his guests to appear before the ballgames started because it was so complicated to get to the broadcasting booth after the game. The player or manager Jack wanted to interview would have to climb over the low red brick wall by the dugout and climb a narrow flight of stairs to get to the press box. Before this particular game Jack asked Hank to be on after the game, and then asked me if I'd subsitute for Hank should something unexpected keep him from making the interview. Hank said he'd go on the show and I promised I'd take his place if necessary. Well, we blew a lead in a late inning when Hank dropped a fly ball after losing sight of it against the sun. It was a terrible defeat, a painful one, and afterwards Hank refused to go on Brickhouse's show. Jack called our locker room and asked me to come instead. I refused, too. No doubt players and managers took losses harder in those days.

The supporting cast around Spahn, Mathews, and Aaron was a colorful lot. My special favorite was Felipe Alou, whom we got from the Giants in time for 1964. Felipe played first base or the outfield, even shortstop on occasion, and never complained about switching positions. He was a true gentleman, respected by all his teammates and a leader on and off the field. I've always thought Alou would make a good, solid manager, a super guy to have in any clubhouse.

But the other Milwaukee Brave player most people remember today is Bob Uecker. I had three catchers—Del Crandall, Joe Torre, and Uke. Uke's main job was to watch the other two play. He kept us entertained on the bench, using many of the stories he tells today. For instance, there was the time Birdie Tebbetts told Uke he would make his first start. He was so excited he left passes at County Stadium for 25 relatives. Just before the Braves left the locker room for the playing field, Birdie asked Uke, "Are you nervous?" "Not a bit," Uke answered. "Are you sure you're ready to go behind the plate?" Birdie persisted. "Yes, sir," Uke replied. "Well, then," Birdie drawled, "I'd suggest you go back to your locker and put your jockstrap *inside* your pants."

Despite the tales he tells about his lack of prowess, Bob Uecker was a pretty good catcher. He had a good throwing arm, one of the best in the National League. But Uke couldn't hit very well, and Crandall and Torre were both good on offense as well as defense. Still, Uke made a genuine contribution to the team, because every club needs a guy to keep everyone else loose and laughing. Whenever we played in Philadelphia, for instance, Uke would tell us his biggest thrill in baseball was seeing a Phillies fan fall out of the upper deck.

When the '63 season began, Del Crandall was still first-string catcher. He'd had many great years with the Braves, a good handler of pitchers who handled the bat well enough to hit second in the lineup—rare for a catcher. Del got along with everybody, but he had the misfortune of having two children with Downs Syndrome. To his credit, and his wife's, the Crandalls did their best to raise their children in a normal home environment. Everyone on the team admired this.

But it quickly became clear in '63 that Joe Torre was simply younger and better than Del. Eventually I had to tell him I was going to make Torre the starting catcher. Del took it well, but asked if he could continue to take batting practice with the starting lineup, maybe half an hour after the extra players took their pregame swings. This would mean he'd have a little more time with his children each day, Del explained. That was fine with me.

After 1963 we traded Del to San Francisco in the deal that brought us Felipe Alou. I didn't see much of Crandall after that until years later, when I was president of the Texas League and Del was named manager of its Albuquerque franchise. He asked for a meeting, and said to me he knew we weren't always in agreement in Milwaukee, but he hoped that was past history. I told him I felt the same way, and welcomed him to the Texas League. Del Crandall is one of the true gentlemen of baseball.

Big Mack Jones was my center fielder, a real character in his own right. In one game we were getting beaten 3-2 in the bottom of the ninth inning, and Jones led off for us with a double. I gave the bunt sign to Denis Menke, our next hitter, but Denis fouled off two quick strikes and I let him hit away. The result was a sharp ground ball to third base, and Mack Jones violated one of baseball's most basic rules by running straight into the third baseman for an out. Instead of a runner on second with one out we had Menke on first; the next two batters made outs and we went into the clubhouse as losers. I called Jones into my office and said, "Mack, would you explain that baserunning maneuver to me?" He said, "Bobby, trying to explain what you don't know is like trying to get back to where you ain't been." That was the end of that conversation.

I enjoyed Mack Jones as I enjoyed most of my Milwaukee players. I felt that way all season, even if our record didn't reflect the talent I believed our ball club to have.

The 1963 Braves finished with an 84-78 mark, a winning percentage comfortably over .500 but still only good enough for sixth place in a 10-team league. Pitching was our downfall; Warren Spahn had a great year, going 23-7 with a 2.60 earned run average. Spahnie was wonderful to watch, a cagey veteran who outsmarted opposing hitters on his bad days and still overpowered them on his good ones. To realize just how great his season was, consider that pitchers Tom Glavine and John Smiley tied for the National League lead in wins for 1991 with 20 victories each. Spahn's 2.60 ERA would have ranked fourth, and his seven shutouts beat the five pitched by Dennis Martinez to pace the league in '91. The 42-year-old Spahn was a workhorse, too; his total of 260 innings pitched would have placed him second in 1991 to Greg Maddux's 263 and well ahead of runner-up Glavine's 246.

But Spahn wasn't even close to the best pitcher in the National League in 1963, a sort of watershed year for excellence. The National League was totally dominant; our league champs, the Dodgers, swept the Yankees in four straight games in the World Series. Sandy Koufax was the best pitcher; his 25 wins led the league, as did his 1.88 ERA. Spahn did edge Koufax in complete games, 22 to 20, but Sandy had 11 shutouts to Spahn's seven and totalled 311 innings pitched to the 260 of my ace left-hander.

The rest of the Milwaukee pitching staff combined couldn't equal most of Koufax's season totals. Besides Spahn, the only starter we had with a record of .500 or better was Burdette at 6-5, and halfway through the season we traded Lew to the Cardinals for Gene Oliver. Lew hung on a few more seasons as a middle reliever and occasional starter, always giving his best. A true old pro if there ever was one.

My other starters were below par, at least in terms of won-loss percentage. Denver Lemaster was 11-14, Tony Cloninger checked in at 9-11, and Bob Henley managed to break in at 9-9. But I was firmly convinced Lemaster and Cloninger were the key to Milwaukee's future, a potential lefty-righty combination to replace Spahn-Burdette. Hendley pitched well enough to be in demand around the league, and we packaged him with Del Crandall to get Felipe Alou away from the Giants after the season ended.

Hank Aaron had a wonderful year, ending up leading the league in home runs and runs batted in with 44 and 130 respectively. Eddie Mathews had solid numbers, but not one of his better years: 23 homers, 84 RBIs and a .263 batting average. The other main bright spot in the offense was Joe Torre: the Fat Kid was named to the All-Rookie team at catcher after a .293 batting average and 71 RBIs. I expected even better from Joe in the future, and he delivered.

It turned out only three National League teams had losing records in 1963. The Pirates stumbled to 74-88, my old pals in Houston were 66-96, and the Mets continued as league whipping boys with just a 51-111 mark. The Dodgers beat the Cardinals by six games to win the league title: the Dodger Big Three of Koufax, Drysdale, and Podres guaranteed their team would never, ever, fall into a long losing streak.

At the end of the season I met with John McHale. He wasn't entirely disappointed, either. Our relationship was just great, and we both believed young players like Torre, Cloninger, and Lemaster would spark a better season for the Braves in 1964. And, too, I believed Warren Spahn had a lot left; one more good season from Spahnie and then the kids would be able to carry the pitching load themselves.

I was so excited about the Braves's prospects that I only spent one month of the off-season in Fort Worth. The rest of the winter found me slogging through Wisconsin snow trying to sell season tickets to a public not nearly as enthusiastic about the team as I was.

JOHN McHALE: In 1962 I was president of the Braves, and a partner in the club ownership. I had been with Lou Perini, who sold the team to a group from Chicago headed by Bill Bartholomay, who'd had some kind of interest in the White Sox. It was a very attractive group of guys—young, well-connected.

In the seasons leading up to Bobby's hiring the team had undergone quite a turnover. When I arrived, Fred Haney was manager during the glory days, very great days for the team—world champs in 1957, league champs in '58, tied for the league lead in '59 and lost a playoff to the Dodgers. It was a very enviable record. But then Haney resigned. He was a network broadcaster for one season, then took over the American League expansion club in Los Angeles. I hired Charlie Dressen to replace Fred. He took over a very talented and very difficult club to manage. There were a lot of stars who each wanted his own way. It took a very strong hand to keep things together. Charlie did well, but near the end of his second season Birdie Tebbetts, who was our executive vice-president, decided he wanted to manage again and Perini thought he'd be better back on the field. So we let Dressen go and Birdie took over; this was mid-1960.

JOE TORRE: We'd just won 10 games in a row. Charlie Dressen went up to that meeting thinking he was going to sign a new contract.

McHALE: But after two fairly good seasons Birdie shocked us; he wanted to go back to Cleveland, to manage there under Gabe Paul, his old mentor from Cincinnati. This left us again without a manager, and I decided to consult with an expert. I met with Branch Rickey and asked him about managers. I wish I'd recorded what he had to say; it was exceptionally entertaining. He would only talk about three: Leo Durocher, Charlie Dressen, and Bobby Bragan. Mr. Rickey said there was no baseball man more instinctively smart than Durocher, but that you needed a firm hand with him, that Leo would get out of control. He talked about Dressen, how smart Charlie was. Then he said that Bobby Bragan was the only manager he knew who could be a combination of the two, combine Leo's baseball brilliance with Dressen's intelligence.

"Besides that, Bobby will have the intelligence and energy to represent your team 12 months a year in front of the public," Mr. Rickey added. He concluded by telling me Bobby Bragan had the potential to become one of baseball's really great managers.

I really didn't know Bobby well. I'd played for the Detroit Tigers and knew a little bit about him when he managed Cleveland. So I did some study and was impressed by Bobby's ability to work with young players. You had to be struck by what he'd done with Maury Wills. We had a Braves farm system at the time that was developing some fine young players, and we felt Bobby would be a perfect fit. We hired him.

Unfortunately, about that time the new team ownership got restless with Milwaukee attendance-wise. They even lost our major television sponsor, Miller Brewing Company. Several seasons before the fact, rumors started circulating the team would eventually move to Atlanta. It had to be a terrible distraction for anybody, a manager or a player.

Well, Bobby being Bobby just jumped in with both feet. He had then as he has now great interest in the promotional aspect of marketing baseball. He got a TV show in Milwaukee and travelled all over Wisconsin making hundreds of speeches. So there were all these rumors the club was going to move, and Bobby right away was out there in front of the public as sort of main team spokesman. The ownership was in Chicago; they didn't have to face the local fans as much. I was behind the scenes trying to keep things under control. Bobby by default immediately became the lightening rod for public opinion. Fans were mad, so they vented their frustrations on him.

Also, some of the mainstay players on the team were on the downside of their careers. It was a tense time, really.

DEL CRANDALL: Bobby Bragan came to manage the Braves at a very difficult time. A lot of us on the team had been there a long time with a degree of success. We were established. Decisions had to be made about whether any of us were on the decline. Who was still good enough to play every day? Who had to go?

With most of us, Bobby Bragan wasn't a very popular manager. Now, as the years have gone by I think we've been able to realize what a bad position he was in, but at that time this wasn't the case. Nobody really wants to admit he's past his best as a player. Bobby recognized this too. I don't think he enjoyed himself much. The front office may have pushed him to do some things. He was a man caught in the middle.

HANK AARON: When anyone would have come in to manage a club like ours that had been successful, there was bound to be resentment. And from the first day Bobby arrived, he was going to do things his own way.

WARREN SPAHN: I had played for several managers. Another wasn't going to make any difference, except we had the feeling Bobby Bragan was there as a hatchet man.

LEW BURDETTE: I would never say anything bad about Bobby Bragan, even though he's the manager who traded me away from the Braves, the son of a bitch. Ah, I'm kidding. They were getting ready to move down to Atlanta, that was no secret, and they wanted new young players for the team down there. They got rid of quite a few of the good Milwaukee Braves and we never got the chance to be Atlanta Braves.

So I only played half a season for Bobby, but he was certainly qualified to manage. We all knew his background with the Dodgers and other players in the league who he'd managed in the minors or majors usually said good things about him. And he let me pitch Opening Day in 1963 instead of Warren Spahn, which was quite an honor. I can't say what the rest of the team thought about him. I do know Bobby got lots of respect from opposing players.

ORLANDO CEPEDA: Even before Bobby managed with the Braves, I knew him. See, Bobby would come to Cuba to manage Almendares every winter. During his career he helped black players like Maury Wills and so many Latin players like Tony Taylor. The blacks and Latins all over baseball took note of this. It was rare. He had that reputation among us of being fair and giving everybody an even chance. Every black and Latin player on his team I talked to said he was a hell of a man.

MAURY WILLS: The Dodgers played Milwaukee in County Stadium for the first time after Bobby was hired as the Braves' manager, and it was cold that day. It was never so cold, even in Candlestick Park. So all of us on the Dodgers put these vinyl windbreakers on under our uniform shirts. It was warm, but illegal. And Bobby Bragan knew every rule in the rulebook, so he made it known to the umpires that we were dressed improperly and insisted we take the windbreakers off.

I said, "Bobby, how can you do this to me? I'm your boy." But he insisted and the umpires said we had to take them off, so I just tucked the arms of the windbreaker back under my uniform sleeves and said I'd removed it completely. And that worked, except every now and then it'd slip out from under my sleeves, and every time Bobby would complain to the umpires and we'd go through the whole thing again.

Finally, Walter Alston got disgusted and made me take the windbreaker off. I nearly froze. After the game I sent Bobby a note in the Braves' clubhouse. The note read, "Now I owe you two losses." And the next day we beat the Braves badly. I played well, and I sent him another note saying, "Now I owe you one." He understood.

AARON: I've always said Bobby was the first one to let me do some things on the field I've always wanted to do. He gave me the green light to run when I wanted. Before, we hadn't had that type of ballclub. We'd just go out and slug away. Bobby showed faith in me. It meant a lot.

CRANDALL: That one season, 1963, I remember a conversation I had with Bobby. I was 33 and Joe Torre had come up. I told Bobby, "Maybe it would be better if you traded me." He looked me in the eye and said, "Okay, you're the Braves' manager. For your club, who do you want on the bench if Joe Torre gets hurt? Del Crandall, that's who, a man who's been one of the best catchers in the major leagues." So I felt better, but ultimately after the season I was traded to the San Francisco Giants anyway.

TORRE: Del Crandall was my idol. My brother Frank had played for the Braves, and when I was in the minor leagues I went out of my way to wear #1 because that's the jersey Crandall wore. I got called to the big leagues in 1961 when Del got a sore arm, and in '62 I caught games on cold days and he caught on warm ones because of his bad arm. In 1963 I guess they decided I could handle the job as a regular. Del made it very easy; he did everything he could to help me along and then he was traded at the end of the season.

DENIS MENKE: In '63 I was having a great time. I was glad I was breaking into the major leagues with guys like Spahn and Mathews and Crandall. That season we used to have team parties and every-one would be there. Spahn was a lot of fun.

SPAHN: I admit our clubhouse was a zoo. Maybe that's where Bragan had a problem with some of us.

TORRE: Because of my brother, I had practically grown up around a lot of those guys. A few of them, Spahn for sure, made fun of me, gave me a lot of abuse because as a teenager I was very fat. I was very sensitive about it, they hurt my feelings even after I was with the club myself, but what the hell could I do about it?

AARON: Spahn was a funny individual. You had to understand Spahn. He was the greatest pitcher I ever saw or played behind, but he had peculiar ways. I didn't have to like them but I thought I understood them.

SPAHN: I did all my work. What could I do on days I wasn't pitching? If asked I would have been more than willing to help out (with the younger pitchers). If Bragan says I was selfish about winning, well, yes. Anyone with pride in his accomplishments is selfish to a certain extent. I'm very proud of my career. I don't think my teammates shared in Bragan's opinion of me. Hey, I can handle criticism. The only way I could hold my job so long was to do a good one. Lemaster and those other guys were the young lions. For years on the Braves I was always the elder statesman. I had to be better than the kids. If I wasn't, it was my job that was going to be taken away.

AARON: As for Eddie Mathews, Eddie has always been one who did what he wanted to do. I couldn't tell you if he and Bragan had any problems. My way was just to worry about myself, be sure I was doing things the right way.

SPAHN: Eddie came to play every day. He never missed a ballgame. I don't know why Bragan comes down so hard on him. I was with the Braves when Eddie came up in '52, and he couldn't stop a ground ball. He worked every day until he became a good fielder.

DENVER LEMASTER: Eddie drank some, but Eddie was a gamer. He was always ready to play no matter what shape he was in. What Eddie did after he left the ballpark I always felt was his own business. Bragan was a teetotaler and didn't think anybody else should drink either.

Bobby had this rule that if you were in the starting lineup, then you had to take fielding practice before the game. There was a $100 fine if you didn't. Well, we were in Pittsburgh and Mathews was sick. Hell, he always played even if he was sick. But Mathews didn't take infield practice, and Bragan came into the clubhouse and told him he was fined $100. Mathews was pissed. He got the clubhouse guy to go over and open the valuables box, then took a $100 bill from his money clip and threw it on the floor. Bragan didn't pick it up and Eddie didn't either. We went out and played a nine-inning game, came back to the clubhouse when it was over and that $100 bill was still on the floor. We all showered, dressed, packed, and nobody would pick that money up. When we left the clubhouse the $100 was still on the floor.

TORRE: Rico Carty was just created in Milwaukee, during his first years as a Brave he looked like a budding star. He marched to his own drummer.

AARON: Rico had an abundance of talent, but he could probably have hit 35-40 home runs a year instead of a dozen or so. He was always satisfied with a single. It could be the last of the ninth, team a run behind, and he'd still try for a single anyway. He was one of the most gifted hitters I've ever seen but he didn't use those skills to the fullest.

And he was different. Very different.

LEMASTER: Carty used to get away with more shit, and Bragan would never reprimand him. Anybody else, and Bragan would have come down on you. One game in San Francisco, Bragan's got him batting fifth in the order. Batting practice, no Rico Carty. Fielding practice, no Rico Carty. National anthem, we're up, we go down one-two-three. And then, you know how in Candlestick Park you get to the field from the clubhouse through a door in the right field stands? Well, right after we go through our side of the first who comes running out that door into left field but goddamn Rico Carty. Nobody says nothin'. We go through the whole game and get beat. Afterwards Bragan calls a meeting in the clubhouse, walking up and down the aisle for 10-15 minutes chewing his big chew and not saying anything. Everybody in there thought, "Good, he's finally gonna hang Rico's ass." So, "Carty," he says, "It's gonna be $500." Carty, he says, "Me no care. Make it a t'ousand." Bragan says, "Okay, it's a thousand." Carty keeps talking back. He says, "Well, why don't you make it two t'ousand." And Bragan says real quick, "No, a thousand's enough." That was the end of that meeting.Geez, what Carty could get away with...

BILLY O'DELL: Well, Rico was quite an individual. He did the most unusual things. He didn't take things as seriously as he should have. But he was so temperamental and so talented, Bragan had to either take it a little easier on him or run him off, and the team was better off with Rico than without him.

LAME DUCKS

I TRULY BELIEVED 1964 COULD BE THE SEASON I'd manage a major league club to a pennant. The Braves had that famous nucleus returning—Aaron, Mathews, Spahn—with our promising pitchers ready to live up to their potential. During the off season John McHale got me veteran knuckleballer Bob Tiefenauer to anchor the bullpen. Gene Oliver and Felipe Alou added years of experience and still-considerable slugging skills. When I matched my starting lineup player-for-player with that of any other team in the National League, I felt we had the edge.

Gene Oliver made a major contribution by bringing the Cardinal system of pitching charts along with his bat and glove. St. Louis coaches had devised a system where each starting pitcher was represented by a different color ink. The idea was to mark where each fair ball was hit off each of our pitchers against each opposing team. We had green ink for Cloninger, red for Lemaster, blue for Spahn, and so on. Then when Spahn pitched against the Dodgers, for instance, we'd look at the blue ink lines for games against Los Angeles and set up our defense accordingly.

Oliver was an interesting man, a thinking ballplayer. At one point during the '64 season we were changing our signs so often that JoJo

White had trouble rewriting the signals on his palms before every game. During one mid-season stretch we had an automatic "take" on for our hitters who got ahead 2-0 or 3-1 in the count *unless* JoJo as third base coach flashed a special "hit" sign. In one game we trailed 4-1 in the eighth inning. With nobody on, Oliver ignored the automatic "take" and swung at a 3-1 pitch. He flied out, trotted back to the dugout, and started putting on the catching gear in anticipation of returning to the field after the inning was over. I said to Oliver, "Why'd you hit that 3-1 pitch?" and he answered, "If you want me to take, put on a "take" sign." "Okay," I replied, "I'm putting the "take" sign on now. *Take* that gear off and let Joe Torre put it on. You're through for the day!"

With a good bench of veteran players like Alou and Oliver, I was able to make more moves in a game than most other National League managers, and to adjust my lineup more to fit the opposing team and pitcher. This is the essence of managing. Almost every player who makes it to the major leagues has a certain amount of talent, and, at least in those days, sufficient knowledge of fundamentals to almost always make the right play. It's up to the manager to keep in mind which hitters do best against which pitchers and vice versa, which veteran needs one day off a week to stay strong where before he might have needed just one day of rest a month.

When a manager gets too committed to the same lineup day in and day out, that means the rest of his players languish on the bench. They get discouraged, disgruntled. Big league ballplayers take pride in their ability. They want to be out on the field. A manager who has a good knowledge of his personnel can make almost every player on the team feel he's making an important contribution —the way Earl Weaver handled the Baltimore Orioles is a good example of that. He once platooned three players in left field, and together they slugged about 40 home runs and accumulated 120 RBIs.

Of course, it's also inevitable that there will be players on every club who, for one reason or another, don't like the manager. It may simply be a clash of personalities, but usually it's because the players don't like the way they're being used. Casey Stengel used to say he had five players who liked him, and that his challenge was to keep the fifteen who hadn't made up their minds away from the five who hated him.

During the '64 season my relationship with Warren Spahn completely soured. There was no question why we weren't getting along: Between 1963 and 1964 the great Spahn completely lost his ability to work effectively as a starting pitcher. He went from 23-7 to 6-13, and he pitched worse than even that poor record indicates. Toward the end of '63 he'd had trouble finishing games, no problem in the reliever-rich tradition of the 1990s but a notable flaw in the 1960s when starting pitchers considered it a point of pride to go all nine innings. I showed Spahn respect by giving him time to work through his troubles if he could, but after 18 mostly ineffective starts I called him in for a conference.

"Your pattern right now is that you can get opponents out during your first time through their lineups," I told him. "But when hitters see you a second time now they tee off and I have to come get you. Considering that, I wonder if it might not be best for you and the team if we made you a reliever."

His response was typical of Spahn: "I know I can still start. I have confidence in myself even if you don't." Well, Warren Spahn was Warren Spahn, a 300-game winner and sure Hall of Famer. You just don't impose your will immediately on such a man. I gave him another half-dozen starts, but the results were no better. As the season moved into July I met with John McHale and told him Warren Spahn was at the end of the road. We were trying to win a pennant. Though Spahn was still a fierce competitor, he had become more rhetoric than sermon. He was sent to the bullpen, and young Bob Sadowski took his place in the starting rotation.

Spahn wasn't happy, of course, and he didn't trouble himself to try to hide his feelings. In his mind, Bobby Bragan was sabotaging a still-brilliant career. Actually, it was the opposing hitters who were doing Spahn harm. By September his earned run average was an awful 5.29.

All of us who respected what Spahn had accomplished hoped he'd retire after 1964. That one poor season in no way overshadowed so many brilliant performances for the Braves. But he insisted he could still pitch, and since there was no place left for him on the

Milwaukee staff we were forced to ask around to see if any other team might be interested in him. The New York Mets were still in their expansion-draft mode of signing fading big-name stars to keep their fans entertained while the New York farm system developed solid young players. When the time came to put a deal together, John McHale paid Spahn the ultimate tribute by selling him to the Mets for one dollar. To take any player or significant amount of money in return would have been demeaning to Spahn. He went to the Mets and had a horrible season in 1965. After struggling to a 4-12 record late in the season, Spahn was released and signed for a few weeks with the San Francisco Giants, who obviously hoped he had some spark left to inspire them late in the pennant race. Spahn went 3-4 in 16 games, and at the end of 1965 he finally hung up his spikes for good.

The 1964 National League race was close throughout the season. Five teams were in contention: the Braves, Giants, Reds, Cardinals, and Phillies. By late August I began to think we didn't have the pitching to hang in to the end. Cloninger and Lemaster were having fine seasons—Tony ended up winning 19 games and Denver got 17 victories—but the rest of our starters had the habit of giving up one more run per game than we could score. And we scored a lot—five of our regulars hit 20 home runs or more—Aaron, Mathews, Denis Menke, Rico Carty, and Joe Torre. Carty, Torre, and Lee Maye each batted over .300 (for one of the few seasons during the peak of his career Hank Aaron didn't).

But it's ultimately pitching that wins pennants, and with aces Chris Short and Jim Bunning it appeared the Phillies eventually had the pennant won. Gene Mauch, an old buddy from Brooklyn Dodger days, was managing Philadelphia, and if I couldn't win the pennant myself in 1964 I was pleased to think another disciple of Mr. Rickey would.

We went into Philadelphia on a road trip with 10 games left in the season. Gene's club still had a comfortable lead, but they'd lost three straight to Cincinnati just before we arrived and the notoriously tough Philadelphia fans were panicking.

We had four games scheduled in Connie Mack Stadium, and when Gene's club took the field before the first contest it should have been natural for the home fans to cheer Phillie stars like Richie Allen and Johnny Callison, who both were having hellaciously good seasons. Instead, the fans rose as one and booed the relief pitchers walking out to the Philadelphia bullpen. There had been some blown leads instead of saves in the Cincinnati series, and the fans chose to focus on those instead of cheering in anticipation of better performances against Milwaukee. Those Phillie relievers looked shell-shocked. Though the day was hot, they wore their warmup jackets over their uniform jerseys in the faint hope the fans wouldn't see their numbers and be able to jeer them by name.

Well, we won the first game by rallying late against ace reliever Ed Roebuck. Ed had a wonderful season, with a 2.21 earned run average and a bagful of saves. But he blew this one, and the fans reacted as you'd expect. Poor Ed Roebuck left the field to a cascade of catcalls. Then we won the second game, too—a reserve outfielder for us named Ty Cline got a couple of key hits. The third game was played on the birthday of Bobby Shantz, a cagey veteran pitcher finishing up a distinguished career with the Phillies. Johnny Callison tried to brake the Philadelphia losing streak single-handed with three home runs, but Rico Carty hit a late-inning three-run triple off Shantz and we won 14-11. The fans helped Shantz celebrate his birthday by cursing him as he left the mound. The whole Philadelphia team was completely demoralized before the fourth game, which we also won to sweep the series and continue the Phillies on their famous swoon which resulted in their losing the pennant to the Cardinals by one game.

After our victory, Philadelphia writers in our clubhouse wanted to know if we played harder against the Phillies than we had for the rest of the season. The answer, clearly, was no. We wanted to win every game the Milwaukee Braves played, whether we were contending for the pennant or if we'd lost every other game that season. But I really felt sick to my stomach for Gene. It was unbelievable to me that fans in Philadelphia on the brink of a pennant could boo their team as if they knew in advance the Phillies would somehow blow it. How did they possibly expect the Philadelphia players to have the heart to perform at their best in the face of that kind of treatment? But Philadelphia is that kind of city with that kind of baseball fans—as Bob Uecker always said, the worst in the world.

In the years since, writers and fans have second-guessed Gene Mauch. He's supposedly overrated, a flawed genius because he never got a club he managed into the World Series. And it is ironic, and sad, that he came so close later in his career with the Angels and still never quite made it. But I'll tell you this: Gene Mauch has to be one of the best managers who ever put on a uniform. Leo is on top, of course, the manager without peer. The second tier is Casey Stengel, John McGraw, Billy Martin—those managers who had the little extra to win games other managers wouldn't have been able to pull out. Mauch is in this group, too, as are Tommy Lasorda, Earl Weaver, and Sparky Anderson. After them, in my opinion, comes Walter Alston. Those are the best managers.

Generally speaking, pitchers almost never make good managers for the simple reason that during their careers they're not involved as much in steal situations, hit and runs, the offensive parts of the game. Catchers, infielders, and outfielders as a rule become the better managers. There are a few exceptions—Fred Hutchinson, Roger Craig, Clyde King, Lasorda, and Bob Lemon, but Lemon was a converted infielder.

Of course, I have some opinions about who might be bad managers. I'd say the one who appealed to me the least was Rogers Hornsby. There was absolutely no communication between him and his players when he managed in Cincinnati and St. Louis. When Grady Hatton played for Hornsby in Cincinnati, he went to then-General Manager Gabe Paul with a complaint. The astute Mr. Paul said to Grady, "Does this have to do with team administration, or is it something in the clubhouse?" "The clubhouse," Hatton said. "Well," Gabe replied, "take it up with Hornsby, the manager." "It's not something I'd like to discuss with the manager," Grady said. "Well, what is it?" Gabe asked. "Mr. Paul," Grady blurted, "In the shower room when the game is over, Hornsby enjoys urinating on his players' legs."

I'm sure some of the Braves' players didn't like me during the 1964 season, but not for that reason.

We finished the 1964 season in fifth place with a record of 88-74. That was only five games behind the pennant-winning Cardinals. My end-of-season meeting with management went fairly well.

McHale wanted to know what the ownership could expect by way of a 1965 finish, and I said honestly that we ought to contend again. I was satisfied with the improvement of our young pitchers, Rico Carty had established himself as a premier hitter, and Mathews and Aaron were still going strong. If we upgraded our pitching a notch, we could be world champions.

I stayed in Milwaukee that winter, getting out to hustle season ticket sales to civic clubs and community groups. There was an extra obstacle to my goodwill efforts in the community; the owner-ship tried to break its lease with Milwaukee's County Stadium and move the Braves to Atlanta for the 1965 season. The county sued, and the owners were forced to keep the team in Milwaukee for one more season.

But now the cat was out of the bag; the team was definitely going to pull up stakes and head south after 1965. The Milwaukee fans had two obvious ways to show their displeasure; they could stay away from games during the Braves' last Wisconsin season, or they could attend and imitate Philadelphia fans by booing and making the situation as unpleasant as possible for the players.

City stores and banks removed Braves' schedules from their counters. Because Atlanta was the home city of the Coca-Cola Com-pany, Milwaukee bars and restaurants stopped selling Coke. It was horrible. The fans booed constantly. In one or two instances civic leaders went so far in 1965 as to claim the Braves were throwing games to get even with the community. One morning I had to have breakfast with a county commissioner named Grobschmidt to try to convince him my team was going all out even though we'd be leaving at the end of the season.

Despite such distractions, I really thought we could give Milwau-kee fans a final National League pennant. As he always did, John McHale went all-out to give me a few additional quality players. Veteran starting pitcher Ken Johnson joined our staff, and we added a nifty middle infielder named Woodie Woodward. During spring training I took a long look at a fellow who appeared to be a career minor league pitcher. Phil Niekro had a fastball that wasn't quite fast enough and a curve that didn't quite break as sharply as it should have.

But I noticed that every once in a while Niekro would fool around with a knuckleball, a good one. I called him in and said, "You need to go back down to Triple A. Concentrate on the knuckler; don't throw anything else. It's the only way you can get to the big leagues and stay there." Phil agreed. He went back down, followed the plan, and by mid-season was back in the major leagues. That knuckleball kept him there for 24 seasons, 318 wins, and, I'm sure, an eventual and well-deserved place in the Hall of Fame.

Our best off-season acquisition was a left-handed pitcher named Billy O'Dell. We got O'Dell from the Giants in exchange for a backup catcher. He was a cool customer from North Carolina, whose slow drawl and calm ways were consistent in any game situation. O'Dell could either start or relieve, and as usual my bullpen needed bolstering. I informed O'Dell he'd be my closer, and he was satisfied to take on that role.

I also got a unique indoctrination from the skinny southpaw.One day in spring training O'Dell took me to his locker; he reached up to the top shelf and withdrew a twig about the size of a pencil. "Bobby, this is slippery elm," he informed me. "It gets real, real slippery when it comes in contact with saliva." Billy broke off a small match-like section and tucked it between his front teeth and lower gum. After a few seconds he put his fingertip into his mouth and showed me a viscous dab of extra-shiny, extra-thick spit. In games O'Dell could actually use the substance to throw the ball toward the batter, get the break on the ball he wanted, and the catcher could receive the pitch, hand the ball to the umpire for inspection, and the ball would be completely dry. It was amazing to see.

Mr. Rickey used to say that in the older baseball days when spitballs were allowed, some hurlers would drench the ball with so much spit that batters would get splashed in the face as the ball passed them by. According to Mr. Rickey, the spitball was really outlawed for sanitary reasons.

There's no doubt: all major league pitchers of modern times know how to throw some form of a spitter or otherwise-doctored baseball. Whitey Ford was often accused of cutting the ball just slightly; supposedly he could force his fingernails into the incision and get that much more break on his pitches. Some pitchers like to use a little vaginal salve; others vaseline or, like Billy O'Dell, slippery elm. The best practitioners in my personal experience were Bob Shaw, Gaylord Perry, and Lew Burdette. Hugh Casey also threw wet ones. The effect of putting spit or another moist foreign substance on a baseball is the same as moving a billiard ball on a pool table. As long as you push downward on the ball with a dry finger, it will spin back. Press down with a wet finger and the ball will roll directly away, because the wetness has eliminated the friction. It's the same thing with a spitball.

It has to be said that 1965 was a tough season for everyone connected with the Milwaukee Braves. The fans who showed up at County Stadium made up for their small numbers with tremendous amounts of invective. Never doubt that players and managers on the field hear the insults hurled at them from the stands. You can pretend not to listen, but you do. I was proud of my team in that each man continued to do his best under bad circumstances.

But the kind of season it was, well, one time one of my starting pitchers did a great job against the Dodgers, allowing just one hit and one run. But Sandy Koufax pitched a no-hitter that game. Our final record was 86-76, good for just a fifth place finish again, but I thought getting the club home 10 games over .500 that last lame duck season in Milwaukee might have been the best managing job I did in my entire career.

Other teams were aware of what we were going through. They were sympathetic, but not to the point of forgiving us for anything. In particular I aroused the ire of the San Francisco Giants for a game the Braves lost to the Dodgers.

Wade Blasingame pitched for us against Koufax; our second baseman, Frank Bolling, powdered a grand slam off Sandy and we had a 4-0 lead early on. After six innings the score was 5-1 and we were on our way to a rare win against perhaps the best pitcher in baseball history. But then the Dodgers started pecking away as they always did, a bunt here, a stolen base there, a scratch single and then some not-so-scratch base hits and I figured Blasingame was losing his stuff.

Like most managers, I had a policy whereby the catcher could dig some dirt out of his spikes and toss the dirt toward me in the dugout, a signal the pitcher had tired sufficiently and needed to be replaced. I trusted my catchers to do this, since I knew from my own experience the receiving end of the pitcher-catcher tandem was in the best position to judge the hurler's effectiveness or lack of it.

Well, in this instance Joe Torre never gave that signal, leaving me to assume the Dodgers were just hitting good pitches. It wasn't until the score was 5-5 that I yanked Blasingame, and we went on to lose. Later on I was criticized good-naturedly by Giants general manager Chub Feeney, whose club was neck-and-neck with Los Angeles in the pennant chase. "What in the hell were you trying to do, staying with Blasingame?" Feeney wanted to know. "I wish I knew," I stammered. I wasn't about to divulge the fact catcher Joe Torre was trying to protect Wade Blasingame, his roomie, by refusing to give me the signal the left-hander had lost his stuff.

It wasn't my season to get along with anyone from the San Francisco Giants. I even had a serious run-in with Willie Mays. I still had a TV show in Milwaukee. It was aired once a week on Saturday mornings; we'd usually film it Friday nights during home stands. During one visit from the Giants to Milwaukee I asked Willie to be my guest on the show, and he agreed. I was pleased because a Mays appearance would draw lots of viewers. Before our game with San Francisco on Friday afternoon, I took our lineup card to home plate for the meeting with the umpires and met Willie there. As team captain of the Giants he usually brought out the lineup card for his manager. "You are still doing my show?" I asked. He said he was.

So that evening at 6 P.M. I sent my son, Bobby Jr., to the Pfister Hotel where the Giants were staying to bring Willie to the TV studio. Bobby Jr. found Willie's room, knocked, and Willie yelled from behind the closed door, "Tell your Daddy I'm down for the night." My son called me at the station to give me the message, and I had to do the show without any guest at all.

The next day I made a point of taking my lineup card to home plate so I could confront Mays there. I said right in front of the surprised umpires, "You know, Willie, every time I've ever seen you in a ballpark or on the street, my greeting to you has been to hold up my index finger to indicate that, to me, among all ballplayers you're Number One. Isn't that right?" Willie nodded. "Well, after your no-show yesterday, you turned out to be a piece of shit. I could grind you under my shoe like this." And I turned and stalked off.

It took maybe two years before Mays and I became buddies again. Most resentments can only be held so long. Now when I see him, like I did at Leo Durocher's funeral when we shared the task of giving the eulogy, I give him the Number One sign, same as always.

And it's true. Out of everyone I played with, played against, managed, or managed against, Willie Mays was the best ballplayer I ever saw. He is the only player who could get fans in any ballpark excited before the game even started. People would come out early to see the Giants' hitting and fielding practices. Willie would hit a few out of the park from the batting cage, make a few of his patented "basket catches" (glove held around his beltline to receive the ball rather than eye- or head-high like other outfielders), and even just run the bases. Mays was the absolute complete ballplayer; not only could he do it all—hit, throw, field, run—he did it with a flourish. In every ballpark where the Braves would visit, some opposing player or coach would point out a spot in the outfield where Willie Mays had made another impossible catch. When Willie went after a fly ball, he never watched the ball once it left the bat. From that fraction of a second of impact, he instinctively knew where the ball would come down. He'd run to that spot without having to look back for the ball, a necessary practice which forces other outfielders to slow down a little. The split second Willie saved there made all the difference between snaring the ball on the fly and picking it up after it bounced off the fence.

It's impossible to even wonder what kind of salary Willie Mays would command in this baseball generation. I'd have to guess salary wouldn't be involved at all—some team would have to make Willie its co-owner. There simply wouldn't be enough money anywhere to pay the salary Willie would require. The only other player I can think of who might be in the same situation would be DiMaggio, the difference being Joe was Enrique Caruso and Mays was Frank Sinatra.

Well, we got through 1965 somehow. There were things to be proud of—we had three hitters with 20 or more homers in Joe Torre, Felipe Alou, and Geve Oliver, while three more cracked at least 30 —Aaron, Mathews, and Mack Jones. Cloninger won 24 games; it seemed obvious he'd be a dominating pitcher all through the '60s and perhaps beyond.

Blasingame won 13, Billy O'Dell won 10 and saved 18 more, but Denny Lemaster was a disappointment with a 7-13 mark. Our lack of staff depth showed.

When the season ended I was 48 years old. My salary was $40, 000 annually. I'd been managing the Braves for three years; the results were fair—no losing seasons—but in my meeting with management after the last game of the year there was no backslapping or anything else by way of congratulations. I got the impression we'd better win more during our first season in Atlanta or I'd once again be out of a job.

In one way, I was excited about the team's move to Georgia. It was closer to my old home grounds of Alabama, and there was certain to be keen Atlanta fan interest in their new team. Surely the Braves' players would respond positively to the better atmosphere.

But I couldn't escape the feeling more might go wrong in the season ahead. I think having the owners more excited about moving to Atlanta than in having me lead the team there was a pretty good clue.

JOHN McHALE: When the team ownership decided to break its lease with County Stadium and move to Atlanta after the 1964 season, there was an antitrust suit filed by the State of Wisconsin. So we stayed in Milwaukee one more year to fulfill the lease. Yes, it was tense.

It had to be extremely hard on the players, and on Bobby. Bobby always wanted to be so positive about everything. And I will say that even in 1965 he gave us an unstinting effort. Bobby's personality and humor were assets for us all. He and I would meet every day before home games during each season, so I knew absolutely how devoted he was to the Braves and how determined he was to win.

DENIS MENKE: It seemed like during the offseasons we got a lot of players from other organizations instead of building up with younger guys from our own farm system. That may have been the problem right there.

DENVER LEMASTER: In 1964 we still had that great camaraderie, and the reason was we were still a winning ballclub, still in contention all the time. All the guys on the team pretty much got along, except for Carty. And in that season Spahn and Bragan were always in each other's face.

JOE TORRE: Spahnie really felt like he was getting the bad end of the stick.

WARREN SPAHN: In 1964, hell, I didn't get a chance to pitch. Bragan or the owners wanted to start the young pitchers. I was relegated to the bullpen. I was not happy; I only got to pitch in mop-up roles. So at the end of the year I went to John McHale and said I couldn't play anymore for Bobby Bragan.

HANK AARON: Some players take coming to the end of their careers very hard. Spahn was like that. He was so good right to the end, a big winner the year before and then it was all gone. Bobby Bragan understood that. He sympathized.

LEE WALLS: Spahn came to me before one game, I was with the Dodgers, and asked, "What's going wrong?" I said, "You got to get an offspeed pitch." See, when a pitcher gets older and loses something off the fastball, if he comes up with an offspeed pitch to throw the batter offstride it also makes his fastball look faster. But Spahn wouldn't see that. He thought he was throwing as hard as ever. And he got rocked all the time and he looked for someone to blame. But it wasn't Bragan's fault. Hell, he was trying to help the son of a bitch.

SPAHN: I let my ego get in the way a little bit when I said I'd go to the Mets. I thought I'd win with them like I always won with the Braves, but the Mets were just the worst team ever. When I was with them, we used to celebrate off days.

I feel like Bragan shortened my career. It was intended that way. I've mellowed toward him somewhat but at the time I thought he was six-faced, much worse than two-faced.

MENKE: After that season, there was a plan to move us to Atlanta but then with a stadium lease we had to wait a year. It was a mess with absentee ownership. I mean, look at what the Brewers are doing today in Milwaukee with local owners. But during 1965 I didn't feel any resentment from the fans. They were mad at management, not the players.

LEMASTER: Those 12 owners didn't care about the city at all. The people there treated me nice, treated all the players nice. Not that I'd ever say anything bad about Atlanta, I ended up making my home there. But nobody on the team really wanted to leave Milwaukee at the time.

SPAHN: The changeover in ownership was behind what was happening. The group that bought the club borrowed the money from banks in Milwaukee but planned to move to Atlanta the whole time. It was a good business move. Coca-Cola offered them more money for their television broadcasts. Obviously, these new owners wanted to get permission from the league to move the club, so they set out to alienate the (Milwaukee) fans so they wouldn't support the club anymore. They did a lot of crappy things like take away beer from the fans at the ballpark.

Bragan was terrible. Getting rid of the veterans was his role. The owners didn't care where we finished those last seasons in Milwaukee. They could go to Atlanta with a young club and draw anyway, no matter how the team played. Mathews, me, Crandall, Bob Buhl, all those guys who'd been frontline players in Milwaukee over the years got sold or traded away. Bragan did the dirty work for the owners.

AARON: More was made about players not wanting to go to Atlanta than there really was to it. It's funny how newspapers put words in your mouth. I said I had kids in school in Milwaukee and didn't want to move them down to Atlanta during the school year, and it came out in the papers that I didn't want my kids in Atlanta. Hey, I loved Milwaukee. It was the city I played my very first professional game in. But I was born a Southern boy; Atlanta was closer to where I came from. So it was fine, the idea of the team moving there.

McHALE: If I had any constructive criticism of his managing during the Milwaukee years, I would say Bobby was too much of a tinkerer. He was never quite satisfied with any lineup he tried, and he tried hundreds of them. The older players on the roster especially resented this. Bobby would go out and win four or five games in a row, and then come into my office and say, in the unique way he growls and rumbles, "Maybe we ought to have Hank Aaron leading off."

LEMASTER: Bragan used to jockey the damn lineup around a lot. I had some knock-down drag-outs with him. One time Rico Carty was brought in to catch me in a game against Pittsburgh, a tough team for me to beat. Bragan got this brainstorm that Carty ought to catch. I think goddamn Carty had caught maybe two other games in his life, none in the big leagues. I couldn't understand why he had to get put behind the plate in a game where I probably would need a real catcher. So I told Bragan, "I can't understand why you're doing this. Just give me one good reason." His justification was, he was the manager and he would do what he damn well wanted.

BILLY O'DELL: Oh, Bobby had some different ideas sometimes, but Bobby was a thinker. He was a gambler. That was always his way. I remember one time I played first base a bit during a game while he brought in a right-hander to pitch to a couple right-handed hitters. Then I went back to pitch to the lefthanders. Well, Bobby wasn't afraid to try anything, and I'm sure if I had been the manager I would have wanted to do things my own way, too.

TORRE: Every once in a while he'd do some bizarre things. When umpires were supposed to start calling every spitball, in one game Bobby told Bob Shaw to throw a spitter on every pitch. He did this because he thought what the umpires were doing was a travesty, calling spitballs against us but not the other team. Bobby had Shaw keep it up until they both were thrown out of the game. I thought that just distracted the course of action in a game.

AARON: You never knew what Bobby might do next.

O'DELL: Slippery elm? Oh, I was in Phoenix during one spring training and saw an old drugstore, the kind with all the bottles of medicine out on shelves, and I happened to look along one wall and there was a jar of slippery elm lozenges. They were what you took years ago when you had a cough. I bought all the jars they had and over the years messed around with using it. There really wasn't too much to it, just messing around with the ball and slippery elm during practices.

LOU BROCK: My memory of those last Milwaukee teams is that they had a lot of hitting but very little pitching. No manager can win without pitching. A .500 record with those teams was no reflection on Bobby Bragan.

MENKE: If you have great talent, like we did with those last Milwaukee teams, well, we should have done better. To me, Bobby was the greatest promoter of baseball I had seen in a long time. I went with him when he was making speeches and he was great. Managing, well, that was a different story.

AARON: I always felt Bobby Bragan was in my corner. I enjoyed playing for him.

LEMASTER: All the players wondered why the front office didn't do something about Bragan.

McHALE: There was never any question. Bobby was coming to Atlanta with us all along. Bobby may have felt or sensed that, well, the ownership was a bunch of young fellows who perhaps began to get the feeling they were more expert about baseball than they actually were. By the time we moved to Atlanta the front office situation was one of everybody running around in all different directions.

FIRED: PART III

No matter what the owners might have thought, I felt I'd done my best job of managing in 1965. The team held together through the Milwaukee-Atlanta distraction and there was reason to hope for better days in a more positive location.

I spent the winter in Fort Worth, enjoying being home with Gwenn and doing everything I could to be prepared for the season ahead. I believed it would take a strong Braves run at the pennant to save my job; a gentlemanly fifth-place finish with a record a bit over .500 wouldn't be good enough. And, again, I felt optimistic.

The Braves' bats would be as potent in Atlanta as they'd been in Milwaukee; the young pitchers—Cloninger and Blasingame, at least —looked solid. If we could avoid injuries I thought we could make 1966 our year.

Once again John McHale did his best to help me with new personnel. Relievers Ted Abernathy and Clay Carroll were acquired to support Billy O'Dell out of the bullpen. Both were talented; Abernathy had a submarine or underhand delivery that kept right-handed hitters off balance. Carroll was a workhorse with a rubber arm. He could pitch two games out of every three if needed.

At spring training in West Palm Beach, two rookies looked especially promising. Felix Millan, a little second baseman, didn't see much action with the team in 1966 but eventually became one of the better players at his position for many years. I also liked the look of a kid named Mike Lum in center field. I told John McHale I wanted to open the season with Lum in the starting lineup, but I was overruled.

A tickertape parade welcomed the Braves to Atlanta. It was a glorious day. The Coca-Cola Company immediately signed up the players, coaches, and me to do a series of commercials, a long way from the cold corporate shoulder we'd endured for the last few seasons in Milwaukee. Gwenn and I found ourselves a nice apartment in Lennox Square; we were informed it was just a 30-minute ride from Fulton County Stadium, Atlanta's new ballpark. What we didn't realize was that 30-minute ride had to be taken on freeways that more closely resembled the Indianapolis 500 Speedway. I disliked the trip to and from the ballpark.

And once I saw Fulton County Stadium I disliked the ballpark, too. The playing field had more distance between the foul lines and the stands than any other stadium in the major leagues. This meant many more foul pop flies would stay in play, a detriment to a team of fly ball hitters like we had with the Braves. Catchers had farther to run while chasing wild pitches and passed balls. If a pitcher heaved a wild pickoff throw towards first base, runners often could get all the way to home plate before the first baseman or right fielder could chase down the ball. For me, it was quite a long hike from the dugout to the mound to remove a pitcher from the game. I could have used a bicycle under the best of weather circumstances, and looking back at some games played under the hot Georgia summer sun I believe I might have left one or two pitchers in to avoid the hot, sweaty trek necessary to relieve them.

A few seasons later, the Braves' management corrected the situation by moving the stands closer to the foul line. This had an advantage for the fans, too, who inevitably want to be as close to the players as possible. Now Oakland-Alameda County Stadium has the distinction of the widest foul territory in big league baseball.

The 1966 season got off to a terrible start in the very first game we played in our new home ballpark. We suffered a 13-inning, 2-1 loss to the Pirates when Willie Stargell hit a home run off Tony Cloninger. The Atlanta media jumped me for the first time (but not the last) the next day, blasting me for leaving Tony Cloninger, my starting pitcher, in for the entire 13 innings. The print outcry grew louder in the weeks ahead as Cloninger struggled in each subsequent outing. I kept quiet and took my lumps, but Cloninger never told me he was too tired to keep going and I never let him go out in the later innings without first consulting Whitlow Wyatt, my pitching coach.

First impressions are often lasting, and the Atlanta media's first impression of Bobby Bragan was that the shorter his stay in Atlanta, the better. Furman Bisher led the newspaper columnists in calling for my ouster. Local TV broadcaster Milo Hamilton enjoyed second-guessing me. As well as the fans, the Atlanta sportscasters, and sportswriters expected—demanded—a winning team immediately, and after the first month of the season we weren't even winning half of our games. Eddie Mathews was struggling; I started to rest him against opposing left-handers. No starting pitcher emerged as a real stopper, a guy you could count on to win crucial games. And Billy O'Dell, my dependable relief closer from the year before, was dealt to the Pittsburgh Pirates. The whole team missed his cheerful personality and common sense.

The media baying was focused on me, not the players who weren't performing up to potential. I thought of a story told by Paul Richards. Supposedly he informed his old crony Lum Harris that if Lum was content to be a coach, Richards would keep him in his job. But if he wanted to manage, then the media would let Lum know when he was through.

I also remembered the day I first walked into Birdie Tebbetts's old office at Milwaukee's County Stadium. There was a note along with two envelopes, numbered 1 and 2, on the desk. The note instructed me to open the envelopes only in case of crisis. I promptly put them both in a desk drawer. Later on that season when we were in the throes of a losing streak, I opened envelope number 1. The note inside said, "Blame everything on me." So I called a press conference and informed the media covering the Braves that Birdie Tebbetts had left me a team primarily of players on the decline. I said I couldn't do anything about that. This got me by for awhile.

Later when word got out the team would be moved, and the fans' cheers turned to boos, I felt it was time to open envelope number 2. The message inside that one read, "Prepare two more envelopes."

Besides the media and the pain of losing there was another aggravation. 1966 was the season Marvin Miller began representing the Players' Association, forcing owners under threat of strike to grant concessions to the players, including a bigger slice of revenue for pension funds and more creature comfort things like requiring clubhouse and bus temperatures to be 72 degrees and giving the players final say in what medicines and liniments were used in the training room. The players even controlled what music was played in the clubhouse. Almost every one of them found something new and irrelevant to bitch about —why the team bus had to leave for the airport at a certain time, why there had to be mandatory infield practice for game starters, why this or that or the other.

It wore me down. Sometimes I didn't even feel I had the support of my own coaches. Once when I assessed a fine during a team meeting, Billy Hitchcock, who'd been hired as third base coach, said in front of the players, "I don't see why you have to fine them." Hell, Hitchcock had been a manager himself, Paul Richards' chosen successor at Baltimore. I replied that maybe he could motivate these players without fines—I sure couldn't.

Losing brings frustration and personally, I wasn't at my best. Trying to make some of my players bear down harder, I resorted often to sarcasm and anger. At one point I held a pitcher's meeting to let my staff know I was disappointed in their recent performances. "We're playing the Dodgers for the next three games," I snarled. "In the first game we're sending Cloninger against Drysdale. Tony's not at this meeting today, but it's okay. He's our shining light on this pitching staff. But in game two we've got Lemaster against Koufax. You know what a mismatch that is." Lemaster, always tense, jumped up and said, "Whenever I go to the mound I feel I'm as good or better than the pitcher going against me." Probably I should have told Lemaster he had the right attitude, but instead I retorted, "I said you couldn't carry Koufax's jockstrap." That was rock bottom for me as a manager—motivation in reverse.

When things go wrong, managers blame their players. Sometimes they're completely right, sometimes they're completely wrong. Usually both players and manager could be doing their jobs better. It just killed me I couldn't get some of those guys to play harder.

My attitude recalled a story Mr. Rickey used to tell about Joe Cantillion, who managed the Washington Senators back before World War I. Teams in those days usually took just 15 or 16 players on a road trip, plenty since starting pitchers were expected to go all nine innings. Cantillion took his club into Detroit on a road trip. They stayed in what was then called the Booke-Cadillac Hotel, just a mile from the ballpark then called Frank Navin Field. It still stands today, and the Tigers still play their home games there, though it's now called Tiger Stadium. Anyway, Washington came to town with a 17-game losing streak. To help publicize the games each afternoon, the team was conveyed to Navin Field in a long horse-drawn carriage. Upon arrival, the team got out and the carriage was parked near the clubhouse until the return trip to the hotel after the game.

For eight innings it seemed like an 18th consecutive loss was in order for Cantillion's team. Detroit took a 3-1 lead into the top of the ninth when, miracle of miracles, the Senators rallied for three runs. Washington even had a couple of more runners on base when a torrential rain suddenly came roaring down. Both teams retreated to their respective dugouts, but then as today the visiting team's dugout was vastly inferior to that of the home team. The roof leaked above Cantillion's bunch, and the Washington manager finally led his squad to shelter in the horsedrawn carriage. Then came a wait of 45 minutes, with the hapless players trying to stay dry and the equally hapless horse getting drenched as it waited in harness. Finally, the Washington players heard the Navin Field loudspeaker boom out, "This game is officially called due to rain. The score reverts to the last complete inning, and the Tigers win 3-1." At the same time, a bolt of lightning struck the horse. Cantillion ran up, looked at the dead animal, raised his eyes and arms skyward, and exclaimed, "Oh God, how can you kill this poor dumb animal and let these donkeys live?" Well, some of my players were performing like donkeys, and in doing so they were making it a cinch lightning was going to strike me.

Six weeks into the season I asked for a meeting with John McHale. "If you think it would be best for the team, I'll step down," I told him. But he replied, "No, Bobby, sit steady in the boat. Everything will be all right." I wanted to believe him. We went on winning two games, losing three, winning three, losing three. It was a slow death by 1,000 cuts. We showed just enough flashes of talent on the field to make it very clear we should be doing better.

At the All-Star break I went to McHale again. I offered to resign and he repeated I had no need to worry. But I did, because almost immediately it was rumored the team owners were about to bring in Paul Richards to call the shots for the Braves. Richards had been taken out of the top Houston spot by Judge Hofheinz; I believe he had been reduced to a roving scout. Eventually the rumor was confirmed; Paul Richards had been offered and accepted an undisclosed front office job with Atlanta. That was the clincher. I'd be leaving.

One hundred and eleven games into the 1966 season and with a 52-59 team record, John McHale asked to see me. "You know your offer, Bobby?" he asked. "I think we should accept it." John was as nice as he could be. We parted friends then and we're good friends today.

I declined John's invitation to attend the press conference announcing Billy Hitchcock's appointment. Hitchcock didn't last very long as Braves' manager. He finished the 1966 season and was fired by Richards with three games remaining in 1967 after the Braves dropped to 77-85. In 1968 Richards did what he intended all along, I'm sure, by making old pal Luman Harris the manager of the Braves. Richards' act hadn't changed one iota in his switch from the Colt .45s to Atlanta.

Anyway, I went home and told Gwenn I'd been fired. She wasn't surprised; in fact, she'd predicted as much when Richards' name first was mentioned. "I can't tell you how happy I am to be out of uniform," I told her. "We'll go home to Fort Worth and get in the radio business or another phase of baseball. I don't plan to manage again." And I meant it. A few years later Peter Bavasi contacted me to see if I'd be interested in managing the San Diego Padres. I turned him down flat—no discussion necessary beyond the answer, "No." The game had changed too much.

The owners saw their teams as investments; the 12 Braves' owners thought they'd turn better profits in Atlanta than in Milwaukee, so they moved the team and to hell with the Milwaukee fans. Instead of feeling privileged to play in the major leagues, the current generation of ballplayers believed it was somehow their right. Managers had to adjust in order to pacify the new order. I lacked the patience.

And yet, the nine innings spent on the field for each game were still beautiful. The science of knowing when to hit and run, the gut check to be taken before ordering the squeeze bunt, calling on decades of intuition in choosing a pinch-hitter or removing a pitcher —these things were the same. If I could have spent my entire managerial career involved in actual ballgames I'd have been happy forever.

But you spend far more time in the locker room and team bus and front office than you do on the field. I'd had my shot at my dream of managing, and now it was time to get on with the rest of my life. Or so I thought.

I went to work for Jack Williams, a Fort Worth Chevrolet dealer. I spent my days doing public relations assignments—a speech here, an appearance there. I soon added two five-minute sports shows a day on radio station KXOL. Gwenn was happy to be home; our West Fort Worth house became a haven for family and friends. The Jack Williams dealership sponsored several youth league teams, and I helped out there; these youngsters were the only ballplayers I felt like being around.

I'd been working for Jack Williams for about nine months when I got a phone call from John McHale. He'd left the Atlanta Braves not long after me, first to take a job in the commissioner's office and then to head up the Montreal Expos expansion team due to debut in the National League in the 1969 season. "Come join me and do whatever you want for the organization," McHale said, echoing what Gabe Paul had said to me after the 1960 season. "You can be in the front office or scout or get back in uniform." The latter was not an offer to manage the Expos. Gene Mauch had already been hired for that job. "I admire Gene Mauch," I told McHale. "I'll be his third base coach." Despite my plans to stay out of uniform forever, I was back in harness. Soon thereafter I got a call from Expo vice-president Gene Kirby asking me what uniform number I wanted. I asked for # 10, but Rusty Staub had already requested it, so I told Gene the jersey number really didn't matter.

I was all set to join Montreal when I heard Hugh Finnerty had resigned as president of the Texas Baseball League, and I never did get back in uniform after all.

B	E	T	W	E	E	N
I	N	N	I	N	G	S

JOHN McHALE: What happened in 1966 was a combination of things. The reality was the Braves were playing very ordinary baseball with lots of talent.

DENVER LEMASTER: I'll say one thing for Bobby Bragan. We used to call him Dr. Jekyll and Mr. Hyde. Standing on a street corner in a business suit he was the nicest—well, he could tell stories and be funny and a hell of a guy. But in a baseball uniform, especially in Atlanta, there was just something in the way he'd come off. His players didn't like it.

BILLY O'DELL: The folks in Atlanta were just like kids with a new toy at Christmas when the team moved there, but they obviously expected to win right away. I felt the writers decided very quickly it was Bobby's fault when that didn't happen.

JOE TORRE: In Atlanta Bobby would agitate a lot of the players and that rubbed some people the wrong way. I always felt the manager was the boss; I respected that. But other people obviously didn't. Overall, though, I'd say I didn't sense much resentment of Bobby from more than a few people.

BOBBY VALENTINE: The days when a manager could say whatever he wanted to where players were concerned was over. You have to use more psychology now. But I don't necessarily agree that a stronger player union started baseball downhill. There were changes that had to be made.

HANK AARON: I'll tell you about that (1966) club. You have to want to win. You have to want to excel, or be as close to perfect as you personally can become. We had a lot of ballplayers on that team who said to themselves, "I hit .280, I had a good year," when if they really tried to bear down they could have hit .300. Pitchers settled for 12 or 13 wins when they could have tried harder and got 16 or 17. There was a lot of talent, but talent alone doesn't do it. Bobby couldn't put heart into players where it wasn't to begin with.

McHALE: At the same time the owners saw, rightly so, that the president and general manager job was too much for one person. They asked me to get someone to handle the baseball end only while I took the business side. Remember this group was from Chicago. They'd become infatuated with Paul Richards during his days as manager of the Chicago White Sox. Noting that, I went to San Antonio on my own to meet with Paul, who was still I believe in some capacity with Houston. He seemed interested in joining us simply as an advisor. Earlier he had been manager of the minor league Atlanta Crackers and he was still a big name in Georgia. So I hired him to do a consulting job, to look at the team's performance and tell us what he saw could be done better. The owners were delighted; they'd had this hero worship attitude towards Paul.

Well, when (Richards) came into the picture, Bobby got uncomfortable. I did not know they had previously had a poor relationship. Of course I did know that during Paul's whole career as a baseball man he had a sort of entourage replete with those he considered his own people, a cadre he took with him wherever he went.

As the season went along Bobby and I talked about making a change as manager. Things just weren't going well, and eventually that is what teams do, though usually managerial changes often don't change much else. With no loss of respect for Bobby's abilities, we made a change. I know Bobby suspected Billy Hitchcock was part of some Richards movement against him, but that truly wasn't so. Hitchcock appeared to be the right choice for a positive change at the time it was determined a change had to be made.

LEMASTER: The players were expecting Bragan to be fired, expecting it and hoping for it. I pitched the first game Billy Hitchcock managed in Atlanta and I beat Sandy Koufax 2-1 when Eddie Mathews hit a home run. It was special because of something Bragan had said to me earlier. I beat Koufax and Bragan was gone and I loved it. Everyone on the goddamn team was celebrating that day.

AARON: I really couldn't tell you what happened when Bobby was fired. I can't remember. All I know is I did my best to play well for him and I did the same for the next guy. You ask me for the name of a manager I played for and learned from and respected and I'll tell you the name "Bobby Bragan."

TORRE: If most of the players didn't like Bobby, then I'd have to say he didn't do a good job, because that's what managing is, getting individual players to work together as a team. But I really don't remember most of the players being unhappy with him.

DENIS MENKE: I remember 1966 as a season where league changes on behalf of the players started happening, and things needed to change. More rights, more say in things. Now, today I think it might have to go back a little the other way. But that season it was good to have more of a voice.

LEMASTER: Look, there were times he was in a good mood and I thought Bobby Bragan was just the goddamndest guy I ever met. And I feel Bragan knew a lot about baseball. I look back, being 50 years old now, and I guess I think Bragan just didn't know how to communicate with players. He just wasn't a ballplayers' manager.

DICK WILLIAMS: Bobby was always an outstanding instructor. There's one simple reason Bobby didn't have a great record managing in the majors—he didn't have the horses. I know from personal experience he was a superb communicator who had so much to offer any player who wanted to listen. Of course, they have to want to listen.

LEO DUROCHER: Bragan was born to be a manager. I don't know where it went wrong for him. Players just stopped listening to managers. It went all to hell.

McHALE: Of course I was anxious to have Bobby with Montreal when that opportunity came, and to this day I have some regret about the way his career went after Atlanta. I remember Mr. Rickey telling me Bobby Bragan had the potential to be one of the great managers, and I agreed even after Atlanta that this potential was there. Bobby got away from managing too soon. He was too young to give it up, but I guess he was one of those people who have problems stepping away from something for just a little while. Casey Stengel didn't become a great manager until he was 56 years old. It's a shame Bobby never managed again. He had so many interests in all aspects of the game, and this perhaps distracted him from what should have been his long-term role as a manager. We'll never know what we, and baseball, missed. And, of course, neither will Bobby Bragan.

AFTERWARDS

I WAS GETTING READY TO JOIN JOHN MCHALE in the front office of the Montreal Expos in 1968 when I got a call from Dick Butler, who was supervisor of American League umpires. Dick told me he understood Hugh Finnerty, president of the Double-A Texas League, was going to resign, and that he felt I could succeed Finnerty if I decided to go after the job. The idea came totally out of the blue; I'd never considered a minor league presidency.

But I talked the possible Texas League job over with Gwenn, and it had one undeniable attraction that being a Montreal coach couldn't match: presiding over the Texas League meant a chance to stay home. Finnerty lived in Tulsa, so the league headquarters was in Tulsa. I figured if I got the job, I'd just move operations to Fort Worth.

It turned out there were just two other candidates for the job— George Schepps, who'd owned the league's Dallas franchise, and Howard Green, a former president of several minor leagues and also a Tarrant County judge. The Texas League owners came to a quick decision: I got the $17,500-a-year job and immediately relocated league headquarters to the Mallick Tower in Fort Worth.

It felt wonderful to be staying in baseball and home at the same time. Immediately after being hired, I called John McHale and Gene Mauch. I told McHale I was grateful for the chance to work with him again in Montreal, but I'd decided the Texas League job suited me better. He replied, "Bobby, if I can help you in any way, please call on me." Mauch had a slightly different response: "Well, I'm disappointed, but I'm not really surprised because you've always been a rebel." It would have been interesting to coach for Gene. As it turned out, my brother Jimmy ended up as his third base coach in Montreal.

But it was also interesting to be in charge of an entire league, with the chance to experiment with things and see how I might be able to spark additional fan interest. At the time I took over, the Texas League's eight franchises were located in El Paso, Amarillo, San Antonio, Shreveport, Memphis, Little Rock, Tulsa, and a joint Dallas-Fort Worth team. The Fort Worth Cats club had more or less gone up in smoke in the mid-'60s.

My job, besides making two trips during the season to each Texas League city and consulting with the owners there, was to initiate any changes I saw fit. One of the first things I did involved my old pals, the Texas League umpires. My feelings for them changed the instant I became league president. I took my umpires out of those deadly dull "pall bearer" black suits umpires in every league had been wearing since Abner Doubleday's era. They were re-outfitted in mix-and-match uniforms of gold, green, and powder blue. Texas League games were called by two umpires, and before each game the ump drawing home plate duties would select the outfit he and his partner would wear - all gold, all green, all powder blue, gold jackets and green slacks, any combination would do so long as both umps wore the same thing. Their caps were tri-color and matched whatever they wore.

The idea of changing umpire fashions soon caught on at the major league level. Just two seasons later the American League gave its umpires maroon jackets, and then the National League put numbers on jacket sleeves so fans could more easily identify who was making questionable calls against their favorite teams. And eventually both leagues let their umpires wear light blue shirts instead of dishwater-dull white.

Another boon to my Texas League umpires was the generous gesture of my previous employer, Jack Williams. Jack provided the league with new cars for the umps to drive from city to city.

I was elected to the Baseball Rules Committee, the group which sanctions or forbids experimentation with traditional ways of doing things. The Texas League applied for and was granted a two-season experiment with the designated hitter, a pet theory of mine for many, many years. I liked the omission of the pitcher's turn at bat in favor of letting a more skilled batter get to the plate. This way the offensive action was continuous. Fans didn't get up to go to the concession stand or the bathroom when the designated hitter came up. Pitchers, even with the wooden stick in their hands, aren't really concerned with hitting and running, breaking up a doubleplay on the basepaths, or stealing a base. On those rare occasions when pitchers do get on, the first thing they do is call time to get a jacket from the dugout. They simply are not offensive players.

So the Texas League was the laboratory where the designated hitter experiment was carried out, and after two seasons we returned to the Rules Committee with a favorable report. Lee McPhail, then general manager of the New York Yankees, immediately made a motion for the American League to adopt the DH rule. I seconded, and the motion was passed. The National League chose not to do the same, and baseball fans have suffered for it. In the American League, the DH rule has extended the wonderful careers of charismatic hitters like Hal McRae, Fred Lynn, and Dave Winfield, not to mention Hank Aaron and Orlando Cepeda. During 1992 the DH rule will allow American League fans to continue to enjoy seeing nine hitters in a lineup. If the National League had a similar common-sense rule you'd see weak-kneed but still top-gate attractions like Andre Dawson add five years to their careers.

Being president of a minor league at this time was a greater challenge than ever before. Major league baseball was continuing to expand, taking away traditional minor league stronghold cities like San Francisco, Los Angeles, Atlanta, and Dallas/Fort Worth. The Dallas/Fort Worth snatch came the year after I assumed the Texas League presidency. Lamar Hunt and Tommy Mercer owned the minor league Spurs, and the team would have to leave the area to make room at Turnpike Stadium (soon renamed Arlington Stadium) for the Washington Senators-turned-Texas Rangers. An indemnity had to be paid to Hunt and Mercer and the Texas League. Commissioner Bowie Kuhn called a meeting in New York to negotiate that settlement. Hunt, Mercer, and I attended on behalf of the Texas League, and a retired judge was named by Kuhn to rule on a proper settlement. Naturally, Hunt and Mercer wanted every dime they could get and the major league owners wanted to pay as little as possible. After much discussion, the Texas League was awarded $640,000— $360,000 to Mercer and Hunt in payment for their franchise being eliminated and $40,000 apiece to each of the other seven teams in the league. We then added Midland as our eighth Texas League franchise.

My favorite part of the job was travelling around the league. It was also necessary to visit cities like Jackson, Mississippi, where there was interest in adding a Texas League franchise whenever a spot in the league might become available. I logged tens of thousands of miles on the highway. Gwenn always accompanied me and we often brought along our grandchildren. The kids enjoyed the motel swimming pools and regional delights like the River Walk in San Antonio or the sight of windblown tumbleweeds on the stretch of road between Amarillo and El Paso.

Occasionally there were bizarre occurences. I got a call at home around 10 P.M. one night from Johnny Cox, the Midland general manager. He told me his field was covered with a swarm of grasshoppers and that most of the women in the stands had run off screaming with grasshoppers crawling through their hair. Could he please call the game on account of insects? I gave him permission.

Cox lived an adventuresome life. One day when Cox's team was idle, his concession manager asked him to take a look at something in the huge cooler. The door locked behind them, leaving the two trapped inside. After her husband didn't arrive home that night, Mrs. Cox called the Midland police. They went to the ballpark and eventually got around to looking in the cooler. There they found Cox and the concession manager calmly sipping beers. The thermostat in the cooler could be adjusted up to 32 degrees, so they passed a chilly off-day by consoling themselves with some comforting brews.

I also had to hand out on-the-spot punishments. At a game I attended in Midland, San Antonio outfielder Gorman Thomas had a dreadful time. He struck out his first two times at bat, and baseball fans who recall Thomas's later glory years with the Milwaukee Brewers will remember that when big Gorman whiffed he made a spectacle of it. So the Midland fans let Thomas know his failures at the plate amused them.

Gorman started to get hot. When he struck out a third time and the fans really let him hear about it, Thomas turned to the stands and made an obscene gesture. The umpires immediately ejected him from the game, and I followed him to the clubhouse. "The fans pay to get in and voice their opinions," I told him. "I don't know what your manager's going to do, but I'm taking $500 from your paycheck." Of all people, I was the one least likely to object to a little colorful behavior on the field, but my pranks with umpires over the years were never intended to cross the line between honest opinion and obscenity. Sometimes fans do get too far out of line, and those who do must be ejected from the ballpark, but in every instance athletes must realize they owe their salaries to the people who pay to see them play.

One of my favorite moments as Texas League president came when I got a phone call from a high school baseball coach in Hooks, Texas. "I'm head coach at this school," he told me, "but I think I can bring more career satisfaction to myself. I'm convinced I'd make a good major league umpire." We talked a while and I liked what I heard, so I told Durwood Merrill I'd do what I could to help. I called Barney Deary, who was in charge of minor league umpires, and asked him to help Durwood get started. I added that I'd like to see Durwood in the Texas League as soon as he was advanced enough to call Double-A ballgames. Well, within four years Durwood was in the major leagues, and he's been one of the very best umpires ever since.

Durwood did spend a season umpiring Texas League games. At the time Cal Ripkin Sr. was managing the Dallas/Fort Worth Spurs, and in a game at Turnpike Stadium a line drive was either caught or trapped by the visiting team third baseman. Durwood called the Spur hitter out, and Cal Sr. came racing out of the Dallas/Fort

Worth dugout and just raised hell. Durwood wouldn't change his call, and Ripkin, exasperated, finally asked, "Will you do me a favor and at least ask the other umpire how he saw the play?" "Be happy to," Durwood replied, and called over Nick Avants, who was stationed at first base. "Nick," Durwood inquired, "did you see what I saw?" "Yes, sir," the quick-thinking Avants answered. Ripkin knew when he was licked and went grudgingly back to his dugout.

Those Texas League years were just a golden time for me. I liked being in charge, getting the chance to be innovative. The travel was great; the only part of the job I hated was the paperwork, and Art Headley, my C.P.A., really did most of the bookkeeping and delivered the annual league financial report. I had no thoughts at all of ever doing anything else; in my third year Peter Bavasi called to ask me about managing the San Diego Padres, and I was not tempted. "The only major league team I'd ever consider managing would be the one in Dallas/Fort Worth," I told Peter. "That's because I'd just be a 20-minute drive from my house when I got fired." Actually, I knew well I'd never be able to adjust to the new "hooray for me" attitude of most players. I was too old to put up with more of that stuff.

My first Texas League secretary got married after just a few months on the job and moved out of town. At the same time, a young man had been repeatedly calling me from Carbondale, Illinois, pleading for a job in professional baseball. Then out of nowhere he appeared at my office door and said, "I'm the one who's been calling you from Illinois. I'm John Dittrich." I told him, "There's a job as my assistant; it pays $400 a month." He blurted, "I'll take it," and we worked together for some time. As I changed jobs, John changed with me. Today, he's part owner and general manager of the Columbus Red Stixx of the South Atlantic League.

But in 1976 Hank Peters resigned as president of the National Association of Professional Baseball Leagues, the umbrella organization for all minor leagues. Hank, the group's seventh president, had been named general manager of the Baltimore Orioles. I got several calls from people around the country urging me to throw my hat in the ring in the search for Hank's successor. Again, I talked the situation over with Gwenn. The minor league headquarters was in

St. Petersburg, Florida, and there probably wasn't much chance I could move it to Fort Worth if I got the job. Also, the competition was going to be tougher than my easy stroll into the top job of the Texas League. I'd have to appear before a gathering of the presidents of all 20 operating minor leagues and get a majority of their votes; eight other candidates would be trying to do the same.

It turned out that my main opponent was George Sisler Jr. Votes were taken in secret, and I won on the third ballot. As I accepted congratulatory handshakes, Sisler was conspicuous by his absence. Afterwards I asked for permission to move the group headquarters to Fort Worth, and, as I expected, the request was denied.

So for my three-year term as president, Gwenn and I split time between Florida and Texas. My salary was $35,000, and the St. Petersburg office was located on the second floor of the city's Chamber of Commerce building. It was not easily accessible, and nearby Al Lang Field was being renovated. The old clubhouses were in a separate building from the ballpark itself. I went before the St. Petersburg City Council and asked for permission to take over the old clubhouses. They agreed, and we spent $75,000 in renovations. Then we leased the building with an annual rent of $7,500 a year for 10 years. Since that time was up, the minor league offices cost the organization just $1 a year in rent.

Gwenn really threw herself into the renovation work, and turned that old clubhouse building into a showplace. There were actually newspaper articles about it; she had that really tasteful touch.

Though I still hated paperwork, the travel end of my new job was outstanding because I got to go all over the country. It was a time of real concern for minor league owners as major league expansion continued to chip away at the traditional minor league fan base. Some leagues were in deep financial straits: in 1949 there had been 59 minor leagues; the number since had dwindled to 20. Overall minor league attendance used to rival that of the major leagues; now the majors drew 30 million and we drew 10 million.

As president of the National Association, I initially made two additions to my staff, John Dittrich and Dick King. King was the Bill Veeck of the minor leagues, a promotional genius. He initiated the trade show portion of the annual baseball winter meeting. Instead of having suppliers on every floor of the headquarters hotel, he arranged for them all to have booths at an adjacent convention center. What he began is bigger than ever today. John Dittrich appropriately enough started a job seekers bureau, so young people seeking career's in baseball as announcers, groundskeepers, administrative assistants, or whatever would be provided with interviews with major and minor league executives. It's still an integral part of the annual meetings.

The American League expanded into Toronto and Seattle during my term as minor league president. Both the new expansion teams were required to operate farm clubs on the Triple-A, Double-A, and A league levels. There were problems about where the two new Triple-A teams would be located. None of the three Triple-A leagues —the Pacific Coast League, the International League, and the American Association—had expansion cities available to them. In desperation I called my old friend Harry Ornest, a Canadian entrepreneur making his home in Beverly Hills. Harry said he would guarantee the operation of two new Pacific Coast franchises in Vancouver, British Columbia, and Portland, Oregon. Since it was against league rules for one man to own two teams, Harry ended up running the Vancouver franchise and his brother Leo took over in Portland.

So there were challenges to be met, but I still knew within a few weeks of starting that I wouldn't want the job beyond my three-year term. Frankly, I didn't much like St. Petersburg. The retired people in Florida live in Fort Lauderdale or Miami. Their parents live in St. Petersburg. It's the only place in the country where the nightclubs have Geritol on tap.

After two years I went to major league baseball commissioner Bowie Kuhn and told him I had no interest in seeking another term. I added I had nothing but the highest admiration for Johnny Johnson, Kuhn's administrative assistant, and that Johnny was the one who should be sitting in my chair. "Of the 20 leagues under my jurisdiction, I can deliver Johnny 19 votes," I told Kuhn. I did, and Johnny Johnson succeeded me a year later.

Meanwhile, Kuhn wanted to know what I planned to do next. "I think I'd like to be sort of your field representative," I told him. "I can represent major league baseball at the collegiate championships,

American Legion playoffs, minor league all-star games, and stand in for you at funerals of notables and so forth." He said he'd check the idea out. Soon he called me to say, "Bobby, you know you're really very employable. Several major league teams said they'd hire you in a second." "But I want to live in Fort Worth," I told Kuhn. "If I work for you I can do that." "How old are you?" he asked, and I told him I was 61. Kuhn went to his executive owners' committee and got permission to hire me for four years at $25, 000 a year. So I came home just as I'd wanted to, and prepared to be the commissioner's extra pair of hands. Within a week I got a call from Eddie Robinson, general manager of the Texas Rangers. "Bobby, I know you had to take a cut in salary," he said. "If you'll add the duties of directing our team speakers' bureau I'll get you back the extra $10, 000 you gave up."

I began doing public relations work for the Rangers, officing out of Arlington Stadium. I'd estimate I spent 90 percent of my time attending to their team business. Bowie Kuhn might call a few times a month, asking me to do things like go represent him at Judge Hofheinz's funeral in Houston or the National Collegiate Athletic Association Baseball World Series in Omaha, Nebraska.

By the time I turned 65, Bob Wirz, Kuhn's director of public relations and Bill Murray, director of baseball operations, had worked out a plan whereby the Rangers were paying the bulk of my salary. On my 65th birthday I became a fulltime Ranger employee and have remained so to this day.

Employment-wise, things had turned out perfectly. I was still involved with baseball without the unceasing aggravation and employment insecurities of managing. I was living in Fort Worth, the city I loved, and Gwenn and I had lots of time to spend together.

This happiness lasted until 1983.

In 1978, Gwenn had surgery in St. Petersburg for a gall bladder problem. She took six months to recover, and needed a special mattress just to ride in the car or to sleep. She eventually got rid of it, but things never did entirely get back to normal.

In 1981 and 1982, Gwenn said at Christmastime she just didn't feel like doing our usual tree-decorating and all the rest of the traditional holiday pomp and pageantry. She just wasn't physically able to do any extra Christmas tasks. So we spent Christmas 1981 at the Holiday Inn in Arlington and Christmas 1982 at the Le Baron Hotel in Dallas. I wanted her to feel like we were having a special time anyway.

Shortly after Christmas in 1982, Gwenn spent time in Fort Worth's All Saints' Hospital; doctors diagnosed cirrhosis of the liver. I got a book and read a lot about the disease. It was supposed to be fatal. I believe Gwenn knew at that time, but we never discussed it.

She came home for awhile. We had a lady named Katie Stanley as an across-the-street neighbor for 25 years. Katie would often come to our home and play the piano. She was sickly and wasted away to the point where she looked practically ethereal, just wafting her way around. After one of her visits, I turned to Gwenn and said, "She's got cirrhosis of the liver; I don't think she'll be here much longer," and Gwenn replied very matter-of-factly, "I'll be going the same way."

We'd been married then for 42 years. I can't once recall her making a complaint about anything. She was a true "people person," and it mattered not the time of day or night if I wanted to bring people over to the house. On no notice at all, she gladly played the hostess, offering coffee and sweet rolls or more substantial fare. Neighborhood kids made our house a regular stop for snacks; policemen running speed traps nearby in hot summer weather were supplied with cold drinks and refreshments.

No matter where my baseball travels took me—Cuba, Pittsburgh, Cleveland, any place—if Gwenn wasn't accompanying me I could always call home and be 100 percent certain she would be there to answer the phone. And I was also sure of one other thing—she was not a baseball fan but a Bobby Bragan fan. She offered her complete support for whatever I wanted to do.

When she got sick, I was naive. I expected her to recover despite what I read about cirrhosis of the liver. When she went into the hospital to stay I slept in the same room. Often I'd be at work when the nurses brought her meals; invariably Gwenn would set aside a piece of cake or fruit for me to have later.

The time came when Gwenn began to have tremendous difficulty getting her breath, and the nurses looked concerned. For the first time I thought she might be nearing the end. Finally I was told April

30 that she must be moved to intensive care. As she was being moved, one of the nurses said to me, "You can dispose of these flowers." "Why?" I asked. "She'll be coming back to this room, won't she?" "Not necessarily," the nurse replied, and I understood her meaning.

That night I slept on a couch outside the intensive care ward. About 11 P.M. a nurse came out to say, "Your wife wants to see you." Though she was sedated, Gwenn was still upset about being in the intensive care ward. She told me there was no need for her to be there. I tried to reassure her, saying the best nurses in the hospital were there with her. After she calmed down, I went back and lay down on the couch. At 5 A.M. a nurse came out to tell me Gwenn had passed away.

For the next six months I could not spend the night alone in the house we'd shared for 34 years. I made certain one of our granddaughters or John Dittrich, who now worked for the Rangers, would be there to spend the night with me. The sense of loneliness was devastating.

I missed Gwenn terribly, but thought I might get through the worst of the grief if I starting going out socially. So in September I began dating Dodie Marshall, a woman I'd met while doing a Little League promotion three years earlier at the bank where she'd worked. I guess I wasn't thinking things through; after several dates, and against the vehement opposition of my daughter and other friends, Dodie and I got married. After three weeks of sleeping with her and her cat, a bedroom fixture in her life, Dodie informed me our marriage wasn't working. I agreed. Three weeks after that she asked if I would call a lawyer or would I prefer it if she called one. She made the call. A couple of days later she called me at Arlington Stadium and said, "I've put all your things in my garage. Come pick them up." During our brief time together we'd been living in a duplex she owned. Dodie's parents lived in the other side of the building. I spent more time with them than with her. At least Dodie and I parted without harsh words or rancor. To this day I've never laid eyes on her again, though I understand she's since remarried and moved to East Texas. I'm sure she took the damned cat with her. I moved back into my house, and once again was glad to be there. I never felt Gwenn was completely gone from it; for six months after she died I sometimes found myself calling the house from my office at the ballpark, somehow hoping Gwenn would answer the phone.

Well, after the experience with Dodie I wasn't anxious to get married again. Besides, things of an exciting nature were happening at Arlington Stadium, and I was right in the middle of them.

Ranger General Manager Joe Klein asked me for the names of the two people I considered the most innovative minor league team owners. Without hesitation I named Jim Paul of El Paso and Larry Schmittou of Nashville. Klein met with both, then hired Schmittou to convert the relatively tiny Arlington Stadium into a facility much nearer average major league standards. Larry erected huge billboards in the outfield, which besides carrying advertising also cut down on prevalent wind currents and immediately converted the stadium from a hitter's nightmare to a slugger's dream. Under Larry's direction a modern DiamondVision screen was placed in dead center field so fans could enjoy replays, and finally oversaw the construction of 50 new luxury suites, 30 more concession stands, and resurfacing of all concourse walkways and the stadium parking lots.

Schmittou, who today owns several minor league teams, brought some talented people with him to the Rangers. Chuck Morgan, once International Disc Jockey of the Year in Nashville, became director of sales and director of DiamondVision. Jay Miller moved from a Class A general manager's position in Salem, Virginia, to assist in the ticket department. Dave Fendrick left his general manager's post at Savannah to become promotions director. Jim Anglea, perhaps the best grounds supervisor in the business, was lured from Cleveland by Schmittou. All have since been given increased authority by new Ranger team owners headed by George W. Bush and Rusty Rose.

I was asked to get involved with selling the luxury suites. They were wonderful but pricey, $300,000 for an eight-seater and $400, 000 for a 12-seater. All were purchased before the season opener. I made calls on all the business executives I knew; one was Vernon Minton, a Fort Worth stockbroker. Minton said he couldn't afford a luxury suite but could give me the names of five different friends who might be interested. It turned out two of the five did buy suites. To thank Vernon, I dropped by his office with some Ranger caps, baseballs, and a few other promotional items. He thanked me for the gifts and then said, "Bobby, I played golf with a lady last week, and I think you two would make a wonderful pair. Call her up." I said, "No, you call her first and tell her I'll be in touch. What's her name?"

A few days later on December 20 I called Roberta Beckman at 9:30 A.M. and asked if she'd like to join me for lunch at Fort Worth's Ridglea Country Club. "That would be nice," she said. "I'll be wearing a blue suit, and my hair is gray." My strategy in inviting her to lunch was simple: the Rangers were having their annual Christmas dinner for team employees at the ballpark's Stadium club that evening, and I thought I might ask Roberta to accompany me there. However, I wanted to check her out before inviting her to join me at this more formal occasion. Over lunch I immediately found myself enjoying her company immensely. A widow, Roberta made nice conversation and enjoyed two of my favorite pastimes, playing the piano and golf. I had no qualms about inviting her to join me again that evening at Arlington Stadium.

"I would love to go with you," she told me. " In fact, this is the only day I have available until January 6th." We had a good time that night, and over the Christmas holidays I sent her a few color pictures so she wouldn't forget what I looked like. On January 6 I knocked on her door, intending to set up another date. "Come Saturday I want to take you to the Paris Coffee Shop here in Fort Worth, where they serve the greatest breakfast in the world including biscuits, grits, gravy and so forth," I said. She surprised me by answering, "I can't do that. My weekends are taken. I've been going with this retired doctor for two years and I spend weekends with him."

I don't give up easily, and I made the same offer for the following Saturday. "I told you my weekends are taken," was Roberta's rebuff.

On the third week I tried a different approach. "Roberta, I've been a member of the First United Methodist Church in Fort Worth since 1949," I said. "For 29 years we had as our minister Gaston Foote, and we felt we had the greatest one ever. Now we have Barry Bailey, and he *is* the greatest. I want you to come with me and hear him preach on Sunday morning." Still I got the same response: "My weekends are taken."

It was time to take more forceful measures. I immediately called a florist and had a dozen roses delivered to Roberta's house on Saturday afternoon. She promptly called me and said, "Bobby, your roses are magnificent. They're the first dozen roses I've ever received, and they're beautiful." I replied, "Make sure the doc gets to smell 'em, won't you?" She said she would. Getting bolder, I asked, "Has that doc asked you to marry him?" "No," Roberta replied, "It's not that kind of relationship." I said, "Will you do me a favor? Tell the doc you and I can get married today, tonight, tomorrow, or whenever you wish." She assured me she would.

On Monday night, the doc came over to Roberta's house and brought a crockpot of food. He cooked dinner for her on occasion. He put the crockpot down in her kitchen and announced he'd go back out to his car and get the itinerary for a vacation they'd be taking in Acapulco. Roberta said, "You needn't bother to do that. I'm going to marry Bobby Bragan." The doc spluttered, "You're what?" and then picked up his crockpot of food and took it back to his car.

The following weekend I was *in* and the doc was *out*.

Eight weeks later, Roberta and I were married by Barry Bailey on March 27, 1985. To date it's been complete marital bliss. We easily blended into each other's family and rarely spend a day apart. Before we met, Roberta had never gone to a baseball game. Now we rarely miss getting out to the stadium when the Rangers are playing at home.

Life is golden again. I make about 250 speeches a year on behalf of the Rangers, mostly in the Dallas/Fort Worth area. I visit the college World Series and help direct the Rangers' annual Fantasy Camp where fans get the chance to suit up and play ball alongside retired pros like Jim Sundberg, Brooks Robinson, Fergie Jenkins, and Rich Billings. I also put together the Rangers' annual Old Timers' Game, which gives me the chance to visit many old friends from my playing and managing days.

For the past 10 years I've also sponsored the annual Bobby Bragan Golf Tournament to raise money for charities. These have included the Boy Scouts of America Longhorn Council, the March of Dimes, and the Arthritis Foundation. Now this tournament, always held in conjunction with the Old Timers' Game so there are plenty of baseball stars to serve as celebrity golf partners, will benefit the Bobby Bragan Youth Foundation, which has been created to help otherwise disadvantaged children who excel in athletics, academics, and citizenship. We're starting out locally, and hopefully will expand to all areas of the country.

It's full circle, you see. When I was a kid, older people took an interest in me and it made all the difference. With my foundation I can do the same thing, and the foundation can continue long after I'm gone—though I have no intentions of going anywhere anytime soon, because I'm having such a good time.

I continue to work towards Leo Durocher's election to the Hall of Fame. Leo's record as a manager should speak for itself —2, 010 wins, sixth most by any manager in baseball history; three National League pennants, and the 1954 World Series championship when the New York Giants swept the favored Cleveland Indians in four straight games. Leo built the Chicago Cubs back into a contender. And more than that, he was one of the very few managers fans paid to see; he was a draw, as much as any player.

In each of the past four years, I've purchased a full page ad in *Baseball America* on the week the Hall of Fame Veteran's Committee meets to elect new members who no longer qualify for the writers' vote. I've contacted every committee member before each vote—as yet, to no avail. But I'll never give up.

As an important part of this book, Jeff Guinn and I called Leo in the fall of 1991 to ask if he'd grant an interview. By then Leo was a very sick man, confined to his Palm Springs home and weakening daily. Even though he was no longer supposed to give interviews, he immediately asked Jeff to come to California to see him. "This will probably be my last interview, Bobby," he told me, and that's the way it turned out. I'm so glad this wonderful man, a real credit to baseball, shares his thoughts with our readers.

Mr. Rickey, of course passed away in 1965. There are many baseball fans and players today who will never realize the tremendous impact he had on the sport as it has evolved. But if you enjoy what you see on modern baseball diamonds, give silent thanks to Branch Rickey.

```
  ┌───┬───┬───┬───┬───┬───┬───┐
  │ B │ E │ T │ W │ E │ E │ N │
  ├───┼───┼───┼───┼───┼───┼───┤
  │ I │ N │ N │ I │ N │ G │ S │
  └───┴───┴───┴───┴───┴───┴───┘
```

DUKE SNIDER: It was funny to think of Bobby as a league president. I came down to manage Alexandria in the Texas League, and at the season-opening banquet he came up to me and said, "This year I'm gonna get some of your money," because I was known to argue with umpires. Bobby Bragan fining somebody for arguing with an umpire! Well, I told him, "You're not getting a cent," and he didn't. I wasn't about to give him the satisfaction.

JOHN McHALE: I could have told the Texas League owners that if Bobby was their league president, Bobby was going to experiment and make things happen.

JOE TORRE: I can't say I'm surprised Bobby chose to be a minor league president instead of getting back into uniform. He didn't like the way the relationships between managers and players was changing. He'd dislike it even more today. Before, if players hated a manager he was in a position to get rid of them, but now if a player with a multi-year contract doesn't like the manager he can just sit back and wait the manager out.

LOU BROCK: I understand Bobby liked being a league president

343

but I think that wasted his abilities. What he should have been was a major league general manager, because he could spot talent like nobody else.

BRANCH RICKEY III: It's true baseball and its minor leagues have been in a state of flux. When my father, Branch Jr., was minor league director of the Brooklyn farm system, the Dodgers had 29 minor league teams. When I had the same job with the Pirates and Cincinnati, I had seven minor league clubs with Pittsburgh and six with the Reds. But many of those agreements in the Brooklyn day were informal. The structure is firmer today; there's greater substance to the major league-minor league relationship than there was before.

My grandfather, Branch Rickey, was involved at the start of the '60s in a role that pushed the major leagues into expansion. He made the effort to develop the Continental League with a theory akin to what happened when the American Football League came into being and challenged the established National Football League a short time later. Rather than mix a few new weak teams into the major leagues with much stronger teams, my grandfather thought he could start a separate league and let the teams in it develop until they were equal to the clubs in the established American and National Leagues and see what happened from there. His supposition was that the U.S. population continued to grow and there would always be new major baseball markets developing. And though the Continental League didn't succeed when the major leagues gave expansion franchises to potential Continental League sites like Houston and Minneapolis-St. Paul, what you see today with Denver and Miami becoming major league cities is that new minor league markets are opening up, too, like Ottawa and Charlotte. The Denver minor league team is looking at moving to New Orleans. There is plenty of room for the major and the minor leagues. There was never a question of the minor leagues being squeezed out of existence by major league expansion.

I know Bobby as Texas League president may have worried about this, but, see, Bobby's heart was and is always so tied to the way the game used to be it's hard for him to accept change. But then and now the minor leagues aren't being crippled, aren't being impinged upon.

STAN MUSIAL: There just aren't any minor leagues any more. It's over, and it's sad.

BASEBALL TOMORROW

IT MUST BE OBVIOUS TO EVEN THE MOST CASUAL OF OBSERVERS: baseball has
to change, radically and immediately. Team owners can act on their
own initiative or delay until decisions are forced on them by the
fans. But one way or the other, change must and will come.

It should begin with interleague play. It simply is not logical that
Jose Canseco might spend his entire career in Oakland and fans in
National League cities might never see him play in person unless
there's a rare occasion at World Series time. American League fans
never had opporunity to see Willie Mays or Roberto Clemente or
Sandy Koufax. National League fans missed the careers of Ted
Williams, Mickey Mantle, and Joe DiMaggio. In each case, half the
fans were deprived. And all baseball decisions ought to be made on
behalf of the people who buy the tickets to see the games.

Interleague play would also be a common sense method of en-
couraging natural rivalries: Mets-Yankees, Cubs-White Sox, Dodg-
ers-Angels, Astros-Rangers. It's nonsense to speculate a few regular
season meetings would spoil the unique flavor of the World Series.
Pro football's Super Bowl remains one of the most immense attractions in all sports even though opponents often have already faced
off during the regular season.

Jealousy between the two leagues is really at the root of their failure to consider the fans first. The National League has usually taken the lead in initiating change—it was first to expand, first to break the color barrier, first to have a domed stadium, first to move to the West Coast, first to build an extensive spring training complex, and first to wear batting helmets. The only thing the American League did first was adopt the designated hitter, which should be utilized in both leagues in order to have continuous offensive excitement. But National League owners have done so much to denigrate the idea it will be difficult for them to turn around and welcome the DH now.

Major league baseball desperately needs divisional realignment. Let's put the teams together in a way that makes geographic sense: East Coast, West Coast, Mid-America. The majority of each team's games should be played within its division. Face it—nobody in Boston can stay up until 2 A.M. on a work night to watch the Red Sox take on Seattle on cable TV.

Every stadium should have synthetic grass. It makes sense from several practical points of view. Consider Riverfront Stadium in Cincinnati: after the Reds put in artificial turf, rainouts practically were eliminated. It can pour rain right up to game time, and then the Reds' grounds crew simply brings out a vacuum and shoots the water off over a fence. Regular grass would be turned into a morass, forcing a postponement. Remember, many people on any one night are probably attending their only game of the season because they have to drive so far from their hometowns to the stadium. Because of work or other commitments, if a game is postponed they can't stay over an extra day. Games must be played as scheduled for the convenience of fans, and artificial turf is one way to do that. (So are domed stadiums, which I love—no rainouts are possible then!)

From a player's standpoint, I'll give you the opinion of Brooks Robinson, perhaps the finest fielder in baseball history. Brooks is an instructor now at all our Ranger fantasy camps, and he always says if he played on synthetic grass "I would have been invincible because there would have been no bad hops." Grass playing fields take a beating during any season. Playing conditions deteriorate as the months go by. Just during fielding practice, a coach might hit

1,000 ground balls to his third baseman over the course of time, and every ball takes a divot out of the grass. On artificial turf 100,000 ground balls won't cause the slightest wear and tear.

Then there's the most important modern baseball issue of all—money, and who gets most of it. There's no question who pays it into the pot—the fans. But owners and ballplayers are violently split on who should get the lion's share of the booty.

For many years in baseball, owners took the profits and players got peanuts. It's a fact; as Stan Musial once observed of Mr. Rickey, "(Owners) thought money and ballplayers shouldn't mix." This inbalance of income was unfair. Then along came Marvin Miller and the players' association, and unbelievable changes resulted. The basic salary structure wasn't changed that much at first—instead, players demanded and got the right to have first class air travel, increased per diem meal money, and control of clubhouse amenities including room temperature and music. The promotion aspect of the sport also mushroomed—through a players' union agreement, even marginal players shared in the wealth from endorsements, baseball card contracts, and other monetary extras.

Free agency and salary arbitration took the balance of power away from owners and gave it to players and their agents. There was no effort to adopt some sort of common-sense compromise. The players were determined to get every cent they could, forgetting the money involved comes not from the team owners but from the fans. It's simply a farce: As Buzzie Bavasi says, an arbitrator might award a $2.5 million-a-year contract to a hitter who can't even run from home plate to first base. The next hitter's agent says *his* client can do everything the first guy does, plus run a little better, meaning he has to get $2.6 million. And under the system of arbitration where both player and club submit contract offers, even if a player loses he usually gets a huge raise, plus the opportunity to say his team doesn't appreciate him because they criticized some aspect of his play during the arbitration hearings. How can anyone think this system makes sense?

Other major sports have found better approaches. The National Basketball Association teams have salary caps. There's free agency in the National Football League, but very rarely does a player involved end up signing with anyone other than the same team he played for in the first place.

Here's a plan to benefit both players and management: give free agency to every player after every season. Eliminate new multi-year contracts and grandfather those currently in existence. Make it like it was and should be again—players get paid on the basis of season-to-season performance. Forget their gripes they work just as hard with multi-season security. How many of these free agents with new mega-bucks, multi-year contracts fall flat on their faces during their first seasons with their new teams?

At the same time, establish a salary cap for teams. All the players go into one pool, and each club can bid for them or not as management chooses. Giving Bobby Bonilla a $6 million contract would mean the team signing him has less money for its other players. Management would have to exercise good judgment. This would be a real test of front office perspicacity. We'd find out who the savvy general managers were fast enough.

All television income, national and local, must go into one pot to be shared equally among teams. Of course a few of the TV-richest clubs would not want to go along with the plan, but something similar has happened before in baseball. For many years clubs took in gate receipts on a home and home basis - the home team got all the money from tickets sold, while the visiting team got nothing. But clubs in smaller markets couldn't make a financial go of it, so it was altered to 60 percent for the home team, 40 percent for the visiting team. Compromise *is* possible.

It's also necessary. Fans won't be able to bear baseball's current financial burden much longer. When a family of four has to spend $100 or so for game tickets, parking, concessions, programs, and maybe a souvenir or two, then Mom and Dad are going to choose alternative forms of wholesome entertainment. In recent years players have complained that fan abuse is becoming cruder, more vehement. Well, if you have to work your tail off just to make ends meet, when you go to the ballpark to relax you expect to see your team's millionaires perform impeccably.

When owners and players start making decisions to benefit fans as well as themselves, they'll find ballpark patrons in much more generous moods. If they don't, and if the costs of running a ballclub keep escalating, which means ticket prices keep escalating, well... tickets to the zoo, bargain movie matinees and putt-putt golf courses will appear more attractive.

Players need to be less ostentatious about their newfound wealth. At the rate things are going, writers in each league will annually have to elect an MVB, Most Valuable Bejewelled, based on the gold chains and earrings and other flashy, expensive accouterments worn on the field.

My criticisms don't in any way mean I've lost my love of the sport. It's no accident I dedicate this book in part to the game of baseball. Baseball has provided me and the rest of the Bragan family continued happiness and enduring friendships —I know this would echo the sentiments of Corinne and George W. Bragan Jr. as well as my siblings Sue, G.W. III, Walter, Lionel, Peter, Marian, Jimmy, and Frank, and all our children, grandchildren, and extended family members.

Personally, it has been my privilege to make a joyful noise while being paid to live out my childhood dreams. No man could ask for more. Baseball continues to change, but no matter what additional changes do come, it is already a radically different sport from the game I loved as a player, coach and manager. If you could somehow reincarnate Babe Ruth or Ty Cobb, those fellows would have trouble recognizing their sport. (I believe Mr. Rickey, though, would welcome the opportunity to return and beat the younger generation at its new operational systems.)

One thing about baseball, though, has never changed. It never will. You can't hit the ball with the bat on your shoulder. I'm grateful for the chances I had to take my swings.

GEORGE W. BUSH: The concept of a salary cap and annual free agency isn't a new one. Charlie Finley with the Oakland A's discussed this years ago.

Of course, we're reaching the limit on salaries. What really hurts teams in smaller markets is that there's just no way to bring in enough revenue to compete with clubs from bigger markets. If there was a salary cap, everybody would be playing with the same rule.

As far as annual free agency goes, that's at least one method of tying performance to compensation. This is the American way; I think fans would be supportive. If a player has a great year, he gets a big raise. If he doesn't perform well, his paycheck the next season reflects this.

Also, current salaries have really estranged the players from the fans, and fans are baseball's most valuable resource. If a fan sees a player with a multimillion-dollar salary, he can't really feel empathy for that player. They have nothing in common. But put that same player on a salary plan where his pay reflects performance, well, anybody who works for a living can understand that.

BOBBY VALENTINE: From the player perspective I can see why they don't think current salaries are out of line. A guy making $5 million a year thinks the current system is just fine. Besides, when you see some guy buy a ballclub and sell it for twice what he paid just two or three years later, you get the idea the owners aren't hurting for cash.

BUSH: One way or the other, things will change. The fans are still the most important element of baseball, and the fans have had enough with the current salary structure. Unless we do things differently, baseball is simply going to price itself out of the entertainment market for most people.

BETWEEN INNINGS
COMMENTATORS

HANK AARON is major league baseball's all-time home run king with 755 roundtrippers. A perennial All-Star, Aaron was the National League Most Valuable Player in 1957 and was elected to the Hall of Fame in 1982, his first year of eligibility. After many years with the Braves in Milwaukee and Atlanta, Aaron concluded his sterling career with two years as designated hitter for the Milwaukee Brewers. He is now an executive with the Atlanta Braves.

BOB ASPROMONTE spent 13 major league seasons as a slick-fielding third baseman for the Los Angeles Dodgers, Houston Colt .45s, Atlanta Braves, and New York Mets. He now runs a Houston beer distributorship with his brother Ken, who was a major league player and manager.

AL BARLICK is a former major league umpire enshrined in baseball's Hall of Fame.

BUZZIE BAVASI is one of the most respected team executives in major league baseball history. As executive vice-president and general manager of the Dodgers in Brooklyn and later in Los Angeles, Bavasi shared in many great moments of baseball history. Later he became part-owner and general manager of the San Diego Padres. He concluded his career as general manager of the California Angels.

CARROLL BERINGER spent 17 seasons in the minor leagues, mostly as a relief pitcher. After retiring as an active player he eventually joined the Los Angeles Dodgers as bullpen coach. Beringer later moved to the Philadelphia Phillies as pitching coach. Players he has tutored include Sandy Koufax, Don Drysdale, Ron Perranoski, Steve Carlton, and Tug McGraw.

RALPH BRANCA, best known for giving up Bobby Thomson's historic home run in the 1951 National League playoffs between the Brooklyn Dodgers and New York Giants, spent 12 years in the major leagues with Brooklyn, Detroit, and the New York Yankees.

LOU BROCK held the major league stolen base record for a single season (118) and a career (938) until Rickey Henderson passed him in recent seasons. Brock spent 19 years in the majors with the Chicago Cubs and St. Louis Cardinals. He was elected to the Hall of Fame in 1985.

LEW BURDETTE had an 18-year major league career, pitching for the Yankees, the Braves in both Boston and Milwaukee, St. Louis, the Chicago Cubs, the Phillies, and the then-Los Angeles Angels. For many years Burdette and teammate Warren Spahn gave the Braves baseball's most feared lefty-righty pitching combination. Burdette twice won 20 games, and led the National League in 1956 with a 2.70 earned run average.

GEORGE W. BUSH is managing general partner of the Texas Rangers. Along with investor Rusty Rose, Bush headed a team of 17 investors who purchased the franchise from Eddie Chiles in 1989.

ROY CAMPANELLA joined the Brooklyn Dodgers in 1948 and went on to win two Most Valuable Player awards during his 10 seasons with the team. His career was tragically ended when Campanella was paralyzed in an auto accident following the 1957 season. In 1969 Campanella was voted into the Hall of Fame.

ORLANDO CEPEDA, nicknamed "The Baby Bull," played in the major leagues for 17 seasons with the San Francisco Giants, St. Louis Cardinals, Atlanta Braves, Oakland A's, Boston Red Sox, and Kansas City Royals. He was voted the National League's Most Valuable Player in 1967. Cepeda led the league with 111 runs batted in that season, and in 1962 paced the National League in both home runs (46) and runs batted in (142).

HARRY CRAFT played six seasons as center fielder of the Cincinnati Reds. He later managed the Kansas City A's, Chicago Cubs, and Houston Colt .45s, finishing seven seasons with a record of 360 victories and 485 losses.

DEL CRANDALL was an all-star catcher for many of his 16 major league seasons with the Boston/Milwaukee Braves, San Francisco Giants, Pittsburgh Pirates, and Cleveland Indians. Crandall managed the Milwaukee Brewers in 1972-75 and the Seattle Mariners in 1983-84.

TOMMY DAVIS led the National League in batting for two consecutive seasons with a .346 average in 1962 and a .326 mark in 1963. He spent 16 years in the big leagues with the Los Angeles Dodgers, New York Mets, Chicago White Sox, Seattle Pilots, Houston Astros, Oakland A's, Chicago Cubs, Baltimore Orioles, California Angels, and Kansas City Royals. Davis also led the league in 1962 with 230 hits and 153 runs batted in.

JOE DIMAGGIO, voted by sportswriters a few years ago as the nation's greatest living baseball player, was the New York Yankee center fielder for 13 distinguished seasons. In 1941 DiMaggio set a major league record by hitting safely in 56 consecutive games. DiMaggio twice led the American League in batting (.381 in 1939, .352 in 1940), was twice league champion in both home runs and runs batted in, and was also acknowledged as one of the finest fielders in baseball history. He was elected to the Hall of Fame in 1955.

LEO DUROCHER spent 17 seasons as a feisty good-field, no-hit shortstop for the New York Yankees, Cincinnati Reds, St. Louis

Cardinals, and Brooklyn Dodgers. He gained his lasting popularity, though, in 24 years as manager of the Brooklyn Dodgers, New York Giants, Chicago Cubs, and Houston Astros. His 2,010 managerial wins are sixth most in major league history. Despite this success, Durocher has not been elected to the Hall of Fame, with some speculation his suspension for the 1947 season by Commissioner Happy Chandler has caused several members of the Oldtimers Selection Committee to adamantly vote against him each year. Durocher died in 1991. His last interview was for this book. Bobby Bragan continues to work toward Durocher's eventual election to the Hall of Fame.

AL GIONFRIDDO became part of baseball lore during the 1947 World Series when his sensational catch robbed Joe DiMaggio of a game-winning extra base hit. Gionfriddo spent four years in the National League, first with the Pittsburgh Pirates and then with the Brooklyn Dodgers. Ironically, his 1947 World Series appearances were his last as a big league player.

DICK GROAT won the National League Most Valuable Player award in 1960, when he led the league with a .325 batting average and the Pittsburgh Pirates won the World Series over the New York Yankees. Groat played 14 seasons in the majors, with the Pirates, St. Louis Cardinals, Philadelphia Phillies, and San Francisco Giants.

JERRY GROTE spent 16 seasons as a catcher for the Houston Colt .45s, New York Mets, Los Angeles Dodgers, and Kansas City Royals. Known for a rifle arm, Grote played on several All-Star teams and in four World Series.

WHITEY HERZOG's major league playing career was relatively undistinguished, spending eight years as an outfielder for the Washington Senators, Kansas City A's, Baltimore Orioles, and Detroit Tigers. He achieved lasting fame as a manager, first guiding the Texas Rangers and later winning division titles with the Kansas City Royals. Herzog then took over as general manager and field manager of the St. Louis Cardinals, winning a World Championship in 1982 and guiding the Redbirds to the World Series on two other occasions. He is now vice-president of baseball operations for the California Angels.

TOM LASORDA never won a game as a major league pitcher with Brooklyn and Kansas City, but more than made up for that in his tenure as manager of the Los Angeles Dodgers. His teams won World Championships in 1981 and 1988.

DON LARSEN pitched the only perfect game in World Series history, beating the Brooklyn Dodgers for the New York Yankees with that 2-0 gem in 1956. Larsen spent 14 years in the majors as a journeyman pitcher for the St. Louis Browns, Baltimore Orioles, Yankees, Kansas City A's, Chicago White Sox, San Francisco Giants, Houston Astros, and Chicago Cubs.

VERNON LAW won 20 games for the Pittsburgh Pirates in 1960 as his team won the world championship. Law pitched in the major leagues for 16 years, all with the Pirates.

DENVER LEMASTER pitched 11 seasons for the Braves, Houston Astros, and Montreal Expos. His career record is 90 wins and 105 losses.

DENIS MENKE spent 13 years as an infielder with the Braves, Houston Astros, and Cincinnati Reds, playing in two World Series. He is presently a coach with the Philadelphia Phillies.

JOHN McHALE played five years with the Detroit Tigers, but achieved more lasting fame as an executive with the Tigers, Braves, and Montreal Expos.

CAL McLISH had the longest full name in baseball history (Calvin Coolidge Julius Caesar Tuskahoma McLish), but his teammates just called him "Buster." McLish's 15-year big league career included pitching stints with the Brooklyn Dodgers, Pittsburgh Pirates, Chicago Cubs, Cleveland Indians, Cincinnati Reds, Chicago White Sox, and Philadelphia Phillies.

STAN MUSIAL won three National League Most Valuable Player awards and led the league in batting seven times during his 22 years with the St. Louis Cardinals. Musial's lifetime batting average is .331. At age 42 in 1962, Musial hit .330 and challenged Tommy Davis for the batting title. One of the finest hitters in baseball history, Musial was elected to the Hall of Fame in 1969.

BILLY O'DELL, who says he only experimented with a spitball in the bullpen, pitched 13 years for the Baltimore Orioles, San Francisco Giants, Braves, and Pittsburgh Pirates. His career record was 105-100.

HARRY ORNEST is chairman of Hollywood Race Track. He and Bobby Bragan produced a 30-minute television special on the career of Branch Rickey, one of the few recorded instances of Rickey candidly discussing his plan to make Jackie Robinson the first black player in the major leagues.

GABE PAUL began his baseball career as travelling secretary of the Cincinnati Reds. He later became the Reds' vice-president and general manager before taking the same position with the expansion Houston Colt .45s. He then moved to Cleveland as general manager of the Indians and eventually served as George Steinbrenner's general manager for the New York Yankees.

JOHNNY PODRES spent most of his 15-year major league career as a pitcher for the Dodgers in Brooklyn and Los Angeles. He concluded his big league tenure with short stints at Detroit and San Diego. Podres's career record was 148-116, and his best-known win in 1955 gave Brooklyn its only World Series victory over the arch-rival New York Yankees.

BRANCH RICKEY III is currently president of the Triple-A American Association. Previously he served as assistant farm director for the Pittsburgh Pirates and later the Cincinnati Reds.

DUKE SNIDER, along with Mickey Mantle and Willie Mays, gave New York three fine center fielders to cheer for during most of the 1950s before the Dodgers and Giants moved to California. Snider played 18 years in the majors, first with Brooklyn/Los Angeles and then for the New York Mets and San Francisco Giants. His 11 World

Series home runs are fourth-most in history. Snider was elected to the Hall of Fame in 1980.

WARREN SPAHN, one of the greatest left-handed pitchers in baseball history, pitched 21 years in the major leagues and won 363 games. Spahn spent 20 seasons with the Braves in Boston and Milwaukee before concluding his career in 1965 with the New York Mets and San Francisco Giants. Spahn was elected to the Hall of Fame in 1973.

CHUCK STEVENS played first base for three years with the St.Louis Browns before playing for Bobby Bragan and the Hollywood Stars of the Pacific Coast League. Stevens is now an officer with the Association of Professional Baseball Players of America in Garden Grove, California, an organization to assist destitute former players.

BOBBY THOMSON hit baseball's most famous home run off Ralph Branca in 1951 to defeat the Brooklyn Dodgers in the final game of a best-of-three playoff series and put the New York Giants into the World Series against the New York Yankees. Thomson spent his 15 major league seasons with the Giants, Milwaukee Braves, Chicago Cubs, Boston Red Sox, and Baltimore Orioles.

JOE TORRE played 18 outstanding seasons as a catcher, third baseman, and first baseman for the Braves, St. Louis Cardinals, and New York Mets. In 1971, his best season, Torre hit .363 and was voted the National League Most Valuable Player. He managed the Mets and Braves, and currently is manager of the St. Louis Cardinals.

BOBBY VALENTINE's promising major league career stalled when he suffered a severe leg injury in 1973. He played several seasons in utility roles for the Los Angeles Dodgers, California Angels, San Diego Padres, New York Mets (where he was released by Met manager Joe Torre), and Seattle Mariners. Later a coach with the Mets, Valentine has managed the Texas Rangers since 1985.

LEE WALLS spent 10 years as an outfielder with the Pittsburgh Pirates, Chicago Cubs, Cincinnati Reds, Philadelphia Phillies, and Los Angeles Dodgers.

DICK WILLIAMS twice turned woebegone franchises into pennant winners, with the Boston Red Sox in 1967 and the San Diego Padres in 1984. Williams also guided the Oakland A's to three American League West Division titles, two league championships, and two World Series victories, in 1972 over Cincinnati and in 1973 over the Mets. Williams spent 13 major league seasons as a marginal infielder-outfielder for the Brooklyn Dodgers, Baltimore Orioles, Cleveland Indians, Kansas City A's, and Boston Red Sox. He managed the Red Sox in 1967-69, Oakland in 1971-73, the California Angels in 1974-76, the Montreal Expos in 1977-81, the San Diego Padres in 1982-85, and the Seattle Mariners in 1986-87. Williams is currently a Padres scout.

MAURY WILLS made baseball history in 1962 when he became the first player to break Ty Cobb's long-standing season record of 96 stolen bases. Wills' 104 steals set the new standard until 1974, when Lou Brock stole 118. Wills won the 1962 National League Most Valuable Player award. His 14 big league seasons included stints for the Los Angeles Dodgers, Pittsburgh Pirates, and Montreal Expos. Wills also managed the Seattle Mariners for portions of the 1980 and 1981 seasons.

DON ZIMMER spent 12 seasons as an infielder for the Brooklyn Dodgers, Chicago Cubs, New York Mets, Cincinnati Reds, and Washington Senators. He later managed the San Diego Padres, Boston Red Sox, Texas Rangers, and Chicago Cubs. Zimmer is currently the Red Sox third base coach.

"DON'T JUST STAND THERE"

You can't hit the ball with the bat on your shoulder,
You gotta get up there and swing.
You'll never hit that apple 'til you start gettin' bolder,
And hittin' the ball is the thing.
For when you get your chance, look the facts in the eye.
You'll never hit a homer if you watch 'em go by.

You know, the boys were playing baseball one evening,
They hadn't hit a ball at all that year.
And every time a player left the dugout
The fans would yell into his ear:
"You can't hit the ball with the bat on your shoulder,
You gotta get up there and swing.
There are ducks on the pond and it's your turn to smile,
Don't be like Casey saying, 'That's not my style'. "

Now he's up there, he's diggin' in, here comes the pitch,
There it goes! It's a home run!
Look at it travel! I'm a son-of-a-gun.

You can't hit the ball with the bat on your shoulder,
You gotta get up there, you HAVE to get up there,
You're PAID to get up there and swing.
So don't let some distraction rob you of the satisfaction
Of knowing at least YOU TOOK A SWING!

(Adapted by Bobby Bragan from "The Baseball Game," written in 1955
by Babe Wallace and published by Zizz Music ASCAP.)